MILITARY RULE IN LATIN AMERICA:

Functions, Consequences and Perspectives

SAGE RESEARCH PROGRESS SERIES ON

WAR, REVOLUTION, AND PEACEKEEPING

SERIES EDITORS: Charles C. Moskos, Jr.
and Sam C. Sarkesian

*Sponsored by the Inter-University Seminar
on Armed Forces and Society*

MILITARY RULE

IN LATIN AMERICA

Function, Consequences

and Perspectives

Edited by PHILIPPE C. SCHMITTER

*This volume was produced in cooperation with
The Center for Policy Study at The University of Chicago*

SAGE RESEARCH PROGRESS SERIES ON
WAR, REVOLUTION, AND PEACEKEEPING

Volume III (1973)

 **S A G E** PUBLICATIONS   *Beverly Hills   /   London*

ACKNOWLEDGMENTS

The Center for Policy Study at The University of Chicago provides a forum for the review and public discussion of major foreign and domestic policy issues. The Center's Arms Control and Foreign Policy Seminar, funded by the Ford Foundation, sponsored an Institute on "Arms Control, Military Aid and Military Rule in Latin America," May 26-27, 1972. The papers by Geoffrey Kemp, James Kurth, Philippe Schmitter, and Jerry Weaver were originally prepared for this Institute. They are printed in this volume by permission of the Center for Policy Study.

The Inter-University Seminar on Armed Forces and Society is a group of scholars from the academic, military, and research fields whose interests include the study of subjects relevant to armed forces and society. Its main purpose is to provide a focal point for the exchange of ideas and viewpoints not only on the internal structure of the military establishment and its relationship with society, but also on a comparative approach to the military in both industrial and developing nations. The Inter-University Seminar is supported by the Russell Sage Foundation. The paper by Alain Rouquié was prepared for the *Revue Française de Science Politique* and is printed here by permission.

For information address:

SAGE PUBLICATIONS, INC.
275 South Beverly Drive
Beverly Hills, California 90212

SAGE PUBLICATIONS, INC.
St George's House / 44 Hatton Garden
London EC1N 8ER

International Standard Book Number 0-8039-0242-5(C); 0-8039-0249-2(P)

Library of Congress Catalog Card No. L.C. 73-77870

FIRST PRINTING

CONTENTS

INTRODUCTION

Philippe C. Schmitter

The publication of yet another volume on the military in Latin America, perhaps, requires some special justification. On no other regional topic have more pages been printed, lectures been given, opinions been voiced, oaths been uttered. To the stereotypic mind, military rule is virtually synonymous with political activity in Latin America and the skewed attention of the area's academic specialists have, no doubt, reinforced this impression. Why, then, risk adding one more voice to this already imbalanced chorus?

One justification, of course, might be *method*—the claim that the essays gathered in this volume represent some appreciable advance in the conduct of inquiry into the nature and role of Latin America's military establishments. While one might argue that some of them are more systematically comparative and explicitly oriented around clearly articulated research hypotheses, and some utilize more complex techniques of measurement and statistical association, this does not markedly distinguish them from several of the most recent scholarly monographs and articles on the topic. The general quality of this literature has improved considerably and we now have solidly documented and historically grounded case-studies of some national military establishments[1] and a few general, systematically comparative inquiries.[2] In fact, much of what is contained in this volume constitutes both a reaffirmation and reaction to these efforts, as well as to those "first generation," broadly speculative and more descriptive studies of the late 1950s and early 1960s.[3]

Another possible raison d'être for this volume might be rooted in *theory*—the pretense that the authors combined herein are engaged in some singular and more advanced conceptional synthesis which unifies the efforts of scholars working across disciplines and methodologies. A cursory glance no further than the table of contents would prove that this is not the case. Eclecticism in vocabulary, approach, case base, data sources, time period and so forth was not only tolerated but encouraged. Beyond the fact that they were selected to represent three broad areas of inquiry: the *political function* of direct military rule, the *policy consequences* of internal military intervention and external military aid and the *prospective impact* of both on regional and global political systems, initially, the authors were left to their own disciplinary and personal inclinations as to how to deal with their broad mandates.

With one exception,[4] the papers collected in this Volume III of the War, Revolution and Peacekeeping Series have not been published before and were aired for the first time at a conference sponsored by the Arms Control and Foreign Policy Seminar of the Center for Policy Study and held at the University of Chicago, on May 26-27, 1972. While the spirited discussion and exchange which occurred there between those giving papers[5] and those serving as commentators[6] may have contributed to some synthesizing of perspectives and mutual responsiveness in methods, themes and inferences, the resultant product is still far from any interdisciplinary and/or interpersonal theoretical unity. At this stage of our inquiry into these topics, any such synthesis would be premature and artificial and probably result in some bland product based on the least common denominator of prevailing "wisdom."

The most plausible justification for this collection of essays rests on *substantive originality* and *critical perspective*—the extent to which they enter previously unexamined areas and/or to which they challenge and force us to revise our presently established understanding of a given topic.

Perhaps, the most obvious manifestation of this sort of recasting and rethinking occurs in Rouquié's article, but its central theme—that a series of recent changes in domestic setting and external context may have greatly modified the political role of Latin American militaries—is echoed by several others. Rouquié argues that previous speculation which tended to identify overt military rule either with preservation of the *status quo* or moderate reform-mongering and to assume that such efforts were exceptional, transient and self-liquidating may be quite out-moded. Relying intensively on the Peruvian and (abortive) Bolivian cases,[7] he specifies a number of conditions which may be affecting nearly all military establishments in the region, encouraging them to play the role of protracted populist authoritarian modernizers, "anti-imperialist revolutionists from above."[8] He even suggests that those more conservative and dependent militaries already in power (e.g., Brazil) may become "Peruvianized" through internal factionalism into a more revolutionary and nationalist perspective.

Another substantive issue raised by Rouquié and analyzed in different ways by Schmitter and Kurth is the nature and impact of external dependence upon national militaries. Here, his argument is quite subtle, suggesting that identical or similar foreign inputs, e.g., equipment, loans, training, strategic "advice," may produce quite divergent outcomes, depending on the presence or absence of relatively autonomous indigenous political factors. He also speculates that recent changes in the balance of power of regional and global international systems are beginning to affect national level behavior, opening up ranges of policy response heretofore unimaginable.

Weaver in his article grapples with one of the most contentious and confused issues in the literature on the Latin American military: its class base. He approaches the problem not through the social origins or ideological propensities of the officer corps, but through an examination of the policy outputs and social consequences of overt military domination of the decision-making process. He shunts aside the simplistic assertions that the military are the guardians of traditional upper class prerogatives or the defenders of new middle class privileges. Through a detailed, paired-comparison of Bolivia and Brazil, he asks what did two types of military regime (populist and anti-populist) actually do with political power once they had seized it and who appeared to benefit from their acts. His finding that in this pair of supposedly different regime-types the same internal and external clients benefited from policy initiatives may not be fully documented and entirely convincing, but it does serve to focus future debate more clearly. Weaver also contributes an extensive and intelligent criticism of another technique which has been used to infer the effect of different regime-types: comparative analysis of aggregate data; and concludes with some suggestions for an improved "political economy model" for assessing policy impacts.

Schmitter's article is, in a sense, an example of how a political economy model and econometric estimation procedures can be brought to bear on analyzing and evaluating policy performance in a specific issue-area. He focuses on levels of domestic military spending as the dependent variable and inductively explores the extent to which they appear to vary with changes in such indogenous variables as resource availability, military intervention and political instability and such exogeneous variables as dependence on foreign (U.S.) military aid and domestic military spending in adjacent, "competing" countries. Replicating his analysis with both cross-sectional and longitudinal techniques, differing data bases and time periods, Schmitter arrives at some fairly compelling empirical generalizations: domestic resource availability predicts most of the variance in domestic military spending, but sporadic military intervention tends to raise it even further; political instability has no measurably significant relation with how much is spent on defense; U.S. military aid is appreciably correlated with higher than anticipated domestic military spending (with one deviant case: Peru); the evidence for widespread dyadic arms spending races in Latin America is weak and inconclusive. When these factors are combined, Schmitter derives a single policy model for military spending in Latin America—generalizable across five of the six units subjected to detailed analysis over time (1950-70)—which tends to reinforce with quantitative evidence some of the previous, more qualitative, remarks by Rouquié and Weaver on the policy significance of military rule (irrespective of sub-type) and external dependence.

Arms control is a prospective regional policy which has barely attracted political or scholarly attention in Latin America. Geoffrey Kemp approaches this issue from a novel direction. Setting aside for speculative purposes the common assumption that failure to gain agreement on regional arms limitations is merely a problem of lack of political will-power and related symbolic concerns, he penetrates to the core of the military-strategic issues at stake and analyzes in considerable detail the force capabilities and geostrategic setting involved. Implicitly, he rejects the notion that Latin American military forces have exclusively symbolic and/or internal repressive functions and suggests the sort of calculation which would have to be made in order to ensure relative balances in external security between neighboring and potentially conflicting countries. In the process, he discusses the rule of external arms suppliers to the region—the U.S., Europe and the Soviet Union—and, in so doing, makes a number of paradoxical and counterintuitive observations about the impact of different types of weapons systems. While Kemp provides no easy formulae for balanced limitation agreements in Latin America, he does succeed in making explicit the geostrategic foundations upon which any eventual agreement must rest.

James Kurth, in the concluding article, emphasizes a factor which has appeared in virtually all the preceeding ones: the nature and impact of external dependence. Explicit attention to the consequences of assymetry in political power, economic exchange and cultural relations between the United States and the Latin American republics has increased of late among scholars, so much so that references to *dependencia externa* have become almost cant. Virtually every observable and conceivable negative outcome within the hemisphere has been attributed to it. Most of this speculation has inverted the concerns of classical theories of imperialism and focused on the impact of trade and investment by central capitalist economies upon their peripheral dependents as the principle culprit. Kurth, after discussing a wide range of foreign policy models and theories for explaining a "weak nation's politics" and "a great power's policies," focuses upon what he calls "hegemonial international systems" as an instrument for analysis. While one element defining these systems consists of unequal economic relations, their historical existence long antedates the emergence of industrial capitalism and, in the contemporary world, includes "post-capitalist" regional arrangements such as that between the Soviet Union and Eastern Europe. These hegemonial systems are composed of a multitude of interrelated cultural, social, economic, political, and military components which jointly serve to "overdetermine" a global relationship of structured inequality. Implicitly, Kurth is suggesting that those who have concentrated exclusively on the institutions and practices of capitalist expansion are overemphasizing one element to the exclusion of a host of others. Also, in so doing, they tend to ignore a range of historical analogues whose analysis might prove insightful for understanding the nature of United States-Latin American relations. Kurth proceeds to analyze the evolution of hegemonial international systems, paying particular attention to levels of economic development and social modernization, and to the degree of polarity in the global international system. He is, thus, able to place the United States-Latin American subsystem in its broadest historical context and to identify certain crucial aspects of its transformation. Interestingly, like Rouquié, Kurth concludes that this hegemonial system is currently in a stage of advanced decomposition and transformation, opening the spectre of wider regime and policy alternatives.

For the editor of a collection of essays—deliberately chosen to emphasize breadth of topical coverage and eclecticism in theoretical approaches—to claim to have discerned in them a substantial convergence of opinion seems manifestly implausible. He, therefore, absolves the assembled authors from any direct responsibility for the following summary remarks and invites the reader after he has completed the articles to judge for himself.

From the mid-1950s through the mid-1960s, Latin American military establishments went through a process of "Americanization." As in the much more intensive, expensive and well-publicized process of "Vietnamization," an external power (the United States) has sought to re-orient the functional role and strategic conception of dependent and peripheral national armed forces and to provide them with the organizational sutructures and military capabilities for exercising these new tasks. Viewed from the donor's perspective, the ultimate purpose of this effort was to ensure the persistence of political systems whose policies would not negatively affect his national interests, whether defined in economic, political or security terms. In addition, such an indirect transformation and penetration would serve to obviate the "necessity" for the more direct forms of intervention, especially physical commitment of troops, which had been used in the past and recently proven so costly elsewhere.

Viewed from the perspective of the recipient defense establishments, this influx of external support not only permitted them to update their military professional capabilities, but also to reaffirm their general functional and political roles. They responded directly by increasing their relative command over national economic resources, and indirectly by demanding greater influence in national decision-making.

In the short-run, this external transfusion of capabilities and tasks was successful for both "contracting parties." The gap between national military establishments and insurrectionary movements (actual or potential) widened to the benefit of the former. For the United States, presumptive Americanization in Latin America could be claimed to have prevented "one, two, three Vietnams" and the subsequent "necessity" for much more costly Vietnamization.

The authors of this volume suggest that this judgment of success may be premature and that the 1970s are likely to pose different challenges. In terms of *political function* and *policy consequence,* there is growing evidence that the recipient military establishments have become increasingly less willing to accept the subordinate and limited strategic posture which has accompanied external support. Having acquired a decisive edge in their capacity to exercise organized violence over civilian opponents (and allies), they are more likely to use their new organizational and weapons strength for different ends. Confronted with internally and externally imposed obstacles to their plans for "modernization from above," they may well respond with policies which diverge considerably from those advocated and promoted by the central, "donor" power, as evidenced most clearly by the Peruvian regime, but also sporadically by the military rulers of Panama, Ecuador, (ex-) Bolivia and (even) Brazil.

On the other hand, the donor, as it winds down its Vietnam commitment and yields to the continued pressure of its military-industrial complex, will find itself with vast quantities of materiel to sell or dispose of. Latin America, with its still basically outmoded and under-modernized military establishments, is likely to provide an attractive market-*cum*-dumping ground for these products.

In terms of *future perspectives,* different Latin American countries responding differentially to these contradictory pressures for increased autonomy and dependence may jeopardize what has, heretofore, been one of the most widely shared assumptions of the Latin American military problem—that national military capabilities will not be used to initiate international violence within the region or to acquire assymetric advantage by threats to weaker neighboring countries. The El Salvador-Honduras "Football War" may be a foreboding of events to come, rather than a ridiculous and irrational accident. As the former U.S. arms monopoly and imposed security umbrella shrinks in a decaying hegemonial system and the disparity in relative military capability increases between Latin American countries, it become difficult to believe that the armed forces of the region will confine themselves to the negative and thankless task of repressing internal dissidents or to the reflexive and unglamorous goal of protecting the continent against an increasingly less credible common external aggressor.

The editor of this volume is indebted to several people for its completion. My colleague, Morton Kaplan, provided the original impetus for convoking a conference on this topic and generously arranged for the necessary funds. Barbara Grau, Suzanne Geis and Barbara Marshall of the Arms Control and Foreign Policy Seminar and the Center for Policy Study guided it to a successful conclusion. The skill and dedication of Lucille McGill is everywhere evident in these typed pages. Without the gentle prodding and active encouragement of James Linger, seconded in the final staged by David Crider, this volume would never have appeared. Stephen Faye provided the translation of the Rouquié article, although the editor is responsible for its abridgment, and for the errors and omissions which, no doubt, persist in this volume.

FOOTNOTES

1. For example, Alfred C. Stepan, *The Military in Politics: Changing Patterns in Brazil* (Princeton: Princeton University Press, 1971); Robert A. Potash, *The Army and Politics in Argentina, 1928-1945* (Stanford: Stanford University Press, 1969); Lyle N. McAlister et al., *The Military in Latin American Sociopolitical Evolution: Four Case Studies* (Washington, D.C.: Center for Research in Social Systems, 1970); Roy Allen Hansen, *Military Culture and Organizational Decline: A Study of the Chilean Army* (Ph.D. dissertation, University of California, Los Angeles, 1967); Luigi Einaudi, *The Peruvian Military: A Summary Political Analysis* (Santa Monica: The Rand Corporation, April 1969); Liisa North, *Civil-Military Relations in Argentina, Chile and Peru* (Berkeley: Institute of International Studies, 1966); Ronald M. Schneider, *The Political System of Brazil: The Emergence of a "Modernizing" Authoritarian Regime* (New York: Columbia University Press, 1971); Marvin Goldwert, *Democracy, Militarism and Nationalism in Argentina, 1930-1966* (Austin: University of Texas Press, 1972); Carlos A. Astiz and José Z. Garcia, "The Peruvian Military: Achievement Orientation, Training and Political Tendencies," *Western Political Quarterly,* XXV (December 1972), pp. 667-85.

2. For example, Philippe C. Schmitter, "Military Intervention, Party Competitiveness and Public Policy in Latin America: 1950-1967," in M. Janowitz and J. van Doorn (eds.), *On Military Intervention* (Rotterdam: Rotterdam University Press, 1971), pp. 425-506; and Eric A. Nordlinger, "Soldiers in Mufti: The Impact of Military Rule upon Economic and Social Change in the Non-Western States," *American Political Science Review,* 64 (December 1970), pp. 1131-48 emphasize policy consequences; Luigi Einaudi and Alfred C. Stepan, *Latin American Institutional Development: Changing Military Perspectives in Peru and Brazil* (Santa Monica, The Rand Corporation, 1971); Elizabeth H. Hyman, "Soldiers in Politics: New Insights on Latin American Armed Forces," *Political Science Quarterly,* LXXXVII, 3 (September 1972), pp. 401-18; Martin C. Needler, "Political Development and Military Intervention in Latin America," *American Political Science Review,* LX (September, 1966), pp. 1131-48 and Robert Putnam, "Towards Explaining Military Intervention in Latin American Politics," *World Politics,* XX (October 1967), pp. 83-110 deal primarily with the background to military seizures of power. Also see Robert E. Dowse, "The Military and Political Development," in C. Leys (ed.), *Politics and Change in Developing Countries* (Cambridge: Cambridge University Press, 1969) and Edward Feit, *The Armed Bureaucrats* (Boston: Houghton Mifflin, 1973) for studies which place Latin America in a more general comparative perspective.

3. For example, John J. Johnson, *The Military and Society in Latin America* (Stanford: Stanford University Press, 1964); Edwin Lieuwen, *Arms and Politics in Latin America*

(New York: Praeger, 1961); *ibidem, Generals vs. Presidents, Neo-Militarism in Latin America* (New York: Praeger, 1964); José Nun, "A Latin American Phenomenon: The Middle-Class Military Coup," in J. Petras and M. Zeitlin (eds.), *Latin America: Reform or Revolution?* (New York: Fawcett, 1968); S. E. Finer, *The Man on Horseback* (New York: Praeger, 1962); I. L. Horowitz, "The Military Elites" in S. M. Lipset and A. Solari (eds.) *Elites in Latin America* (New York: Oxford University Press, 1967), pp. 146-89. A useful summary of this literature is Lyle N. McAlister, "Recent Research and Writings on the Role of the Military in Latin America," *Latin American Research Review,* II (1966), pp. 5-36.

4. Alain Rouquié's essay initially appeared in the *Revue Française de Science Politique,* Vol. XXI, Nos. 5 and 6 (October and December 1971), pp. 1045-69, 1234-59.

5. Limitations of time and space prevented utilization of the two other papers presented at the conference: Stephen S. Kaplan, "United States Military Aid to Brazil and the Dominican Republic: Its Nature, Objectives and Impact" and James L. Payne, "Some Determinants of Military Coups in Latin America."

6. Discussants at the conference included David V. Edwards, Edmund S. Finegold, Michael Mihalka, Richard C. Rankin, John Saxe-Fernández, César Sereseres and Miles D. Wolpin. Michael Francis and Morris Janowitz served as panel chairmen.

7. In his initial article M. Rouquié also dealt extensively with the Panamanian military regime and its policy initiatives.

8. For a suggestive treatment of earlier such regimes (in Japan and Turkey), see Ellen Kay Trimberger, "A Theory of Elite Revolutions," *Studies in Comparative International Development,* Vol. VII, No. 3 (Fall 1972), pp. 191-207.

I

CHANGING FUNCTIONS OF MILITARY RULE

MILITARY REVOLUTIONS AND NATIONAL INDEPENDENCE IN LATIN AMERICA: 1968-1971*

Alain Rouquié

FROM "NATIONAL REVOLUTIONS" TO "REVOLUTIONARY NATIONALISMS"

Military interventions in the political life of
Latin American nations seem to have changed recently.
It was the Peruvian coup d'etat of October 3, 1968 which
first appeared to open the way to a new type of military
regime. General Ovando's rise to power in Bolivia on
September 26, 1969 confirmed the Peruvian experience.
In a very different geopolitical setting, the style of
action adopted in Panama by the government of the
"National Guard," born in October, 1968, showed enough
similarities with the foregoing regimes for one to
attribute a continental dimension to a phenomenon which
might have seemed geographically limited.

---

*Due to space limitations, the editor has had to
abridge portions of this article and to eliminate
numerous footnotes. In particular, several interesting
portions dealing with Panama have been removed, as well

2

The original character of these new military governments was not due to the mechanisms of seizure of power.[1] In the three cases concerned, the army intervened as a unit and as an institution, just as it had Argentina in 1943 and 1966. These were "institutional coups d'etat" and not "pronunciamentos" in favor of a daring general or a popular colonel. Finally, although apparently standard since the Brazilian "Revolution" of 1964, the protagonists of these "institutional coups d'Etat" never considered their intervention in political life as provisional, or rather they refused to present the government they had installed as a transitory regime between two civilian administrations. Rejecting elections and rapid return to "constitutional normalcy", those responsible for these regimes set their goals more or less precisely and intended to give themselves enough time to reach them.

In fact, the apparent novelty of the Bolivian and Peruvian regimes lies elsewhere. It hardly matters that in the Peruvian case a junta of generals is both a collegial-type executive and a council of ministers, while in Bolivia the army delegated electoral and sole

---

as a lengthy section on the public policy ramifications of military rule in Peru and Bolivia. These can, of course, be found in the original version of the article which appeared in two parts in the Revue Française de Science Politique, XXI, No. 5 and No. 6 (October 1971 and December 1971), pp. 1045-69, 1234-59.

constituent powers to a president chosen from its own
ranks who then surrounded himself with civilian ministers. That these regimes would call themselves "revolutionary" is not new either, since the word "revolution"
has long been the noble term for "political discon-
tinuities" or "unconstitutional changes in government."
The effort of these governments to define themselves as
"nationalist" and to place themselves on the ideological
left is more significant. In practice, these new
military regimes attempt to control foreign economic
penetration, recuperate natural resources, and undertake certain reforms of existing structures in order to
accelerate social development. They show themselves to
be only moderately repressive vis-a-vis popular organizations: unions and parties on the left are neither
prohibited nor systematically persecuted. Finally, they
proclaim their desire to pursue international policies
more flexibly and less strictly aligned with the U.S.
Before examining more closely the real import of this
roughly sketched orientation, some remarks are in order
which place the meaning of these new regimes in the
context of the political interventions of Latin American
armies since 1960.

If one views the last decade, it seems evident
that the content of these "nationalist" regimes can not

be confused with the goals of those anti-revolutionary
coups d'Etat which marked Latin American history from
1962 to 1968. "De facto" governments established
themselves in Brazil and Argentina in April 1964 and
June 1966 by different means and in very different
social climates and brought together political contraction and social counter-revolution. Consequently,
they immobilized the existing order and limited popular
participation. These politically authoritarian and
economically liberal "national revolutions" opened their
doors to foreign interests and made themselves the
champions of an anti-communist crusade within, as well
as beyond, their borders. These supporters and loyal
allies of the dominant power freely identify their
fight against subversion with opposition to social
change. In this way one can understand why numerous
observers have been struck by the relative novelty of
military regimes in Peru and Bolivia.

In another way, the rupture with the recent past
is particularly flagrant in Bolivia where the army had
held power since November 1964,[2] and did not seem to
exercise it in a particularly progressive direction.
Are not the military, today's "revolutionaries" and
"nationalists" responsible not only for the execution
of Ernesto Guevara in October 1967, but also for the
bloody repression on numerous occasions in 1965 and

1967 of the miners of the Altiplano? General Ovando
Candia, who was placed in the presidency as a result of
the September 26, 1969 coup d'etat, had effectively
shared power with General Barrientos, head of State
since 1964. There is no doubt that by his presence he
gave his approval and that of the army to the repression
of the mining camps, just as he had done to the policy
of granting concessions to foreign companies which
characterized the presidency of Barrientos.

In Peru, one may recall the role that the army
played in squelching rural guerrillas in 1965. Certainly,
the previous military coup d'etat (July 1962) had been
ambiguous and if it is sometimes given a reformist
orientation, or at least an affirmed goal of modernization,[3] (especially after the eviction from the Junta
of General Pérez Godoy), it seems that within the
Peruvian army the active and radical wing found itself
a minority. This was shown by the failure of General
Juan Bossio Collas, Minister of the Interior for the
Junta, to rally support among his colleagues for his
projected "nationalist" reforms. Elsewhere, the
decisive support given by the army to Belaunde – Terry,
the "conservative-reformist" candidate of the Popular
Action Party during the 1963 elections, and the advantage he enjoyed in having the Peruvian Left placed "out
of the running" illustrates well the mood of the Peru-

vian general staff who were attracted to the wise
pragmatism of this moderate planner.[4] This at least
confirms that, also in 1962, the Peruvian army was
fairly removed from the the Nasser-like temptation with
which it was credited.[5]

Judging from the predominant political orientations
of the nine "successful" military coups d'Etat that
stretch from March 1962 to March 1968, it would appear
that Latin American armies were directly linked with
dominant social groups and others concerned with the
preservation of the status quo. In effect, of the nine
cases, only that of Bolivia, in 1964, could be considered politically ambiguous, if not neutral, in that
it involved personal conflicts and did not immediately
entail significant modification in the government's
behavior. In all the other cases, the army preventively
eliminated any government believed to be too weak
towards popular movements or communism, or else accused
of wanting to carry out "subversive" reforms as in the
Dominican Republic and Brazil.

These comparative indications are admittedly
summary. Nevertheless, one must not forget that Latin
American armies are less than prepared to direct progressive movements in the style of Ataturk or Nasser
since the definition of their specific mission within
an inter-American defense system notably weakens their

nationalist motivations--in some cases to the point of
obliteration. In effect, since the change of hemispheric defense strategy by the Kennedy Administration
in mid-1961 in response to Cuba, the emphasis placed
on internal security and the fight against subversion,
at the expense of the usual defense policy directed
against external aggression, transformed the military
institutions of Latin American countries into forces
of control and social conservation.[6] Admittedly, the
Western Hemisphere armies are not organically integrated, but their close practical coordination (which
does much further than the fairly loose instrument pre-
scribed by formal treaties) and relative dependence in
matters of equipment have reinforced a domination by
the Pentagon which takes many forms: training and
instruction of Latin American officers in specialized
schools in the U.S. or in the Canal Zone; technical
advisors and permanent military missions; financial
aid; sale, loan or rent of weaponry; and joint manoeuvres.
Finally, the diffusion of counter-guerrilla techniques
and of an "anti-insurrectional" military doctrine by
these diverse methods does not predispose these armies
to the role of a "popular avant-garde," or agent of
social progress and national liberation. The theory of
"ideological frontiers," elaborated jointly by the
Argentine and Brazilian staffs in 1965, is the logical

conclusion to such a process of "denationalization."[7] The nebulous "Western, Christian World" seems to have replaced the Nation-State in the hierarchy of loyalties to which the officer is professionally subjected.

Certain commentators have not hesitated to draw an extreme conclusion from this situation. If the Latin American armies are unconditionally opposed to all transformation and reform, it is conceivable that the modernization of Latin American societies and the social necessities of development will take place only through their elimination. Notable historical precedents give this thesis a certain plausibility; in Mexico, Bolivia and Cuba the only three agrarian revolutions were associated with the disappearance or dissolution of regular armies. Is the rupture of military support for social immobilism the necessary prerequisite for changes of some breadth or for the opening up of such archaic societies?[8]

Those in agreement with this thesis, however, seem to overlook the heterogeneity of the officer corps. Neither the professional defensive reflex, nor the immoderate taste for order and hierarchy, nor the counter-guerrila doctrine and apprenticeship at the school of Fort Gulick have made Latin American militaries uniformly and monolithically hostile to necessary reforms, or indifferent to national independence.

Within the period under consideration (i.e., without going back to Brazilian tenentismo or to the socialism of the young Chilean military during the 1920s, or to the durable alliance of the working class and the Argentine army under the guidance of General Perón), the presence of progressive sectors, of groups open to change or sensitive to popular pressures within the ranks of the Latin American armies is undeniable. Thus, in Guatemala, the "M.R. 13" and "F.A.R." guerrilla movements led by former lieutenant Yon Sosa and former second-lieutenant A. Turcios respectively, originated in 1960 from an unsuccessful military putsch against the conservative regime of Ydígoras Fuentes.[9] One could also cite the "Castrist" revolts of the Venezuelan navy in May 1962 at Carupano and in June of the same year at Puerto Cabello. It was an important fraction of the Dominican army that rebelled in 1965 under the command of Colonel Caamaño Deno against the Right wing triumvirate to reestablish the constitutional president, Juan Bosch, in power. Outside the Caribbean zone, it is worthy of mention that after the Brazilian coup in 1964, at least a thousand officers considered as outright "nationalists" or partisans of the "laborite" president were removed from the ranks and sometimes denied their civic rights for a ten-year period. Among them were a field marshal, more than a dozen generals,

and five admirals.[10]   Also, is it not surprising that
regular military officers have been relatively numerous
among the revolutionary cells fighting the dictatorship
of the field marshals.[11]

As the events have shown in each case, the
absence of political homogeneity in the armed forces
did not change their collective orientation or their
actions. Left-wing officers, when placed in subaltern
positions, must either submit or resign since internal
discipline is the main strength of the military institution in Latin America as elsewhere. Hence, these
officers, even in higher ranks, remain a minority and
are rejected by the defensive system with which they
conflict.

Under what national and international conditions
have nationalist military regimes emerged? How did the
"body guards" transform themselves into the "avant-garde
of the people?" Has one really gone from the defense
of "ideological frontiers" to that of "economic borders,"
and for what reasons have the military governments
become the champions of national independence while
justly accused at the same time of being particularly
sensitive to entreaties from Washington? If one chose
to characterize the military in Peru as "not like the
others," how is this national singularity possible when
"nationalist" officers are also in power in Bolivia and

Panama? Is this an exception to a new rule? It is
very tempting to extrapolate and draw some attractive
generalizations; even more so since, for once, it would
not be groundless. In effect, beyond irreductible
national peculiarities, the similarities of officer
corps in recruitment and training, as well as in their
common professional orientation and coordination of the
national staffs, invite posing the problem in continental terms.

However, this approach raises many questions. In
effect, if one is witnessing a general evolution of
Latin American armies, it is right to ask oneself, not
only what is the scope and size of such developments,
but also if the "palace or barrack revolutions" which
cropped up in Brazil and Argentina are really part of
this same mutation. Afterall, should not one see in
this phenomenon simply the local expression of a continental movement towards nationalism of which the
most significant manifestations might be the Joint
Declaration of Viña del Mar (May 1969), the resolute
defense of the 200 mile limit for national territorial
waters, and even the electoral victory of the People's
Unity coalition in Chile--among others?

To answer these questions, it would obviously be
preferable to analyze economic, social and political
situations country by country, to examine the position

of armed forces in each national situation, and to
locate the "military class" in the social configuration
as well as in the actual functioning of the political
system. However, we will limit ourselves to placing
the changing political role of the Latin American
armies within a framework which takes into account the
specificity of military institutions.[12] The functional
definition of armed forces, as the nation's instrument
of defense and the upholder of its foreign policy, warns
against separating their study from the international
context. Too many "eminent" descriptions and comparative interpretations have forgotten this cardinal
dimension of the problem.[13]

We believe on the contrary that in the last
analysis, external contingency is the decisive variable
in the orientation of military interventions. This is
neither a paradox nor a truism, nor even less an attempt
at a monist explanation. If one takes into account the
"extroverted" character of Latin American societies as
well as   the existence of roughly parallel historical
evolution within the region, beyond the diversity of
the nations and their political isolation, one cannot
help considering that external factors have played a
determining role, at least with regard to long-term
orientations. One can single out two major periods of
differing political orientation since the beginning of

the "military era" (1930): on the one hand, a pre-
dominantly "nationalist" period from 1930 to about
1952-53 coincides with a series of international events
(Great Depression, World War, Korean War) which
increased the bargaining capacity of Latin American
countries and the autonomy of their armies; on the
other hand, after 1962--with a short "demilitarized"
interval--the hemispheric climate of the cold war
tended to distract armies from independent national
projects. From 1968 on, we are perhaps witnessing a
distinctly new phase, the scope and the causes of which
remain to be determined through the analysis of processes linking the characteristic internal components
of each society and the dynamics of external forces.

REVOLUTIONARY NATIONALISMS AND MILITARY DOMINATION

> [Here the editor has removed a lengthy analysis
> of the domestic and foreign policies followed
> by the Peruvian, Bolivian and Panamanian
> military regimes.]

NATIONAL DEADLOCKS AND CONTINENTAL DETENTE

The determination of the new Latin American military regimes to defend national independence can be
accounted for by the particular situations of the armed
forces in their respective societies. Certainly, a
cluster of internal changes made the evolution of the
armed forces possible and gave it a "nationalist"
direction. But it no less true that this mutation goes
far beyond the arena of national political systems in

both its causes and its effects. Perhaps, instead of
thinking of the "military sector" of the state apparatus as one of the many groups competing for the control
of power in societies without a hegemonic elite,[14] it
would be better to concentrate on the decisive and
dynamic contradiction between the mission of Latin
American armies (which is by definition national) and
their distinctive character as transnational institutions confronted by the exigencies of development.[15]
This is, at least, the perspective through which we
will examine the situation of the armies in Peru and
Bolivia.

THE PERUVIAN REALITY AND THE MISSION
OF THE ARMED FORCES

It would be tempting to rewrite the contemporary
history of Peru by asking what would have happened if,
hypothetically, dramatic events such as the Trujillo
massacres in 1932, had not definitely poisoned the
relations between the most powerful Peruvian political
party, the APRA, and the military. This apparently
inexpiable and reciprocal hate between the popular party
and the military was certainly important to the political course of the Peruvian Army. The memory of the
Trujillo massacres was never forgotten by the army in
whose view the APRA appears as a violent and totalitarian revolutionary organization from which Peru must
be protected. This memory is nurtured in military

school[16] and the "anti-aprism" remains lively among
young officers to whom the Trujillo incidents mean
nothing. APRA, the "first Peruvian party," did not, in
effect, hesitate to foment putsches and to encourage
junior officers and troops to rebel against their
leaders in order to get out of the "catacombs" of
underground politics. In the early 50's, APRA thus
appeared to the army as an element of "dissociation"
and of indiscipline--a direct threat to the military
institutions.

However, in 1956, APRA decided to adopt a policy
of cordiality towards the right in order to move out
into the open. While this policy of "coexistence"
compares with that adopted by most of the "social-
democratic" parties of the continent which thus have
moderated their revolutionary zeal and suppressed their
anti-imperialism,[17] it does also reflect the evolution
of the social forces behind the APRA. The Party of
Haya de la Torre moderated its public demands, and the
old "Revolutionary Alliance," which proposed to liberate
"Indo-America" from imperialism enjoyed the sympathy
of U.S. government circles along with other "anti-
communist" reformist parties of the continent, as shown
by the attitude of the American government during the
July 1962 coup aimed at barring the head of the APRA
from the presidency.[18]

It is interesting that the army kept its distance
in relation to both the oligarchy and the status quo
while the "wiser" APRA fell into the hands of traditional managing groups and received the approval of the
U.S. This political run-around is not one of the lesser
peculiarities of the Peruvian situation. Today, the
tenaciously bitter military oppose their veto to the
"Trojan Horse of Imperialism" just as they fought the
"Sect of Native Bolchevism" in the past. Of course,
the evolution of the army was not determined by simple
opposition to its historical adversary. There cannot
be any mechanical correlation between the position of
these two dominant organizations of the Peruvian
political system, but one should not assume that the
anti-Aprista reflex--a powerful element in the unity of
the Peruvian army--necessarily waned as nationalist
tendencies waxed. In fact, nationalism and "anti-
Aprism" are inseparable. Furthermore, one cannot overlook the fact that other political groups define themselves essentially as a function of and in relation to
the APRA and that the relations between Peruvian officers
and political circles always come back to this fundamental cleavage.

In this way one can grasp the important role
attributed by many observers to the famous CAEM (Institute of Superior Military Studies) which some have seen

as the main source of changes in attitude among officers
and as proof of the singularity of the Peruvian situation. It is true that this center of learning and
research, which has served to complete the general
knowledge of superior officers and the military
knowledge of important functionaries since its incep-
tion in 1952 under the presidency of General Odria,[19]
has helped to reconcile officers with civilian political
circles and to make them aware of Peruvian economic and
social problems. However, one should not be misled
since similar institutions exist also in Rio and Buenos
Aires and their ideological influence in a progressive
sense has been modest. It is only due to the presence
of a majority of "radicalized" intellectuals among the
professors and civilian collaborators of the CAEM that
this institution was able to play a decisive role in
the enlightenment of military circles to the problems
of external dependence and social development. If one
studied the political complexion of civilians taking
part in the CAEM, one would not only find a reflection
of the power relations which exist at the heart of the
Peruvian "intellectual class," but above all the
absence of representatives or sympathizers of APRA.
This ostracism leveled against the largest Peruvian
party allowed a reconciliation between the "uniformed
intellectuals" and the "little left wing," or "hot

heads," of the Popular Action Party of President
Belaunde.

The military preferred to deal with politicians
attached with those parties which decided to carry the
"Aprist torch" against the APRA from 1956 on, such as
Popular Action, Christian Democracy, and the Progressive
Social Movement. Perhaps one can see here also that
the "radicalization" of the involved intellectuals, if
it corresponded to the correct tensions of Peruvian
society, is also not unrelated to the spectacular
reorientation of the APRA. Of course, this does not
underestimate either the appeal to the military by
reformers who had lost hope of coming to power by way
of elections, or the deep affinities which may exist
between the organizing mentality of the Peruvian
colonels and the technocratic impatience of an ideological pressure group like the Progressive Social
Movement.[20]

Among the immediate causes of the mutation of
Peruvian militarism, the activity of the ex-president
Belaunde, who was thrown out by the military in 1968,
has been justifiably emphasized. The political style
of Belaunde, "the architect," combined a rhetorical
exaltation of national identity and the ideology of
development which could not have left the military
indifferent. Whether they were slogans or realities,

incantations or programs, "Fertilization of the Economy,"
"Peru for Peruvians," "the Winning of the Interior"
were themes which were endlessly repeated from 1956 on
and which helped to bring together the officers of
 Popular Action and to hasten the "nationalitarian"[21]
maturation of the Peruvian army.

All these converging phenomena are situated in
and take their meaning from the great changes taking
place in Peru during the sixties.[22] Here, one can distinguish two inverse processes whose coincidence is
enough to make the critical differences of Peruvian
society into explosive issues. On one hand, progress
in all forms of communication provided mobility and a
growing "homogenization" of a very divided nation by
drawing into contact formerly isolated social sectors,
facilitating the awareness of a common destiny, and of
forgotten problems and awakening aspirations to progress and immediate change. Simultaneously, on the
other hand, the imbalance between the listless and
archaic interior and the narrow, prosperous coast was
dangerously enhanced.

The blindness of the "coastal" elites to the gap
between the "two Perus" was all the more evident to
the cadres of the army who through their garrisons all
over the territory and their direct contact, through
conscription, with Indians excluded from national

life[23] had reinforced their conviction that the "dualism" of Peruvian society was an element of national weakness, notably in terms of defense and security. In addition, one should take into account the geographical origins of Peruvian officers who are mostly provincial and distrustful of the managerial classes in Lima whose irresponsible frivolity they disapprove of.[24]

A great number of these internal elements are ambivalent and could have made the cadres of the Peruvian army lean in the direction of a vigilant defense of the status quo when faced with the dangers and tensions of unequal development. This did not happen because a new element intervened to reemphasize the role of the military. The fight against rural guerrillas was that new element. Not that the "guerrilla trauma" was for so many officers a "Road to Damascus" at the end of which their new mission appeared to them, but it did catalyze an otherwise improbable reaction.

Let us review the facts.[25] Starting in 1960, sporadic peasant agitation was intensified in the Sierra and was accompanied by the occupation of land and of establishment of unions, notably in the valley of the Convención where they were headed by Hugo Blanco, a Trotskyite. These were not guerrilla movements, but "invasions" of haciendas did not proceed without violence and the movement spread to create a fully insurrectional situation[26] which partially escaped the control of the police and the Civil Guard. The army, forced to intervene, openly expressed its disdain for police functions, which were inevitably unpopular and which "went beyond the limits of their specific mission."[27] Things went differently after the establishment of some guerrilla _focos_ directed by young dissidents of the APRA and the Communist Party in 1965. Military circles themselves pressed the president to take exceptional measures in order to repress the "Castrist" attempts as soon as possible. The Peruvian army, according to its official spokesman[28] and their opponents,[29] used the most modern techniques of anti-subversive warfare (psychological activity, bombing, napalm) to liquidate the guerrillas. However, the Peruvian military remained relatively discrete about their victory accomplished by means and methods out of proportion with the firepower and persistence of their opposition.

An army which refuses to be reduced to a role of police must have experienced feelings approximating professional humiliation when it discovered the true nature of the anti-subversive war in the field. The ideological illusion of a national war against an enemy infiltrated or directed from abroad did not stand up in reality. To the extent that one is able to reconstruct the motivations and the proceedings of its cadres, the Peruvian army became aware that "revolutionary war" is a form of civil war and that the doctrine of anti-guerrilla combat learned at Fort Gulick or in the U.S. was elaborated by the North American army for operations abroad where the entire population is identical with the enemy. There is little information on the discomfort which apparently existed among the troops, composed of peasants, during these "pacification" campaigns. Regardless, the Peruvian officers, their corporate honor and national sentiment having been affected, became doubtful of the nature of their mission. For the old members of the CAEM, it was clear that the military methods were not enough to suppress agrarian rebellion. It was necessary to go to the root of the disorder to defuse the peasant powder keg.

The questioning of anti-communist ideology brought by the military missions, joint manoevres, and counter-guerrilla training is all the more natural since the Peruvian military, like their counterparts in other countries of the lower-continent, have a professional reason to be discontent with the U.S. policy. In effect, since the redefinition of the hemispheric defense strategy, the U.S. refused unconditionally to deliver heavy, modern armaments which would have given their southern "allies" an acceptable level of technical

effectiveness by international criteria. The North
American governments, on the basis of their new policy
of continental defense, refused to sell until recently
anything more than light arms and vehicles intended for
the maintenance of public order.[30] Supported in this
matter by Congress and public opinion, they refused to
deliver classical and powerful armaments which could
serve, in their view, to disturb the peace of the
hemisphere and, therefore, to weaken their flanks.

In 1965, the Peruvian army (which thinks of itself
as under-equipped), had difficulty accepting the subordinate functions which the interamerican division of
military labor seemed to assign to it. A certain resent-
ment towards the U.S. resulted and this is certainly
not unrelated to their definition of a national project
of development. The response of the Peruvian general
command to the U.S. refusal and then to their later
agreement to furnish certain types of armaments was the
first stage of a policy of national affirmation. The
Peruvian response was to turn to Europe to obtain
modern armaments.[31] In this way, not only did Peru
free itself of its only supplier of military equipment,
but the purchase of advanced weaponry helped to weaken
the antisubversive obsession and divert the army from
internal security. Formerly, this had led it to
identify its military objectives with the preservation

of the status quo or, in other words, with the
interests of the local oligarchies and foreign companies.
Paradoxically, the alternative of "butter or guns"
seemed excluded by the logic of the situation. "Un-
productive" expenditures, by reinforcing the State and
strictly national motivations, may accompany social
progress in a so-called "underdeveloped" country under
military domination. It goes without saying that this
variable cannot be isolated from the global situation.
Purchase of Mirage planes is no proof of nationalist
political orientation.

THE BOLIVIAN ARMY BETWEEN THE CHACO AND COLD WARS

The political history of the Bolivian army summarizes the general stages for most of the armies of
the southern continent and illustrates their actual
contradictions by magnifying them. The National
Revolutionary Movement (MNR) dispossessed of its
electoral victory by a military junta in 1951, came to
power in 1952 during a rebellion in which some units of
the regular army were beaten by an improvised militia
of miners and urban workers. The first act of the new
president, Paz Estenssoro (head of the MNR), was to
practically dissolve the army considered as the supporter
of the "tin barons" and the mainstay of the unpopular
regimes which had governed the country for the previous
six years. After the retirement of 80 per cent of the

officers and the closing of the military school, the
army disappeared to be replaced in a quasi-spontaneous
fashion by a militia of miners and peasants who intended
on defending—and, if need be, accelerate—the revolution. But fear that these militia might escape the
control of the party in power moved the government,
under the influence of the right wing of the MNR, to
restore the regular army. The government of Paz
Estenssoro claimed it meant to preserve the accomplish-
ments of the revolution from a resurgence of reactionary
militarism by various procedures such as recruitment of
officer candidates according to social and political
criteria, and the organized political instruction and
implantation of the party in the army.[32]

The economic situation quickly made these wise
precautions inoperative. A dramatic drop in price of
tin in 1953 having provoked an exceptionally serious
financial and economic crisis, the government solicited
U.S. aid without worrying about its nationalist pro-
clamations or its revolutionary objectives. From
that date on, the U.S. contributed directly to the
reduction of the Bolivian budgetary deficit. Obviously,
this aid was matched with certain conditions: the
monetary stabilization plan of 1955, the Oil Code and
the "triangular operations," which from 1961 onward
have financially salvaged the nationalized tin mines

(COMIBOL) with the help of American and German capital, are some examples. The tin crisis that broke the pact between the government and the miners made the rapid reorganization of a regular army all the more necessary. North American instructors were closely associated with this task which was facilitated by generous credits made available by the Pentagon.

After the coup d'etat in November 1964, which removed the MNR from power, the "reinstating" military did not return to the "revolutionary" identity (as promised in 1952), but to repression and the economic "realism" of the old tin magnates.[33] The Bolivian army maintained this attitude until 1969, even if the solemn "pacts" of the military with the peasants gave the impression of an "agrarian populism"[34] which was inconsistent and unsettled despite the personal presence of General Barrientos in Cochabamba. In 1961-1962, the essentially anti-communist (and more generally counter-revolutionary) orientation of the North American military aid program grafted itself onto this national situation and was reinforced by the subsequent appearance of a guerrilla foco.

It is no less true that another image of the Bolivian army exists. In this view, the antimilitarist reflex is not widespread in the civilian population and the nostalgia of an alliance between the army and

the mining and peasants is evoked among numerous
officers. The Chaco war, where the Bolivian army was
defeated by Paraguay (1932-1935), still represents the
brotherly and heroic ideal to which nationalist officers
aspire. The equality and reciprocal discovery of con-
scripts from the small urban bourgeoisie, miners, and
Indian peasants, and the social mixing which took place
on the battlefield did much to further the formation of
a Bolivian national conscience.[35] Although it was the
veterans and reserve officers of Chaco who started the
Nationalist Revolutionary Movement (whose history
identifies itself since then with that of Bolivia),
nevertheless the humiliation of the defeat has affected
even officers who did not live through it.[36]

This political tradition of the Chaco--popular,
reformist, anti-oligarchic, and tainted with xenophobia
--was piously maintained at the heart of the army.
General Barrientos, himself an old militant of the MNR,
never ceased to invoke the "martyrs" of national independence, Busch and Villaroel, henceforth inscribed in
the National Pantheon, even while opening the country up
to foreign penetration and smothering miner demands
with violence. The discrepancy between this "patriotic"
cult and the actual role of the Bolivian army after
1961 is striking. Reorganized and instructed by U.S.
missions, formed by counter-guerrilla courses, this new

army sent its rangers against the discontented miners
in the name of the fight against communism before
wiping out the "guerrillero" center of "Che" Guevara
with the help of American counselors.[37] Their well-
founded impression of having lost contact with the
popular masses made military officers fearful of being
pulled down with the regime founded in November 1964
and of risking, if a new revolution intervened, the
dissolution of the army which, this time, might not be
temporary.

If the nationalist wing of the army won in 1969,
it was not only from opportunism but because of the union
of new political facts with old reflexes. Thus, one
misunderstands the agreement of its different tendencies
on an independent oil policy if one does not evoke once
again the mystique of the Chaco and the extreme sen-
sitivity of Bolivian opinion, and of the military in
particular, to mentions of oil since the bloody conflict with Paraguay in which the issue of oil was clear
to everyone.[38] Since 1966 for the first time oil
represents an important export product. By virtue of
the liberal legislation of the new code, the royalties
are distinctly inferior to the heretofore classical
"fifty-fifty" split, and the Bolivian treasury
extracted meager profits from this new national production. When announcing the nationalization of the

Bolivian Gulf Oil Company, General Ovando did not miss
the opportunity to point out that, following this
revolutionary decision, "the blood spilled on the sands
of Chaco were not in vain."[39]

The discovery of guerrillas in the first months of
1967 and the exceptional interest taken in them by the
North American security services because of the presumed
presence of the most illustrious of the guerrilleros,
constituted a new element of discontent and of unity for
for the Bolivian army. In effect, from 1967 onward the
direct presence of U.S. advisers in the field was added
to the U.S. aid which had made the rapid reorganization
strength of the Bolivian armed forces possible.[40] Perhaps forgetting the Bolivia is one of the countries
most dependent on U.S. aid for its military expenditures in Latin America,[41] Bolivian officers, and those
from the Chaco in particular who were still numerous in
the staff headquarters, had their professional pride
hurt by the interference of foreign officers in operations which the national army could have, in its view,
carried out on its own. In addition, the poorly tolerated presence of numerous American functionaries (information services, "technical advisers," Peace Corps,
A.I.D., etc.) which gave the impression of overriding
ministeries and even of penetrating the Presidency,[42]
created a certain discomfort even among those officers
least suspect of systematic antiyankism." "The incred-

able affair of the diary of Guevara and of the presence of a questionable person suspected of being a
double agent at the head of the Ministery of the
Interior sufficiently confirmed the strange climate of
Bolivia during "the hour of Che."[43]

If Ernesto Guevara did not succeed in creating
"many Viet Nams" in Latin America as he had wished, his
strategy at least resulted in engaging Bolivia in a
process of an enlarged Vietnam type of "military col-
laboration." The engagement which leads to civil war
with foreign participation was clear to the Bolivian
staff. The professional nationalist reflex, even if
negative, was no less concerned with the future.

THE INTERAMERICAN "THAW" AND THE INTERAMERICAN
MILITARY SYSTEM

In fact, these parallel evolutions towards an
increased autonomy of national defense systems were
produced in a favorable external contingency. The
mutation that we have described would have undoubtedly
been impossible without a prior change in the
atmosphere over the continent. It was the new configuration of forces acting in the Western Hemisphere
which permitted the undeniable growth of nationalism
which ran through the southern continent and liberated
the progressive sectors at the core of the national
armies.

This hemispheric "thaw" corresponded to modifica-

tions in the local strategy of the two great powers,
and more precisely to changes in attitudes of the two
poles of tension: Cuba and the U.S. Without under-
estimating either the diplomatic importance of the
solution adopted by the American states at the Caracas
conference in 1954 on the Communist problem, or
"Operation Guatemala" which put it into practice a few
months later, one could say that the cold war didn't
really make its appearance in Latin America until the
very moment when a first period of "peaceful coexistence" was initiated in the worldwide diplomatic system.
The first serious differences between Havana and
Washington were in effect contemporaneous with the
Krushchev-Eisenhower talks at Camp David in September
1959. Castro's breaking off with the U.S. and the
reconciliation of Cuba with the Soviet Union opened an
entirely new and unexpected diplomatic era among the
American countries. The existence of a state tied to
the socialist camp within 90 miles of Florida, henceforth, affected all inter-American relations and, in
particular, the military system of the U.S. and its
"southern allies." The tension provoked by this new
international situation produced some critical situations, such as the Bay of Pigs invasion of 1961 or, even
more so, the missile crisis of October 1962 which had
repercussions in all of the states in the region.

Furthermore, since the Caribbean crisis of 1962, this tension has not appeared to subside despite an agreement between the U.S.S.R. and the United States which banned all Soviet military establishments within the U.S. security zone. The U.S. intervention in the Dominican civil war, in order to avoid "another Cuba," is proof enough of this.

The Cuban government, which since 1960 has been accused of "exporting" its revolution, seemed by 1967 to want to "embrace less in order to grasp more." The conference of the Latin American Organization of Solidarity (OLAS) held in July and August 1967 reduced its ambitions for revolutionary ecumenism on the American continent. One could say that the OLAS conference was in fact an end-point--an official consecration of the many attempts to establish "guerrillero" cells according to Castro's Latin American strategy--and not a point of departure or, even less, an effective war machine. Furthermore, the failure in Bolivia of the attempt to make the Andes a South American Sierra Maestra marked the beginning of a Cuban retreat and symbolized the end of an era.

On the revolutionary calendar instituted at the entry of the "rebel army" into Havana, each year is given a name suggesting Cuba's main objective and policy. 1968 was the "Year of the Heroic Guerrilla."

Henceforth, Cuba embarked on policies of withdrawal.
Although in 1965 international problems and continental
policy prevailed over internal problems, this movement subsequently was reversed. 1969 was the "Year of
the Critical Effort;" 1970 that of "Ten Million Tons"
of sugar; 1971, "the Year of Productivity." Castro has
abandoned, at least temporarily, the hope of creating
"many Vietnams" or of establishing a second Cuba in
Latin America. Instead, under the pressure of serious
economic difficulties, he has rallied his forces to
build "socialism in a single country."

The pressure of the U.S.S.R., whose economic,
financial, and military aid is basic to Cuba's survival
and which publicly showed on numerous occasions, through
the voice of orthodox communist parties, its disagreement with the Cuban "adventurist" policy, accounted to
a great extent for the suppression of the OLAS and for
the search for an unacknowledged modus vivendi with the
North American "imperialism." Of course, Cuban rhetoric
has remained the same and the principles are reaffirmed
with even more force, now that they are not being
applied. But these last militants in the rural
guerrilla cells on the continent today pass bitter
judgment on the new course of Cuban foreign policy
which they claim has sacrificed the "principles of
international proletarianism" and of "revolutionary

continentalism."[44]   However, Cuba's alignments with the
Soviet Union and its "tacit coexistence" with the
United States are not without advantages, even from the
diplomatic point of view, as is shown by the many recent
declarations by Latin American governments which have
proposed the return of the island into the OEA,
if not the renewal of diplomatic relations with Havana.

In the U.S., where Richard Nixon's election
coincided within a few weeks with the Peruvian Coup
d'Etat, the involvement in Viet Nam and the endless
Middle East crisis have obscured the "threat of Castro"
even if the existence of a communist state in the
Caribbean has not been forgotten.   Furthermore, because
of the lassitude of American public opinion, whether
pacifist or isolationalist, the new administration has
broken with the worldwide activism of the democratic
president who preceded it.   The low profile policy,
which sought to limit the world responsibilities of the
U.S. because "hegemony is demoralizing" (H. Kissinger)
imposed an attitude of discretion and circumspection
towards Latin America.   Henceforth, the Department of
the State has shown an undeniable spirit of concilia-
tion to avoid direct confrontations with the Southern
Republics even when North American economic interests
are at stake.

The democratic opposition to President Nixon spoke

out against this passivity or lack of foreign policy;[45]
it would be more correct to remind those awaiting the
definition of a new global U.S. policy towards Latin
America, that Republican administrations are generally
recognized for their indifference to explicit and long
term programs[46] and prefer to treat problems bilaterally
rather than multilaterally. The actual U.S. policy
towards Latin America is essentially pragmatic: it is
characteristically selective and gradual in its approach.
It does not attempt to apply universal principles and
adapts itself according to the situation and interests
at stake. Thus, the government in Washington took
serious retaliatory measures against the civilian and
moderate government of Equador which maintained its
fishing rights and territorial waters of 200 miles
against California tuna fishermen. However, under
similar circumstances, Washington threatened and took
limited action against the Peruvian military junta.
In the same way, Nixon's administration does not intend,
it seems, to defend the private economic interests of
its nationals in every case or with all possible means.
Henceforth, the Department of the State has given
priority to vital, long-term strategic interests, beyond
the disputes provoked by American investment, which can
always be negotiated and do not have to imply political
rupture. It seems that the Cuban crisis has born fruit,

as further shown by the reactions of polite and dis-
creet discontent towards the first measures of the
"Marxist" Chilean government. As pointed out in a
recent article by the former Secretary of State for
Latin American affairs under President Johnson, it is
in the national interest of the U.S. to ignore its
traditional "diplomatic function of protecting private
North American economic interests."[47] It is true that
the diversification of these interests has facilitated
the adoption of a more selective and flexible diplomatic
policy.

In effect, it seems clear that the investment in
primary production and extractive industry, which are
politically more conspicuous and economically less
remunerative than other investments, have become the
weakest link in   American capital in the southern
continent. The uncontested "Chileanization" of the
copper mines by Christian Democrat President Eduardo
Frei as well as the moderation of the Americans towards
the nationalization of the IPC testify to this fact.
Whether one attributes this change to a mutation in the
composition of American investments, of which the most
dynamic sector is comprised of "multinational" companies
of manufactured products and of services whose branches
work for local markets, or to the effectiveness of
lobbying by these industrial corporations (which comes

to the same thing), it is certain that the United States are ready to give up certain sectors in order to guarantee others. Considering that the most influential economic circles believe that the best partner for an industrialized country is another such country. American diplomacy has definite reasons to think that a "branch country"[48] is more advantageous because it imposes less responsibility than a "banana republic" or a semi-protectorate.

This slightly cynical realism implies also and above all the abandonment of a certain "paternalism." The "Trade not Aid" formula is diametrically opposed to the Kennedy Alliance for Progress which, in exchange for modest and poorly oriented aid, advised sovereign states about necessary reforms and the ideal form of their government. The self-centered withdrawal of the great industrial power is perhaps being concealed under the alluring image of more egalitarian relations, but the margin of operation for the Latin American states has increased anyway. It is in the name of this same realism that the United States discreetly adapted to the wave of nationalism which has swept the continent or to the military tide unleashed on the South American capitals. Thus, Secretary of State William P. Rogers announced in January 1971 that "nationalism is a good thing in Latin America" and added: "the fact that the

Latin Americans feel responsible for their future and
are proud of their national identity is a good thing.
It is natural that this national pride at times takes
the form of antiamericanism . . ."[49] One cannot find
a more explicit affirmation of the will of the United
States to disengage from the Latin American situation.
In the same way, one sees the U.S. placing its political
interests over its democratic credo by dropping the
anathema held a short while ago against those governments which did not come to power through elections.
From the resigned acceptance under the Kennedy administration of military coups d'etat because of their
generally conservative and anticommunist functions,
advisers of the Department of the State and of the
President now hold to the theory of "salvation by the
military" who are seen as forces of progress and agents
of orderly modernization. Proof of this evolution
dating from the presidency of L.B. Johnson is the very
official Rockefeller Report. The special representative
of President Nixon in Latin America, who spent a long
chapter dealing with this problem, was not only very
impressed by the new military regimes and sympathetic
with the military reformers, but he did not hesitate to
describe them as "the essential force of constructive
social change."[50]

These interconnected developments point to the

breakdown of the tensions which, since 1961, have maintained throughout the continent both the active solidarity of Cuba with the armed revolutionary movements
and the counter-revolutionary obsession of the United
States. This relaxed atmosphere is particularly evident
at the level of the armed forces which are no longer
permanently mobilized in an anticommunist crusade.
Furthermore, after the abandonment of the project for
institutionalizing an Inter-American Peace Force in
1967--linked to the Dominican crisis--and the progressive phasing out under President Johnson of the
Alliance for Progress, "the good neighbor policy is
from now on in the hands of the military" as observed
one officer in the Military Review a few years ago.[51]
The main theme of the Eighth Conference of the Chiefs
of Staff of the American Armies, which was held in Rio
de Janeiro in September 1968, under the symbol of
"unity and development," seems to agree with him.
Furthermore, the important speech given on this occasion
by the North American representative, General Westmore-
land, former commander in chief in Viet Nam, placed
emphasis on the economic and social aspects of insur-
rections, with an especial emphasis on "the activity on
the social and political levels aimed at extirpating
the causes of frustration" that is "more critical than
the actual military action."[52] This reformulation, by

and for the military, of the recommendation of Punta
del Este has without a doubt been extended to Peru,
Panama and Bolivia. Is "Pentagonism," which the former
Dominican President, Juan Bosch, denounced as the
"substitute for imperialism,"[53] now under the new name
for the Alliance for Progress?

Certainly, one should not hastily conclude, as
did some irredentist guerrillero groups or certain left
wing intellectuals in Peru and Bolivia[54] (if not in
France), that the current "military revolutions" constitute the "second wind of imperialism"--an infinitely
clever maneuver by the U.S. to insure their control
of the Latin American countries at a minimal cost.
It would be excessive to believe that the conflicts
between these "military revolutions" and the United
States are factitious--and that the panegyrics directed
by Fidel Castro to the Peruvian regime[55] or the critical
support of the Communist Party given to the military
junta from the first weeks of its existence[56] have
received the approval of the Department of the State,
even if one recognizes the momentary convergence of the
political objectives of the United States and the
U.S.S.R. in Latin America. However, it must be admitted
that the continental thaw has corresponded with a
policy of Inter-American security which is both defensive and indirect and which coincides with the principal

aspirations of the armed forces in many of the countries on the continent.

CONCLUSION

At the conclusion of this study during which we have placed the emphasis on the singularity of national situations confronted with a continent-wide phenomenon, it would be useful to single out certain common traits of the societies concerned. We have seen how the "military revolutions" have appeared in an international context which demands a redefinition of the political role of the armies. The national aftermath has brought to light the reforming and modernizing functions of the armies which the cold war and the logic of counterrevolutionary struggle had banished for the past ten years. Does there exist, nevertheless, any pertinent characteristics shared by the countries in which this transformation took place?

First of all, the new military regimes only came into being in the nations where the army played an hegemonial role, whether it had been directly in power for a number of years or constituted the first political party and the supreme judge of public life. This being so, if we limit ourselves to the cases under consideration (Peru and Bolivia; Panama was also treated in the original article-PCS), the revival of reformist militarism takes place under the following conditions:

1. In countries considered as socially very
    unstable and potentially explosive because
    of extreme social and racial unbalance and
    the existence of disenfranchised majoritarian
    sectors or severe limitations upon sovereignty.

2. In societies where the weakness of the middle
    classes leaves the military, who are themselves
    situated in the middle social strata, great
    flexiblity in their operations, when the
    "radicalization" of these weak middle strata
    does not push them to change.

3. In economies of substantial external dependence
    even when it is functionally weak, as in Peru.
    This is perceived with a particular keeness
    by public opinion and is especially con-
    spicuous because it is direct and primary; it
    is expressed in the possession of land by
    public or private foreign interests, if not
    related to the exploitation of the subsoil.

4. In polities where the armed forces (including
    the National Guard in Panama) were among those
    Latin American military institutions,
    which depended most on financial aid from
    the U.S.

5. In countries where, for different reasons,
    the State was politically weak and finan-
    cially poor. In this context the reinforcement
    of decision-making and economic intervention
    powers becomes a necessity for development
    and part of the modernization process.

May one conclude that the continent-wide phenomenon
described above has only affected countries exhibiting
these characteristics? In other words, has this détente,
which seems to have made the emergence of progressive
neo-militarism possible, also modified the course of
conservative military regimes?

To answer this question would involve lengthy
discussion and would be material for another article.
We must limit ourselves to a few brief remarks. It

is undeniable, for example, that Argentina, a relatively
developed country with a complex social structure, has
been affected by the evolution of the general politico-
military context. Although Argentina is a socially
stable country--in flagrant contrast to its chronic
political instability--endowed with strong middle
classes, removed from the problems of primary external
dependence because of its geographical position and its
resources, and the recipient of the smallest proportion
of North American military aid in the entire continent,
it does not seem to have escaped the new atmosphere.
Of course, this was not apparent the day after the
army's overthrow of General Ongania, the defender of
the "ideological borders," on June 1970. But by the end
of the year the Argentine government had broken from
economic neo-liberalism, made a 180 degree turn in
relation to its former policy of financial orthodoxy
and monetary stability, and headed in the direction of
moderate "economic nationalism." Public authorities
resolved to give their support primarily to Argentine
enterprises, both private and public, and put an end to
the wave of "denationalization," i.e., the sale of fail-
ing enterprises to foreign companies. The administrative and financial measures taken in opposition to multinational food processing companies and international
companies, and in promotion of a major national petro-

chemical industry with public funds were some of the
aspects of this discrete revolution within the "Argentine Revolution" which occurred during the brief
administration of General Levingston. His fall in
March 1971 and replacement by General Lanusse, who
passed for more conservative and is well connected to
agrarian circles, opposed governmental economic intervention, does not, however, appear to have involved any
immediate modification of this new policy, which is
popular within the ranks of the army, even if it is
improbable that the new "de facto" president will move
further in a nationalist direction.

The situation has been very different in Brazil
which remains fixed in the shadow of the cold war and
where the military government has carefully maintained
an atmosphere of counterrevolutionary struggle. The
purges of the army which eliminated most of the
nationalist and progressive officers, the attachment of
the Brazilian military to a privileged and intangible
alliance with the U.S. and even the influence of the
middle classes in the developed southern area of the
country--their desire for protection in an "inarticu-
late" society having neither a partisan tradition nor
strong structures of association--only partially explain
Brazilian isolation and the progressively more repressive nature of the regime, unjustified by any social or

economic crisis. Explanation in terms of the gravity
of the tensions generated by accelerated and dependent
industrialization, an argument which paradoxically has
been put forth both by President Garrastazu Médici in
his speeches and by left wing commentators, does not
account for the creation of an enlarged repressive
apparatus whose social costs are out of proportion to
any internal or external economic benefits expected by
its presumed promoters.

The analysis of relations between the policy orientation of contemporary military regimes, the regional
context, and the hemispheric defense policy of the U.S.
necessarily suggests some doubts about the future course
of political systems so sensitive to international fluctuations. Would a tightening of the attitude of the
Pentagon or Department of the State towards progressive
Latin American experiments or some historical incident,
renewing the cold war (which Chile and Cuba are both
capable of initiating) suffice to break the fragile
balance of a precarious detente and modify the direction
of those governments supported by armed forces? Certainly, the possibility of creating a new, more durable
stability in the relations between the north and south
of the continent is not out of the question. Faced
with the undeniable rise of economic nationalism among
Latin American countries, whose deception towards the

U.S. is proportional to the great hopes raised by the
Alliance for Progress, it is probable that the U.S.
will pursue an "particularistic" policy in Latin
America, dealing country by country. This could protect the "nationalitarian" political regimes even in
the event of a general tightening of nother-south
relations. Nor is it impossible that the North American
diplomacy will stop looking at Latin America through
the "distorting prism" of the Caribbean,[57] and, by
distinguishing a number of sub-regions in the continent in the future, adopt a distinct general policy
vis-a-vis each of these which is a function of permanent strategic interests. It is no less true that
the temptation to recreate, through the establishment
of "friendly governments," a southern zone of influence
where, as in the past, American interests could enjoy
freedom from nationalization or from laws limiting foreign
investment, still exist.

One can ask whether in the long run these "military
revolutions" (and we have seen they are more military than
revolutionary) whose primary objectives are the strengthen-
ing of state decision-making capacity and the growth of
national production, will be able to create a revolutionary dynamic which can surmount all obstacles or eventual

accidents in their path. It is obvious that each national situation is very different. However, this revolutionary experience may fail in the hour of need, even in Peru, primarily because the hierarchical conception of military power does not facilitate the mobilization of masses. The difficulty that military regimes have in "institutionalizing themselves" politically, to "civilize" themselves, is not one of their lesser weaknesses. By refusing to create parties or official trade-unions, fearing the temptation of populism, and seeking to avoid the predominance of an uncontrolable popular leader, the progressive regimes which grew from "institutional coups d'etat" may produce an isolation which renders them particularly vulnerable to external pressures. Their leaders are often aware of this danger without, however, daring to provide themselves the political means needed to acquire a social basis for their own legitimacy. In fact, only the future will show whether these "revolutionaries" in uniform have thought enough about Tallyrand's classical remark on the proper use of bayonets.[58]

FOOTNOTES

1. In 1954 out of 20 Latin American Nations, twelve had governments originating from military coups d'etat. By 1961, as the result of a wave of "democratization" and "demilitarization" over the southern continent, only one such government remained in power and this in a small country (Paraguay). In 1962, a new series of coups d'etat started with the overthrow of Argentine President

Frondizi. This time the military tide reached the largest nations and, by 1970, had covered three-quarters of the South American population.

2. On the attempts to "civilize" and give a democratic facade to the 1964 coup d'etat, see J. P. Bernard, "Deux Années de Politique Bolivienne," Problèmes d'Amérique Latine, 17 (September 14, 1970), pp. 5-6, and T. M. Millington, "Bolivia under Barrientos," Current History (January 1969), pp. 27-28.

3. This point of the view is supported by certain authors, notably, Lisa North, Civil-military relations in Argentina, Chile and Peru (Berkeley: University of California, Institute of International Studies, 1966), p. 55, and Henri Favre, "Reformismes civil et reformisme militaire au Pérou," Politique Etrangère, 34, 3 (1969), pp. 351-352.

4. For a succinct description of the 1963 elections, see Hugo Neira "Pérou," Tableau des Partis Politiques en Amérique du Sud (Paris: A. Colin, 1969), pp. 299-300, and the analysis of Belaunde's rise to power in François Bourricaud, Pouvoir et société dans le Pérou contemporain (Paris: A Colin, 1967), p. 290.

5. Notably in Anibal Ismodes Cairo, "La conducta política de los militares peruanos," Panoramas, No. 1963, pp. 61 and 67; and, with many nuances and insistance above all on the reformist potential of the Peruvian military power, F. Bourricaud, op. cit., p. 282.

6. No systematic study of this change in U.S. policy nor on its causes exists, but one may find some discussion of its strictly military consequences in Willard Barber and C. Neale Ronning, Internal Security and Military Power: Counter-Insurgency and Civic Action in Latin America (Columbus: Ohio State University Press, 1966), and B. E. Glick, "Conflict, Civic Action and Counterinsurgency," Orbis, X, 3 (1966), pp. 899-910.

7. Clarin (Buenos Aires), August 26, 1965.

8. For a detailed, but polemic, agreement of this thesis, see John Gerassi, The Great Fear in Latin America (New York: Macmillan, 1965), pp. 316-317, as well as Alberto Ciria, "Cuatro ejemplos de relaciones entre Fuerzas Armadas y poder político," Aportes, VI (October 1967), pp. 41-42.

9. For the military roots of "Castrism" in Guatemala, see Luis Mercier Vega, <u>Techniques du contre-état</u>, (Paris: Belfond, 1968, p. 146.

10. <u>Le Monde</u>, April 24, 1964.

11. In an interview, Carlos Marighela, the recently murdered revolutionary leader, agreed with official statistics which stated that of 150 guerrillas arrested in 1967, 20 per cent were military or ex-military. Cf. Carlos Marighela, <u>Pour la liberation du Brésil</u> (Paris: Aubier-Montaigne, 1970), p. 67.

12. In other words, we reject the elegant paradox offered by Edwin Lieuwen who states that "to understand the nature of military intervention in Latin America today, it is useful to shrug off the deeply rooted myth which considers the armed forces as being above all military institutions." <u>General vs. Presidents: Neo-militarism in Latin America</u> (London: Pall Mall, 1964), p. 95. That the effective role of Latin American armies has ceased to be military does not imply that their function and profession are purely political.

13. For a critical analysis of theories and interpretations of Latin American "militarism" see our commented bibliography,"Le rôle politique des forces armées en Amérique Latine," <u>Revue Française de Science Politique</u> (August 1969), pp. 862-885.

14. The concept I have borrowed from Antonio Gramsci <u>Notes sur Machiavel, La politique et l'Etat moderne, Œuvres choisies</u> (Paris: Editions Sociales, 1959), pp. 246-251 to characterize "the crisis of hegemony of the managerial class" when no social group has the means to impose a policy. This is often used by sociologists to describe the recent situation of a number of Latin American countries. See Jose Nún, "América Latina: la crisis hegemonica y el golpe militar," <u>Desarrollo Económico</u>, Nos. 22-23, (July-December, 1966), pp. 355-415, and F. Bourricaud, "Voluntarismo y experimentación. Los militares peruanos mano a la obra," <u>Mundo Nuevo</u> (December, 1970), p. 4.

15. In particular, see Irving L. Horowitz, "The Military Elites," in Seymour M. Lipset and Aldo Solari (eds.), <u>Elites in Latin America</u> (New York: Oxford University Press, 1967), p. 146 who insists on the multiple contradictions of the Latin American military and,

notably, on the dependence of institutions responsible for warranting national sovereignty on
foreign aid. In fact, the dependence is more
worldwide and the relations with the dominant
power less asymmetrical than he thinks.

16. According to Lisa North, op. cit., p. 49, the
testimony of a former commander (major) of the
Peruvian army who militated in the ranks of the
APRA during the forties: Victor Villanueva,
Nueva mentalidad militar en el Peru? (Buenos
Aires: Ed. Replanteo, 1969), pp. 165-166.

17. As shown by Susanne Bodennheimer in her article,
"La crisis del movimiento social-democrata en
América Latina," Estudios Internacionales,
(January-March, 1970), pp. 544-567.

18. This is analyzed at length in F. Bourricaud,
Pouvoir et société, esp. p. 278. For a direct
testimony of the sympathy of the American govern-
ment towards Haya de la Torre, see Arthur M.
Schlesinger, Jr., Les 1000 jours de Kennedy
(Paris: Denoel, 1966), pp. 7040705.

19. See Luis Valdez Pallete, "Antecedentes de la nueva
orientación de las Fuerzas Armadas en el Peru,"
Aportes, 19 (January 1971), pp. 175-178.

20. See Hugo Neira, "Pérou," op. cit., p. 310 and Ruiz
Eldrige, (leader of the MSP), "Quienes orientan
la política peruana," La Nación (Buenos Aires),
July 17, 1969.

21. We have borrowed this term from Anouar Abdel-Malek
Egypte société militaire (Paris: Le Seuil, 1962),
p. 9 who makes a distinction with "nationalist"
and uses it to mean "the taking in hand of the
nation and of the national State." "While the
'nationalist' movement appears especially" writes
Abdel-Malek, "under a negative aspect, often
accompanied by an imperial volition, the
'nationalitarian' effort is intended as a process
of autonomy and identity building--a veritable
reconquest in depth of identity itself."

22. See Anibal Quijano Obregon, "Tendencies in
Peruvian development and Class Structure," in J.
Petras and M. Zeitlin, Latin America, Reform or
Revolution? (Greenwich, Conn.! Fawcett, 1968)
pp. 289-328, and Alcira Leiserson, Notes on the
Process of Industrialization in Argentina, Chile,

<u>and Peru</u> (Berkeley: Institute of International <u>Studies</u>, University of California, 1966).

23. The Constitution does not give electoral rights to illiterates and Indian peasants speaking native languages are almost all illiterate.

24. According to V. Villanueva, <u>Nueva mentalidad</u>, between 1955 and 1965, 82 per cent of the army generals are provincials, and 49 per cent of this group were natives of the "Sierra." According to our calculations, out of the fifteen members of the junta--which we do not consider as a representative sample--two-third were provincials and only two members were born in the coastal region. One should also note that the junta has four representatives of the air force and two from the navy, while the decisive political force has been, of course, the army, which is least "coastal" in its origins.

25. See the testimony of one of the guerrilla leaders, Hector Bejar, <u>Les guerillas peruviennes de 1965</u> (Paris: Maspero, 1969), and the analyses of Hugo Neira, "Le castrisme dans les andes peruviennes," <u>Partisans</u>, Nos. 26-27 (1966), pp. 77-85, and James Petras, "Revolution and guerrilla movements in Latin America: Venezuela, Colombia, Guatemala, and Peru," in J. Petras and M. Zeitlin (eds.), <u>op. cit.</u>, pp. 329-69.

26. See Adolfo Gilly, "Révolution au Pérou: Hugo Blanco et le mouvement paysan," <u>Partisans</u>, No. 13 (December 1963-January 1964).

27. As witnessed, for example, in the article by Lieutenant Carlos A. Moreira, "El militar y los políticos," which appeared in <u>Revista Militar del Peru</u> (July 1961) and which accused politicians of using the armed forces after they failed in their mission of resolving national problems.

28. Ministerio de Guerra, <u>Las guerrillas en el Peru, su represion</u> (Lima: 1966).

29. Hector Bejar, <u>op. cit.</u>, p. 83.

30. According to certain rumors, the U.S. refused to deliver any napalm to Peru for antiguerrilla operations in the fear that this incendiary product would be used against a neighboring country. This was also true of Bolivia which, because of

the border conflicts with Chile, did not receive
any napalm either.

31. In October, 1967, Peru decided to purchase 15
     Mirage fighter planes from France. Edouard Bailby,
     "L'affaire des Mirages en Amérique Latine,"
     Le Monde diplomatique (November 1967), p. 10. The
     further acquisition of Exocet sea-to-sea missiles
     by Peru is a continuation of this armament policy.

32. Theoretically, half of the new cadets would be
     recruited among sons of miners, peasants and
     workers and the other half among the sons of MNR
     supporters from all other social strate based on
     certain conditions of seniority within the party.

33. See, for example, David Rios Reinaga's book,
     Civiles y militares en la revolución boliviana
     (1943-1966) (La Paz: Difusión, 1967). The
     author, who is ferociously hostile to the MNR and
     very sympathetic to the three "tin kings" (Patino,
     Hoschild and Aramayo), did not hide the future
     hopes he placed in the "democratic" action of the
     military.

34. Cf. Thomas M. Millington, op. cit., p. 25.

35. As is rightfully pointed out in the study of
     Richard W. Patch (ed.), "Peasantry and national
     Revolution: Bolivia," in K. H. Silvert (ed.),
     Expectant People (New York: Random House, 1963),
     pp. 95-136. Carlos Montenegro, promoter of
     Bolivian nationalism, wrote in a now classic book
     in 1943: "It is in Chaco that the Bolivian national
     sentiment, which has disappeared for a half-century,
     will awaken." Nacionalismo y Coloniaje (Buenos
     Aires: Pleamar, 1967), p. 221.

36. As shown in the interview of General Juan Jose
     Torres by Ph. Labreveux, Le Monde (October 22,
     1970). The Bolivian President recalls, to justify
     his action: "In the thirties we had a much more
     important conflict with Paraguay than with the
     guerrillas--a fratricidal war instigated by
     imperalist oil interests. My father was killed.
     He was fighting for the defense of the national
     territory."

37. Their presence was recognized by both Ovando and
     Barrientos. La Nación (Buenos Aires), April 3,
     1969. Their number is unknown, but it was on the
     order of a few hundred--at least 200 according to

North American sources. See J. Amalric, "La disparition de Che Guevara," Le Monde diplomatique (November 1967), p. 9.

38. The Bolivians believed that they fought for Standard Oil (N.J.) and the Paraguayans believed they were fighting for Shell. Cf. Charles J. Kolinski, The Story of the Paraguayan War (Independence or death) (Gainsville, Florida: University of Florida Press, 1965).

39. Speech by General Ovando on October 17, 1969. Text published in "Bolivia. La segunda revolución nacional?" Cuadernos de Marcha (Montevideo), (October 1969), p. 62.

40. The Bolivian armed forces were limited to 8,000 men before 1952; comprised about 18,000 men at the time of their reorganization in 1953-1955, and had reached more than 30,000 men by 1965 including 41,000 men in the Civil Guard, according to D. Wood, Armed Forces in Central and South America (London: Institute for Strategic Studies, Adelphi Papers No. 34, 1967), p. 24.

41. In 1965, according to our calculations and to the extent that the statistics of military expenditures furnished by the countries involved are reliable, the U.S. contributed more than 14 per cent of the Bolivian military budget. (Ibid, tables 1 and 3). Alain Joxe (Las Fuerzas armadas en el sistema político chileno (Santiago: Ed. Universitaria, 1970), pp. 103-104 places Bolivia in the higher bracket of countries whose military budget is 15-20 per cent dependent on U.S. aid. One must point out that, at least in the case of Bolivia, these calculations are not very significant since the budget of the State itself depends directly on American aid.

42. Cf. the statement to the press by the personal secretary of President Barrientos on the role of exiled Cubans, agents of U.S. intelligence service within the administration. "La ingerencia de la CIA en Bolivia," La Nación (April 3, 1969).

43. Antonio Arguedas, former Minister of the Interior and personal friend of Barrientos, claimed on numerous occasions to have been a trusted man of the CIA before becoming a "correspondent" of the Cuban government during his stay in office. See his account to Carlo Cocciolo, L'Express, (June 29,

1970), pp. 41-43. This is related to the discrete explusion on February 25, 1970 of some
North American functionaries accused of spying.
This measure was not followed by any form of
public protest from Washington.

44. Cf. in Le Monde (July 17, 1970), the interview by
Douglas Bravo granted to Georges Mattei.

45. See "In Search of a foreign policy," Newsweek
(December 14, 1970), pp. 12-20.

46. Osvaldo Sunkel, "Esperando a Godot: América latina
ante la nueva administración republicana de los
Estados Unidos," Estudios Internacionales
(April-June, 1969), pp. 23-24.

47. T. Olivier Covey, "Ha habido alejamiento de la
realidad," Visión, (January 2, 1971), pp. 24-25.

48. On Latin America and the danger of "branchifica-
tion," see Osvaldo Sunkel, "Política nacional de
desarrollo y dependencia externa," Estudios
Internacionales (April 1967), pp. 43-75.

49. U.S. News and World Report, "Changing Role of
U.S.," Interview with William P. Rogers,
Secretary of State (January 26, 1970), p. 34.

50. La calidad de la vida en las Américas (Nelson A.
Rockefeller Report), p. 19. (Informe presentado
por una Mision presidencial de los Estados Unidos
al Hemisferio Occidental, 30 agosto 1969), s.l.,
s.d., multigr., p. 19.

51. Lieutenant-Colonel Harry Walterhouse, "Good
Neighbors in Uniform," Military Review (February
1965), p. 12.

52. Le Monde (September 29-30, 1930) and El Espectador
(Bogota) (September 27, 1968).

53. Juan Bosch, El Pentagonismo, sustituto del
imperialismo (Mexico: Siglo XXI, 1968), pp. vii-151.

54. For Peru, see the interview of Hugo Blanco by M.
Niedergang, "Le syndicaliste Hugo Blanco conteste
que le régime péruvien soit revolutionnaire,"
Le Monde (January 29, 1970), and the texts of the
Committee of National Opposition and Resistance
(CONDOR), formed by students close to the MIR, of
which certain parts have been printed in France in

the <u>Bulletin du Comité francais de solidarité avec</u> <u>les victimes de la repression au Pérou</u>, No. 30 (Paris: January 1970), pp. 1-13. On Bolivia, see all of the E.L.N. statements (Army of National Liberation).

55. Castro praised the Peruvian military regimes for the first time on July 14, 1969 during a speech to 30,000 sugar workers on the occasion of the beginning of the harvest of ten million tons.

56. If the Peruvian Communist Party (P.C.) is today one of the strongest supporters of the "anti-imperialist" and "antifeudal" policies of the junta, it also quickly approved its nationalist measures. Cf. "El Péru de pie ante la intromision yanqui," <u>Unidad</u> (P.C.P. publication), December 12, 1968.

57. As emphasized by T. Olivier Covey, <u>op. cit</u>.

58. As this article was on its way to press, the Bolivian government of General Torres was over-thrown by a rightwing military rebellion on August 21, 1971. At the very moment the U.S. has decided to take the initiative in foreign policy and tighten its attitude towards Latin America in economic matters, will this victory of the military champions of anticommunism and conservatism be a warning, if not the first sign, of the end of the cycle of "revolutionary nationalism" which started in 1968? In fact, this expected backswing of the political pendulum illustrates the indecision of the Bolivian army. For it was above all pro-fessional motives which drove the great majority of officers into the right wing. The irresponsible initiatives and permanent outbidding of an Assembly of Popular Forces, which General Torres tolerated without ever receiving its support, played a decisive role in this respect. It is then per-missable to suppose that, in spite of this temporary unity, the confrontation between the partisans and opponents of change will continue within the army.

II

CONSEQUENCES OF MILITARY RULE

AND MILITARY AID

ASSESSING THE IMPACT OF MILITARY

RULE: ALTERNATIVE APPROACHES*

Jerry L. Weaver

> "The centralization of the state that
> modern society requires arises only on the
> ruins of the military bureaucratic govern-
> mental machinery which was forged in
> opposition to feudalism.
> Karl Marx

Marx' attack on the stultifying affect of the
military-based French state might well have been made
by an observer of current regimes in Latin America.
Having aligned itself with the middle class during the
1950's to break the hold of the landed oligarchy and
its lackeys, the contemporary Latin American military
subsequently became a force for defending the status
quo by preserving middle-class domination against
efforts by the working and peasant classes and progressive politicians to democratize Latin societies.

Had you read this hypothesis prior to the advent
of the current or recent "populist" military regimes in
Bolivia, Peru, Panama, and Ecuador, I suspect that it

would have aroused little interest and disagreement.
Indeed, it was widely agreed by the mid-1960's that the
Latin military was a midwife for the birth of middle-
class rule in Venezuela, Peru, Argentina, Guatemala,
Brazil and elsewhere. But the recent populist regimes
have revived interest in the consequences of military
rule. "Populist" seems to indicate, for those accustomed
to seeing the term in its American or Russian context, a
marked departure from middle-class rule in favor of
organizations and practices extolling the virtues of
the peasant and worker: democratic political participation, consumer protection, economic policies that
benefit small enterprises, nationalism cum nativism,
and decentralization of political power and administrative control. Have similar procedures, institutions
and policies emerged under the Latin American "populist"
military regimes?[1]

What have been the social, political and economic
consequences of the re-emergence of direct military
rule, populist or antipopulist, since the mid-1960's?
What similarities and differences mark the current
Brazilian (antipopulist) and Peruvian (populist)
military governments? How do the present military
governments of Panama, Argentina, Ecuador and
Guatemala differ from their military predecessors of
the late forties and early fifties?

GENERAL STATEMENTS CONCERNING MILITARY RULE

In order to determine the consequences of military
rule, we shall examine both empirical case studies and
quantitative aggregate data analyses of Latin American
societies governed by military elites. The analysis
will be organized around a series of hypotheses concerning the consequences of military rule. These hypotheses reflect research and thinking about military rule
during the 1950's; by testing them with data from contemporary military regimes we shall evaluate their
predictive and explanatory utility.[2]

The following is neither an exhaustive nor
exclusive collection of hypotheses; for each one offered
there are alternatives--often contradictory ones--
employing the same variables. The presence of alternative formulations must be borne in mind lest the
reader mistakenly conclude that the following represent
the consensus judgment about earlier military rule. We
consider these statements merely points of departure
for organizing our research.

Military as Non-reformers

I. No military regime has elevated living
standards or made significant headway toward
solving socioeconomic problems.[3]

I.1 The armed forces are a conservative,
antirevolutionary institution standing
in the way of the achievement of
evolutionary social change by democratic
means.[4]

I.2   The military in politics is a tool of
the oligarchy and as such delays the
country's attainment of political
maturity.[5]

I.3   There is little evidence to support a
view of the military as a democratic
force.[6]

Armed Forces Protect Middle-class Hegemony

II.   The armed forces align with the middle class
and agree on industrialization, state
capitalism, economic nationalism, and put a
low priority on agrarian reform.[7]

II.1 In the economically advanced countries
of Latin America, the armed forces
assume the responsibility of protecting
the economic and political privileges
of the middle class.[8]

II.2 Military elites stand in the way not of
economic development, but of those
reforms which entail a threat to the
higher civil bureaucracy and officer
corps.[9]

Armed Forces Support Imperialism

III.   Military establishments tend to produce
governments which support United States
foreign policies and protect the economic
interests of U.S. and other foreign
investors.[10]

III.1   Because of their inherent conservatism
military regimes protect United States
extractive and industrial interests
from expropriation by "radical"
politicians.[11]

III.2   Through numerous close ties with high
military officials in Latin America
via training schools, exchange visits,
military assistance and advisers, the
United States can indirectly veto
potential presidential candidates
perceived as threats to what U.S.
policymakers consider critical
interests.[12]

Military Budgets

IV. Military budgets and costs of foreign
assistance loans and equipment contribute to
conflicting economic pressures which further
strain Latin American social systems.[13]

IV.1 United States military aid programs
exacerbate endemic rivalries and mutual
suspicions among Latin American republics
and give rise to arms races.[14]

To operationalize these hypotheses we must first
agree upon empirical indicators of the major concepts.
Hypothesis (I) and its corollaries seem to present
little difficulty: military regimes (the independent
variable) are regimes in which the elite of the military
sector (usually the senior officers of the armed forces,
militia or national police) declare public policy,
either as formal office holders or as a veto group.
Social and economic consequences of military rule can
be evaluated within two contexts. The first is associated with the regime's policies in such areas as
public health, education, social security, infrastructure, industrial and agricultural production, and
reflected in its formal allocation of public resources
(outputs). The second context is the actual consequences (outcomes) of allocations as seen in changes
of literacy, morbidity and morality rates, income
distribution, and other social and economic well-
being statistics. We would consider hypothesis (I)
supported if, for example, we found that after a decade

of military rule, census data revealed that the per cent of the nation's population classified as illiterate remained unchanged (the actual situation for Guatemala).

Hypothesis (II) introduces the notion that the armed forces may govern in concert with the middle class to preserve that class' social and political privileges and interests which, in turn, are rooted in an economic system characterized by import-substitution industrialization, tariff protection and tax exemptions, and high profit-to-investment ratios. The policy goals of this alliance are fairly easily indexed; however, the concept "middle class" requires some consideration, both from an ideological perspective which might challenge the existence in Latin America of "classes," and from the ambiguity of "middle." As used by most writers (and in the present case), the middle class includes bureaucratic, professional, managerial and entrepreneural groups (including the officer corps). We would consider hypothesis (II) supported if, for example, a military regime provided loans, technical information and tax exemptions to commercial farmers and processers of agricultural products while denying funds, equipment, and land to campesinos and minifundistas.

Hypothesis (III) suggests that, because of close

ties to the United States military, Latin American
officers who come to power tend to support and protect
the political and economic interests of the U.S. government and U.S. investors. U.S. political interests may
be defined as supporting the U.S. position in the O.A.S.
(e.g., voting to condemn "communist" penetration of
Guatemala at the 1954 Caracas O.A.S. meeting or sending
troops to the Dominican Republic in 1965). Support for
U.S. economic imperialism is reflected in policies that
allow U.S. moneylenders and businessmen to gain control
of natural resources or major industries. For example,
we would consider hypothesis (III) supported if a
military regime lent support to U.S. intervention in
the affairs of a sister Latin American state, if a
military regime did not take steps to curtail the
remission abroad of profits of foreign-owned businesses,
or if the regime awarded concessions to foreign companies when local enterprises were available.

Military budgets and the overall costs of maintaining a military establishment are extremely difficult
to measure since without exception Latin American governments hide military appropriations in several budget
categories (the Ministry of the Interior or Justice
expenditure, for example, may conceal funds ostensibly
programmed for military-controlled "public safety");
moreover, debt repayment and service charges on loans

made to military and counterinsurgent programs, or for equipment, are usually not included in the formal accounts of the armed forces. In many countries, the armed forces operate factories, engage in roadbuilding, provide medical and wide range of social security services to their members and other bureaucrats: should these services, capital expenditures, and maintenance coasts be considered military expenditures? Similarly complex questions arise in cost-accounting military equipment: are new weapons systems to be charged to the purchasing fovernment, or seen as investment which periodically must be renewed, and therefore, should be amortized over ten or twenty years? Nevertheless an approximation of the direct costs of military operations can be found in the annual budgets. Using this admittedly incomplete indicator we may hypothesize that military regimes will tend to spend proportionately more public resources on the armed forces; in particular, military regimes are likely to increase the overall dollar amounts allocated to the armed forces budget. Now we have a handle on hypothesis (IV.1): _if_ rivalries exist, and if new purchases exacerbate them, then an increase in the military spending of regime "A" will produce an increase in the military allocations (or a symmetrical change in weapons' configurations) in regimes "B", "C",. . . "X". In addition we shall examine the relationship between

military rule and armed forces' expenditures by
analyzing the patterns of defense appropriation. We
would consider Hypothesis (IV) supported if a direct
association is found between military rule and an
increase in military spending over the level of previous
civilian regimes.

CASE STUDIES OF MILITARY RULE

During the 1960's numerous case studies of Latin
American military appeared. Historical monographs were
complemented by North American social science research
and by an occasional piece by a Latin American scholar.
While these efforts reflect varying research methods,
normative orientations and epistemological assumptions,
they offer a first approximation data base for testing
hypotheses concerning military rule. I say "first
approximation" in order to underscore the inherent
limitations in attempting to build middle range theory
in this manner. We have no way of knowing what the
original scholar saw but failed to report. Also, case
studies generally impose limitations on range of
issues, amount of background and number of actors
incorporated. Thus, such a study may ignore the role
of forces beyond the immediate scene of action or
overlook broad trends whose effects are not noticeable
in a short period.

Mindful of the selective perceptive and other

limitations involved in using case study materials, we
shall analyze two contemporary military regimes: Brazil
and Bolivia. Both came to office in 1964 after overthrowing civilian regimes; both have continued programs
and policies of their predecessors while introducing a
wide array of new measures, especially attempts to
revitalize and stabilize their economies; both have
faced and overcome political opposition; and both have
experienced several changes of chief executive since
the inauguration of military rule. The Bolivian regime,
at least until the 1971 coup by General Hugo Banzer
and a coalition of conservative MNR and Falangist
civilian politicians, might be called "populist." In
contrast, the rule by the Brazilian generals has
witnessed the political demobilization of the worker
and peasant classes in what might be called "antipopulist" politics. Since both regimes have faced similar
economic and political problems, the techniques and
results offer an opportunity to compare and contrast
the consequences of their allegedly different political
styles.

Bolivia

Ironically, the present Bolivian military regime
came to power by overthrowing a civilian regime that
had earlier all but abolished the Bolivian Armed Forces.
The first MNR government of Victor Paz Estenssoro

destroyed the Bolivian Army shortly after coming to power in 1952. But the second MNR government led by President Hernan Siles Suazo began, with U. S. assistance, to rebuild the armed forces after 1958. This policy stemmed from the decision to redirect the Bolivian revolution by shifting the costs of national development from the middle to the lower classes. This redirection entailed reducing inflation and stabilizing the currency by cutting subsidies to public utilities, freezing wages of miners, and increasing efficiency of the nationalized mines. With the miners strongly opposed to this policy and organized into armed militias, their pacification necessitated an armed force subservient to the government.

As Hobbes notes, when players cannot decide which suite will be trump, clubs are always trump. The MNR attempted to shuffle itself a winning hand. Although the military did not displace the civilians until November 1964, officers joined MNR politicians as determiners of public policy at the beginning of the decade.[15]

Analyzing the post-1964 regime in terms of our four central hypotheses, we find the following patterns: the Barrientos government not only increased dramatically the budget of the armed forces, but lavished other resources on the military. The military government's first armed forces budget (1965) was \$20.9 million, an increase of 33 per cent over the last MNR budget.[16] (But appropriations for the armed forces soon dropped to pre-1964 levels—and below; see Table 1) Military officers were accorded symbolic honors and prestige by the government as indicated by new uniforms, public recognition along side the President and flattering references to the revolutionary tradition of the Bolivian Army. Through grants and purchases the armed forces received new equipment, and numerous officers were sent to U.S. training facilities in Panama and the United States. The acclaim heaped on the Ranger Battalion after the capture of "Che" Guevara is illustrative of the government's desire to retain the confidence of the military elite.[17]

The presence of U.S. military advisers in great numbers—leaving aside the large scale involvement of the CIA and Special Forces during the pursuit of the Guevara foco—is indicative of the overall greatly expanded U.S. presence after 1964.[18] Another indicator of the new U.S. influence is the commitment of the Government of Bolivia to a very conservative, U.S.-sponsored, monetary and fiscal policy.

This monetary and fiscal policy apparently did not stimulate foreign firms to invest or reinvest Bolivian-earned profits. Between 1965 and 1968, for

TABLE 1

EXPENDITURES ON DEFENSE AND AGRICULTURE AS A PER CENT
OF TOTAL EXPENDITURES BY THE GOVERNMENT OF
BOLIVIA, 1961-1970

Year	Defense Expenditures as Per Cent of Total Government Spending	Agriculture Expenditures as Per Cent of Total Government Spending
1961	16.2	2.4
1962	14.6	2.0
1963	11.7	2.1
1964	16.7	3.3
1965	17.3	5.4
1966	11.1	2.9
1967	11.2	4.3
1968	7.4	1.8
1969	8.8	3.9
1970*	10.4	3.0

Source: U. S. Agency for International Development.
Summary Economic and Social Indicators 18
Latin American Countries: 1960-1970
(Washington, D.C., April 1971), pp. 43;46.

*Preliminary

example, net private foreign investment decreased by

$12.5 million to an estimated minus $2.8 million.

During the same period remission of profits increased

from $1 million to $10.5 million. Foreign loans,

increasing from $14.2 million in 1964 to $52.0 million

in 1968, kept the economy afloat.[19]

While encouraging the proliferation of U.S.

military advisers and mortgage brokers, the Barrientos
government took steps to encourage foreign private
investment. New mining laws introduced private contract mining at previously nationalized sites and
obliged unemployed miners to work for private contractors
without the protection of the labor code. U.S.-owned
Gulf Oil was granted extensive new leases and its
production soared while the national public petroleum
corporation, Y.P.F.B., lagged.[20]

Public investment in education, highways, build-
ings and commercial agriculture, complemented by leap-
ing rates of private investment in basic and consumer
industries, proved a windfall for the middle and upper
classes. With the currency stabilized and inflation
checked and with abundant new jobs and consumer goods,
local managerial, entrepreneurial and professional
elements enjoyed a remarkable rise in their standard
of living.

While salaries for public employees rose to become
the second largest budgetary appropriation during 1964-
68, the miners and campesinos continued to receive
short shrift. Breaking the political power of the miners
was a policy ruthlessly pursued by the Barrientos
regime. During 1965 Barrientos signed a series of
labor decrees which resulted in massive layoffs, salary
reductions of roughly 50 per cent and reductions in

benefits. When the miners struck, the military attacked the mines, smashed the strike and disarmed the worker militias. Labor leaders were either killed or driven into exile; in their place the government appointed tame figureheads and then bolstered them by placing the major mines under permanent military occupation.

It is a cruel irony of Bolivia that the peasants who along with the armed forces supported the eradication of the mine unions have faired no better than their victims. After the overthrow of the MNR government, expenditures for agriculture, as Table 1 reveals, averaged less than 3 per cent of the total budget; and the bulk of these funds and USAID loans to develop agriculture went to large commercial producers of sugar, rice and cattle. Moreover public funds for road construction and colonization largely were invested in areas of commercial, not _campesino_, farming.[21] While Barrientos masqueraded as a champion of the peasants, his government drastically curtailed land reform and redistribution programs: during 1964-68, an average of 16,000 campesinos received titles to land parcels compared with an annual average of 40,000 during the previous five years.[22]

The post-1964 military regime has pursued a strategy of attempting to mobilize the middle and upper classes through a complex and massive investment of public resources. The two principal segments of the lower classes, the miners and the peasants, have been handled differently (the former with force and economic sanctions, the latter with symbolic acts of good will--especially by Barrientos--reinforced by minor and selective allocations of goods and services). The military government wanted to demobilize popular sector commitment to left/progressive reference groups (such as Lechin's unions) while substituting the government, armed forces (through "civic action") and private patrones as the legitimate sources of expectations. Deference, submission and quiescence comprise the behavior pattern sought by the regime from the lower classes. Peasants, miners and others of the lower classes were treated with authoritarian contempt; parties and unions that might mobilize the lower classes or represent their interests of the rules were disbarred and their leaders exiled or forced underground.

Brazil

The current Brazilian military regime is a model of antipopulist politics. It may be instructive, therefore, to compare and contrast the policy consequences, rather than rhetoric, of the Brazilian and Bolivian military governments.

Both regimes formally seized the presidency in a
period of economic crisis and political fragmentation.[23]
Both undertook to stabilize the economy through orthodox
monetary and fiscal policy. The Brazilian military
regime apparently succeeded in restoring a measure of
economic order and growth--if increases in GNP growth
rates and checking inflation are accepted as indices of
order and development (see Table 2).

TABLE 2

INFLATION AND ECONOMIC GROWTH IN BRAZIL
DURING THE 1960'S

Year	Inflation Rate (Per Cent)	GNP Growth Rate (Per Cent)
1961	34	10.3
1962	51	5.3
1963	41	1.5
1964	92	2.9
1965	66	2.7
1966	41	5.1
1967	31	4.8
1968	22	8.4
1969	22	6.6
1970*	21	8.0

Source: U.S. Agency for International Development,
         Summary Economic and Social Indicators 18
         Latin American Countries: 1960-1970
         (Washington, D.C., April 1971), pp. 7; 93.
*Preliminary.

Many elements of the Brazilian population paid
heavy (if short-term) prices. Attacking inflation
through lagging salary and wage increases behind
increases in the cost of living, eliminating deficits
in state-owned utilities, and reducing subsidies to
inefficient businesses in effect reduced the real wages
of the urban (most inflation-ridden) population by 20
to 25 per cent during 1964-67. Restrictions on credit
and reduction of the money supply hit many Brazilian
businessmen hard, forcing some locally-owned businesses
to liquidate--occasionally to the benefit of North
American and foreign corporations. After 1966, the
government instituted a new support program for the
coffee growing industry, the result of which was to
reduce this once-dominant sector's public subsidy. To
complement their cost-cutting programs, the Brazilian
technocrats turned to direct taxation as a means of
raising revenues: the number of income tax payers rose
from 470,000 in 1967 to more than 4 million in 1969.[24]

These measures produced widely different economic
and political results. For example, while coffee
producers found their subsidies cut, industrialists
and other entrepreneurs received major subsidies such
as tax write-offs for investing in the Northeast, wage
stabilization, and protection from strikes. Businessmen and capitalists received additional support through

the expansion of the credit market: the government effectively encouraged the growth of the domestic stock shares market, and handed investors a bonus, by providing a 12 per cent deduction from personal income tax for buyers of stocks. The success of economic reform both in terms of increased consumer goods and new jobs for workers, technicians and managers, is evidenced in the booming Center-South region and is exemplified by the rapid expansion of the Sao Paulo automobile industry.

The consequences of the economic stabilization and growth programs for the Brazilian middle and lower classes must be seen not only in terms of jobs and stable currency but from the perspective of the overall standard of living. The government consolidated and expanded the social security coverage by enrolling virtually the entire wage-earning urban population of Brazil: from military officers and bureaucrats to shop clerks, gas station attendants and journalists. By compulsory union membership, the individual found his way to pensions, health services and often subsidized housing and food shops, job retraining and even recreational facilities. This state-encouraged corporatism provides an important source of non-monetary income, in the form of services, which goes largely untouched by inflation. Certainly a political consequence of this social security system is to undercut

potantial unrest by mitigating the economic hardship
of wage-earning and salaried citizens.

Although many of Brazil's military elite publicly
proclaim themselves economic nationalists, the military
regime has followed a course of encouraging foreign
penetration of the economy. Early in the regime,
Castello Branco signed a decree repealing the remit-
tance-of-profit law enacted in 1962. The controls on
remittance had been vigorously opposed by foreign
investors and the United States embassy. The repeal
was offered as proof to the international lenders and
the U.S. government that Brazil was firmly committed to
the "free world" economy. Symbolic of Brazil's
"internationalism" was Castello Branco's approval of
concessions to the Hanna Corporation to exploit and
transport iron ore.

The ramifications of the Hanna deal, however, were
felt beyond the private sector. In an effort to appease
economic nationalists among the officer corps, the
government agreed to increase public investment in
Brazil's state-owned iron ore "monopoly," the Rio Doce
Valley Corporation. This statist policy underscores the
government's quiet but significant expansion support of
public corporations. Returns from the public sector,
as a per cent of GNP, rose from 18 per cent in 1963 to
approximately 30 per cent in 1970. And although the

regime has maintained a vigorous pro-private enterprise,
anti-statist public posture, no major state corporation
has been dismantled; instead, existing corporations
have been reorganized to increase production and
efficiency and new ones have been created.

It is well known that the United States Government
opposed President Goulart; USAID and other foreign
assistance funds were withheld from the federal government.

In a policy known as "islands of sanity," U.S.
aid went only to state governments and federal agencies
independent of Goulart and the "communists." The overthrow of Goulart produced a quick reversal of this
policy--within two years the United States had
massively increased both military and economic assistance (to the federal government) so that the USAID/
Brazil mission had the third largest U.S. staff in the
world.[25] During fiscal years 1967-1969, approximately
1,300 Brazilian military and civilian personnel from the
military service and National War colleges attended
"courses" or were given "orientation tours" in the
United States.[26] Military Assistance Program grants
totaled $58.0 million and U.S. military sales to Brazil
amounted to $67.9 million during 1965-70.[27]

The post-1964 military regime did not extend its
belt-tightening policies to the armed forces. In 1965,

the armed forces budget, as a per cent of GDP, was
increased by nearly 50 per cent over the previous year.
The Brazilian armed forces continues to enjoy a bigger
slice of a considerably expanding GDP.[28]

In the realm of political participation, the
Brazilian military regime has been characteristically
antidemocratic. While there appears to be policy
debate and alternative views within the officer corps,[29]
this tolerance is not extended to civilians. Strikes,
demonstrations and similar active manifestations of
opposition are repressed, often harshly. Elements
marked as "extremists" are "enemies of the state" to
be destroyed by "internal war." Students, priests,
nuns, female relatives of suspects and other "enemies"
have been subjected to the most barbarous torture.[30]
Censorship and suspension of civilians' political rights
are widely used alternatives to physical forms of
intimidation. Peasant leagues and labor unions, once
major bases of mass politics, have been purged and
allowed to retain their organizational existence only
under strict control.[31]

BOLIVIA AND BRAZIL AS TESTS OF THE HYPOTHESES

The review of the two military regimes offers
uncompromising support for hypothesis (I.3) that
military rule is not conducive to the growth or survival of democracy. But to assert, as hypotheses (I.1)

and (I.2) do, that the military are tools of the oligarchy or wedded to the status quo is not supported by either case study. In both Bolivia and Brazil the military regimes have introduced policies that have brought social and economic changes. Corporatism, new urban construction, technology-based import substitution industries and other economic programs have brought prosperity and a high standard of living to professionals, managers, technocrats, skilled laborers, and, of course, local and foreign capitalists. And in so far as new factories, urban expansion, and expanding service industries offer jobs and improved living conditions to workers and peasants, the lower classes, especially in urban areas, perhaps have benefitted from the economic policies of the military regimes.

The basic characteristic of the policies of both regimes is that they are not redistributive. That is, while education, health and other social services are expanded, and industrial and commercial enterprises are protected and encouraged, nothing is being done to increase the participation of the masses in politics, in the economy, or in the society. This characteristic is illustrated by the Bolivian government's limited efforts at land redistribution or assistance to subsistance agriculture. In Brazil, the proscription of peasant organization and antimilitary, counterelite

political activities reveals the unwillingness of the
regime to expand power to the lower classes. The range
of policies pursued by the two regimes is biased to
protecting the privileges and property of the middle
and upper classes.

But I must hasten to add that this does not mean
that the military is the guardian of the middle class.
Before this hypothesis can be fairly tested, the social
elements which constitute the "middle class" must be
clearly determined. If as Nun and others seem to say,
the middle class incorporates everyone between the
traditional landed oligarchy, on the top, and the wage-
earning industrial and plantation workers, on the
bottom, the middle class includes military officers,
priests, radio repairmen, bank presidents, lawyers,
physicians, accountants, owners of dress shops, school-
teachers, production-line foremen and thousands of
other occupations. Clearly policy consequences of
military rule in Brazil and Bolivia have not favored or
even reflected the interests of many of these elements.
Owners of small commercial farms, shopkeepers, bureaucrats and other petty bourgeoisie in Bolivia and Brazil
have seen credit tightened, wages lagged behind rising
costs of living, and large foreign corporations cut
further and further into domestic markets. Are we
willing to confine "guardianship" merely to keeping

lower classes without political power, economic opportunity and social status that might challenge the
privileges of the propertied? If so, we must admit
that the current military regimes differ hardly if at all
from the civilians they displaced in the extent to which
they "guard" the middle class. The "military-as-guardian-
of-the-middle-class" hypothesis is simply too indiscrimi-
nate about what constitutes the middle class and what
guardianship implies in policy terms to be a useful
predictor of the outputs of military rule.[32]

Hypotheses (III) and (III.1) are apparently supported in both cases: the Bolivian and Brazilian
military governments have opened their economies to
foreign corporations (particularly from the U.S.), have
been encouraged to accept and have accepted large amounts
of U.S. military and economic assistance. The
Brazilians supported U.S. foreign policy at one of its
most controversial moments--the invasion and occupation
of the Dominican Republic. Why the military are so
supportive of U.S. interests is not clear. Since both
regimes are recipients of a variety of military
assistance (advisers, mobile training teams, training in
Panama and the U.S. as well as new playthings and money),
the interpretation given by hypothesis (III.2) ("through
numerous close ties with high military officials . . .")
at least is not without face validity.

The issue of military budgets is not resolved by our case studies. Although the advent of direct military rule was marked by temporary sharp increases in the budgets for the armed forces, it is not at all clear what these increased expenditures meant to the national economy. Cost/benefit analysis of military expenditures is extremely difficult since appropriations and expenditures are concealed, often go to capital goods (such as factories or highways), and in some unknown extent are spent locally for salaries, supplies and administrative overhead. Even flashy new super-sonic jets, aircraft carriers and tanks are difficult to cost-account since the purchase price may be far below their production cost and they may represent replacement of outmoded, worn out equipment. Appropria-tions for the armed forces rose immediately with the advent of military rule; but, as we shall see below, it is difficult to attribute such increases to the unchecked glee of rapacious solders.

QUANTITATIVE MEASURES OF MILITARY RULE

Although several efforts have been made to analyze the relationship between situational variables (e.g., economic depression) and incidents of military seizures of power,[33] much less attention has been given to the problem of the consequences of military rule for social and economic processes. In this section I shall review

selected examples of the latter type of research.
Works will be analyzed that deal with Latin America at
large and which employ aggregate data as indicators of
outputs and outcomes of military rule.

Robert Putnam[34] offers a series of hypotheses
concerning military intervention (M.I.) in Latin
America.   Intervention is indexed by an interval scale
(0 = apolitical, minor pressure group; 1 = civilian rule,
military significant in nonmilitary matters; 2 = mili-
tary-civilian coalition, autonomy for both groups; 3 =
military regime, civilians supplicants or tools of the
military) for each country over a ten year period
(1956-65), thus yielding a zero-to-thirty point range.
Sources on which the author based the ratings are
appended to his article.   While Putnam is principally
concerned with examining the relationships of intervention to social mobilization and economic development, two correlations lend themselves to our analysis
of the consequences of military rule: the relationships
between M.I. and strength of political infrastructure,
on the one hand, and internal characteristics of the
military establishment, on the other.

Using data from the Cross-Polity Survey,[35] Putnam
constructs four scales to measure the strength of
political infrastructure: (1) extent of articulation
by political parties; (2) extent of interest articula-

tion by voluntary associations; (3) stability of the
party system; and (4) extent of interest aggregation by
political parties. His analysis indicates that the
correlation between the level of M.I. and different
forms of interest articulation is negligible: .04 for
parties and -.19 for associations. The stability of the
party system is negatively correlated with M.I. (-.36).
The extent of aggregation by political parties and M.I.
are strongly and negatively related: -.63. Putnam
concludes that "These figures, especially the latter
one, strongly suggest that in contemporary Latin America,
political parties and military regimes represent
mutually exclusive mechanisms for reaching political
decisions."[36]

An alternative explanation of the negative correlations is that the political infrastructure scores
reflect assumptions by the scorers about the impact of
the military on politics. It is not at all clear that
the presence of viable parties and an active military
are not seen by these analysts as mutually exclusive.
If military rule is _assumed_ to be antithetical to
strong political infrastructure, then the correlation
would be negative because the rankings reflect
tautological reasoning. Unless it is established that
interest aggregation and military intervention are
based on independent measures, Putnam's correlations

are potentially spurious and therefore meaningless.

In light of the hypothesis (and longitudinal evidence from Brazil and Bolivia) that military regimes increase appropriations for the armed forces, it is noteworthy that Putnam finds defense spending as a per cent of GNP correlates cross-sectionally with M.I. at .55. Two other characteristics of the armed forces which might be assumed to correlate with the direction of expenditures, military personnel as a per cent of the adult population and size of the standing armed forces (in thousands), fail to conform to expectations. They were .07 and -.24, respectively. Perhaps the military elite are more interested in money than bodies in uniform. Putnam thinks increases in sophistication and professionalism, which relate to appropriations more than to size, are reflected in these three dissimilar correlations.

Another cross-sectional analysis of the impact of military rule on social and economic change is offered by Nordlinger.[37] His computations employ an interval scale of military control "according to the 'political strength of the military'." This scale, and his socioeconomic data, are taken from Adelman and Morris[38] and cover the period 1957-62.

Table 3 summarizes the relationships between military power and selected indicators of economic

TABLE 3

CORRELATION OF POLITICAL STRENGTH OF THE MILITARY AND ECONOMIC
CHANGE OF FOUR GEOGRAPHICAL REGIONS

	Latin America	Middle East North Africa	Asia	Tropical Africa
Mean size of Middle Class	71	62	51	37
Mean Level of Economic Demands	66	47	37	27
Rate of GNP	.01	-.28	.03	.45
Change of Industrialization	.16	.03	-.02	.42
Change Agricultural Productivity	-.06	-.03	-.39	.60
Expansion Education	-.43	-.12	-.07	.07
Investment Level	-.38	-.32	-.26	.06
Leaders' Commitment to Economic Development	-.43	-.16	-.17	.08
Mean Correlation	-.18	-.14	-.17	.29

Source: Eric A. Nordlinger, "Soldiers in Mufti: The Impact of Military Rule Upon
Economic and Social Change in the Non-Western States," American Political
Science Review, 64:4 (December 1970), p. 1146.

development. In Latin America, as in the Middle East, North Africa, and Asia, "soldiers in mufti," as Nordlinger calls officers who have seized control of governments, either fail to contribute to economic change or oppose modernizing demands and efforts where these exist. The negative coefficients for Latin America indicate that as the political strength of the military increases, economic development and modernization either decline or increase at progressively lower rates. For example, the Gross National Product growth rate remains constant regardless of military or civilian predominance; the average ratio of gross investment to GNP declines quickly with increased military power; military rule does little to spur increase in average annual industrial output; and enrollment at the secondary level of education as a percentage of the age group fifteen to nineteen decreases steadily with increased military strength. Only in tropical Africa is military strength positively related to economic change. In Latin America, the extent to which governments demonstrate concern for, and efforts toward, economic development, varies inversely with degree of military strength. That is, the stronger the military, the less likely is it that a government will be involved in direct or indirect central guidance of the economy; will be purposely attempting to alter institutional blocks to development goals; and will have a national plan or planning group within the administration.

These correlations clearly challenge the notion that the Latin American armed forces are guardians of middle-class economic interests. Since economic growth affords the middle class new jobs, consumer goods, improved social services, and overall higher standards of living, the finding that increased military strength is inversely related to economic development seems to attenuate the guardianship hypothesis. But Nordlinger arrives at the opposite conclusion.

Nordlinger finds that the size of the middle class seems to be an important predictor of the negative military development correlations. Apparently once a middle class which constitutes over 10 per cent of the economically active male population emerges, officers in mufti act to conserve, not expand, economic opportunities. The author hypothesizes that further expansion is seen by the military as involving the redistribution of economic privileges. Since the officers represent part of a middle class which has secured a relatively comfortable standard of living, there is little or no motivation to undertake strenuous programs which might increase their own tax burden, bring on inflation, and create more competitors for consumer goods and middle-class jobs. Viewed from this perspective, rapid and comprehensive economic development may be a threat rather than a boon to the middle class. Nevertheless, Nordlinger's coefficients and arguments actually support the claim that the guardianship hypothesis is based on too sweeping a notion of the middle class and middle class interests. Who constitutes the middle that benefits from restricting or curtailing of economic growth? Real estate investors and speculators? Administrative and technological personnel employable by import-substitution and local market-oriented industries? Owners and employees of retail and service enterprises? Graduates of school of business and faculties of economics? Hardly. These and other "middle-class groups" find little solace from factories unbuilt, schools not expanded, investments foregone, and agricultural and industrial production left dormant in order to preserve "their" economic privileges. These occupations comprise part of what might be called the "new middle class." Their economic health rests on expanding markets, mobilizing capital, securing tarriffs and tax incentives, finding skilled tractable employees. To these ends, structural impediments and traditional practices, be they lack of infrastructure or three-hour luncheon breaks, must be overcome. Perhaps members of the traditional professions along with bureaucrats,

owners and employees of export and extractive
industries, and of course the higher officers of the
armed forces, are frightened by economic growth. I
doubt, however, if many Fiat dealers in Buenos Aires,
managers of Sears Roebuck stores in Lima, production
engineers in Sao Paulo, or owners of construction
companies in Panama City hold the same negative attitudes. Rather, these and other members of the new
middle class support modernization and growth--and
very well may be the civilians who look to the "populist" military officers to break the hold of civilian
politicians who came to power after World War II when
the traditional middle class, with the assistance and
support of their cousins in the officer corps, wrested
political power from the landed oligarchy, social
notables, and senior generals of the army.

The most extensive treatment of the policy consequences of military rule is offered by Schmitter.[39]
Using both cross-sectional and time series methods, he
examines the relationship between M.I. and policy
outputs and outcomes (ca. 1960-65) by analyzing up to
126 variables. This remarkable exercise is too complex
and detailed to summarize here; instead, I shall
abstract from it those findings which seem to bear on
the present hypotheses.

Military rule, he infers from the patterns of

scatterplots and residuals, has little impact on expenditures for social services, education or public health programs. Direct taxes tend to be less, indirect taxes (especially on exports and imports) are likely to be higher as a per cent of central government revenue under military regimes, even when controlling for the level of economic development. The more party competitive and less military regimes are, the more they seem capable of extracting resources for the pursuit of public policies, again regardless of development level. Civilian regimes definitely spend less on defense than do militarized ones, but only when they are not plagued by frequent military inter-ruptions and threats. They also spend more on welfare. Long term military regimes spend more of their budget (but less of their GNP) on the military, have the lowest levels of expenditure per soldier and, yet, the highest rates of increase in their defense budgets. Those Latin American countries with the most politically quiescent military establishments spend less on defense even after all other factors have been considered.

The works of Putnam, Nordlinger and Schmitter are sophisticated attempts at testing significant and interesting hypotheses. They are clever in conception (and Schmitter's is brilliant in execution); however, their findings and the interpretations the authors

place upon them are acceptable only if one keeps in
mind three caveats. First, the data they use in the
construction of their indices are often highly
questionable. Relying on the <u>Cross-Polity Survey</u> or
Adelman and Morris (both volumes largely rely on the
opinions and intuitions of "experts"[40]) brings the
analyst pre-condensed classifications. This is not a
serious problem when dealing with reasonably "hard"
statistical data such as growth of GNP. But when such
"soft" subjective indicators as political strength of
the military are being established, relying on
evaluations by informants unknown to the user raises
questions about validity and reliability. Adelman and
Morris employ a three-cell taxonomy of the political
strength of the military: (a) direct political control;
(b) important political influence but not direct
control; and (c) little or no political influence.
Within these broad categories, countries are further
distinguished by (+) and (-).[41] Schmitter avoids the
limitations of relying on predigested input by forming
his own data bank. But like the others he is confronted
with primary data of dubious credibility. Much of the
data Schmitter processes is accurate and precise, but
I simply do not share his belief that error and inaccu-
racy is randomly distributed and, therefore, of little
<u>statistical</u> significance.[42] I have looked closely at

the data collecting and reporting procedures in one
Latin American country and have found both random and
systematic errors in every governmental reporting
unit.[43] Inaccurate data are not a problem when computations are heuristic exercises; when computations
are offered as statistical tests of substantive
hypotheses, sempre disputandum est.

The second caveat concerns the use of concepts such
as "apolitical," "essentially civilians," and "competitive." These concepts are so subjectively loaded
and operationally imprecise as to call into serious
question attempts to use them as bases for constructing
scales. Schmitter attempts to concretize "party competition" by defining it in terms of spread in per cent
of votes between the first- and second-place candidates
in presidential elections, ca. 1960. But this technique
ignores the voter's range of alternatives and the
honesty of the vote count, and assumes that elections
are, in fact, important for Latin American politics.
That "party competition" is a valid measure of popular
participation in politics is, at best, dubious.

At issue here is a broader problem common to the
works by Putnam, Nordlinger, and Schmitter: the tendency to see military rule in terms of military intervention. Tanks at the presidential palace; manifestos;
and, shortly, a be-medalled officer, surrounded by

grim-faced, often machine-gun-carrying, comrades,

accepting the Executive Sash. To conceptualize

military intervention thusly is to reflect a notion

of politics as essentially a formalistic series of

public actions.

An alternative view sees military rule as simply one

manifestation of military intervention. This view

reflects an understanding of politics as the formula-

tion of public policy and holds that the military may

intervene in varying ways, at various places, and

through varying actions. The three authors' ears are

attuned to gunfire and pronuncimientos and are insen-

sitive to the vibrations of brown oxfords walking to

and from cabinet rooms, whispers in the ear of Opposi-

tion legislators, rumbling from the strategic garrisons,

and the sound of the first rather than just the other

combat-boot dropping.

The third warning has to do with the use and abuse

of aggregate scores. One issue is comparability of

aggregate scores based on dissimilar periods. Nord-

linger states that half his economic indicators are

based on 1950-62 whereas the military scale covers only

1957-62. Consequently, some (what degree?) of Nord-

linger's aggregate economic indicators are actually

attributable to regimes not included in the military

scale. Are nations so unaffected by inchoate social,

political and economic forces that we are warranted to juxtapose these scales and then attribute variations in 1950-62 consequences to the actions of 1957-62 governments?

The issue of collapsing scores of differing value into an overall indicator is raised by Putnam's calculations. Here the analyst has used aggregate military intervention scores for each of ten years for twenty Latin American republics. With this aggregate score as his independent variable, he computes the association of military intervention and selected social, economic and political characteristics. By basing his analysis on the aggregate M.I. score, Putnam actually obscures the nature of the associations since scores vary from year to year in many countries. Far from increasing the confidence of his findings, he has raised doubts about the impact of variations over time and has lost an opportunity to learn about the association between M.I. and selected characteristics. He has reduced his data from 200 to 20 cases.

How serious is this contraction of data? If the changes in annual M.I. scores are rather evenly distributed or are of a small order, then it is entirely possible that the associations remain largely unaffected by the contraction. But Putnam uses a four-value scale so that a shift of even one category

represents a variation of 25 per cent. Moreover, the
aggregate scores mask the varying strength (and presumably, varying impact) of the military at particular
points during the decade. For example, Ecuador,
Honduras, Argentina, and Venezuela all have M.I. scores
of 23. But, as we see, Venezuela experienced military
regimes at the beginning, Ecuador at the end, and
Argentina and Honduras intermittently during the decade
1956-65:

	1956	1957	1958	1959	1960	1961	1962	1963	1964	1965	M.I. Index Score
Ecuador	2	2	2	2	2	2	2	3	3	3	23
Honduras	2	3	2	2	2	2	2	2	3	3	23
Argentina	3	3	2	2	2	2	3	2	2	2	23
Venezuela	3	3	3	2	2	2	2	2	2	2	23

By assuming that each of the four countries has been
effected identically by military intervention, we may
have missed important characteristics stemming, for
example, from differential levels of economic prosperity
or social unrest in each country during the decade, or
in the association between M.I. and economic development, social mobilization, and political infrastructure.[44]

An alternative correlational technique to the one
employed by Putnam is cross-sectional analysis: comparisons on a year-by-year basis of one variable (or
more) in two or more countries. For example, comparing

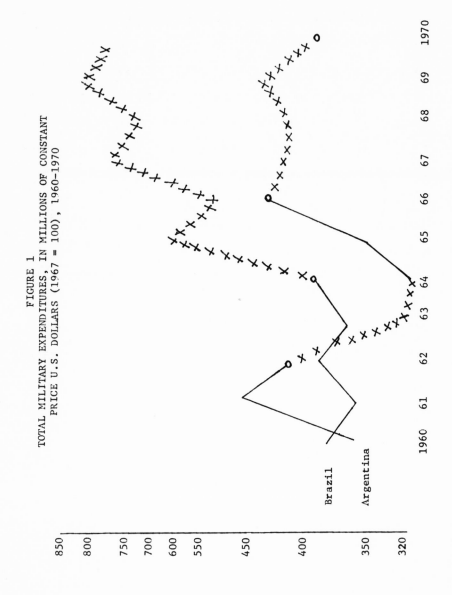

FIGURE 1

TOTAL MILITARY EXPENDITURES, IN MILLIONS OF CONSTANT

PRICE U.S. DOLLARS (1967 = 100), 1960-1970

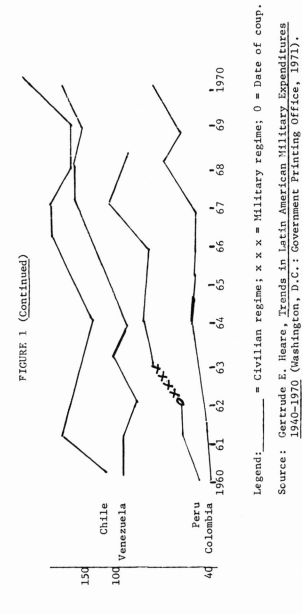

FIGURE 1 (Continued)

Legend: _____ = Civilian regime; x x x = Military regime; 0 = Date of coup.

Source: Gertrude E. Heare, Trends in Latin American Military Expenditures
1940–1970 (Washington, D.C.: Government Printing Office, 1971).

military budgets for Argentina and Brazil in 1965.
When we have two or more points in time (cross-sections)
for each country and variable, trend (or longitudinal)
analysis is available. (Comparing Argentine and
Brazilian expenditures in 1964, 1965 and 1966.) Such
trends allow comparisons both at particular points in
time as well as across a broad period.

Figure 1 presents a longitudinal comparison of
dollar expenditures for the armed forces in six Latin
American countries. Periods of formal military rule
are shown by "x"s; circles along the trend lines
indicate a successful golpe. Chile, Colombia and
Venezuela, which have had over a decade of civilian
rule, serve as contrasts to Argentina, Brazil and Peru.
These trend lines provide bases for (1) comparing
levels of spending by military and civilian regimes;
(2) analyzing the relationships between level and
direction of military expenditures and golpes; and
(3) examining the "contagion-effect" of increases/
decreases in spending in rival countries.

The time-series data in Figure 1 reveal that
increases in appropriations for the armed forces are
more frequently associated with civilian than military
regimes. While the contemporary Brazilian military
government dramatically increased armed forces'
expenditures after 1964, the Peruvian and Argentine

military did not when they seized authority. With the
exception of Brazil in 1964, the appearance of military
regimes is not associated with quick, steep rises in
military appropriations.

But using dollar amounts as an indicator of military
costs to the economy is deceptive: if an economy is
booming, larger dollar expenditures may hide an actual
reduction in the armed forces' per cent of total
public spending. Similarly, if dollar expenditures
remain constant over a period of contracting public
revenues, the drain on the economy may actually be
much greater than revealed by a trend line reporting
millions of dollars expended. For these reasons, a
more sensitive indicator of the impact of military
appropriations is the armed forces' per cent of Gross
Domestic Product (GDP). Using per cent of GDP we are
protected from distortions introduced by short-run
fluctuations in the economy. Also per cent of GDP is
a more reliable guide to the burden of the military on
the economy; it is the concept of burden on the economy
that is the central concern of Hypothesis (IV). With
this caveat in mind, we shall look again at the relationship between increased appropriation and military
rule.

Figure 2 reveals that for Argentina and Peru, two
republics which have alternated military and civilian

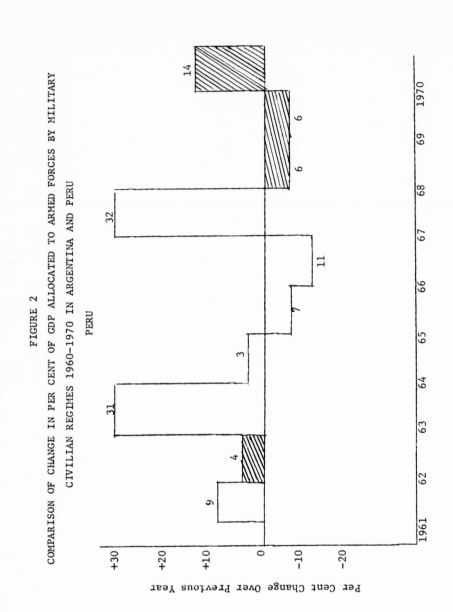

FIGURE 2

COMPARISON OF CHANGE IN PER CENT OF GDP ALLOCATED TO ARMED FORCES BY MILITARY

CIVILIAN REGIMES 1960–1970 IN ARGENTINA AND PERU

PERU

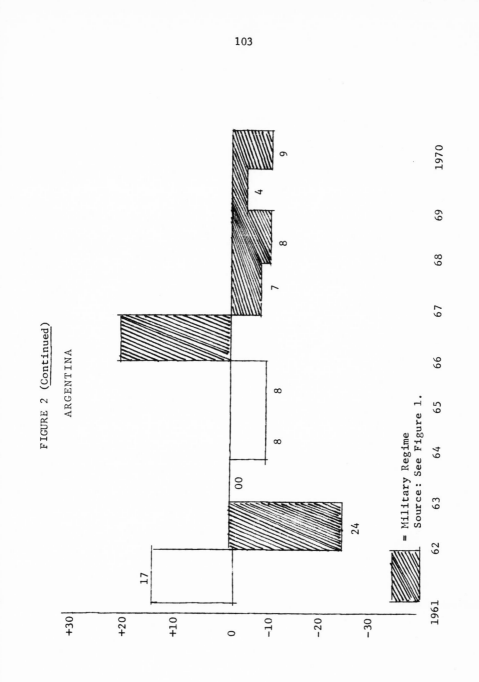

FIGURE 2 (Continued)

ARGENTINA

= Military Regime
Source: See Figure 1.

rule during the sixties, there is no clear pattern of
military rule being associated with increases in the
military's per cent of GDP. For Argentina military
rule seems to produce decreases in per cent of GDP over
the previous year: a civilian regime increased the
military's share 17 per cent in 1961 over what it had
received in 1960; but when a military regime came to
power in 1962, the per cent fell 24 points under 1961.
In 1966 the Argentine military regime increased by 23
per cent the armed forces' slice of the GDP; the same
military regime reduced the per cent of each of the
next four years. Data from Peru reveal that the two
most spectacular increases in the armed forces' per
cent of GDP took place during the civilian regimes.

Hypothesis (IV.1) suggests that the acquisition of
new weapons systems in suspicious or rival republics
acts as a spur to military appropriations. Figure 1
seems to lend support to this contention. The budgets
of Brazil, Chile and Argentina closely follow each
other through peaks, plateaus and troughs. We sought
to test this contagion hypothesis by correlating the
per cent of GDP spent on the armed forces in pairs of
rival neighboring republics. Table 4 indicates the
hypothesis is not supported in several cases.

The support of the rivalry-contagion hypothesis is
indicated by positive coefficients. Table 4 reports

TABLE 4

CORRELATION OF PER CENT OF GDP SPENT ON ARMED
FORCES IN RIVAL LATIN AMERICAN STATES
1960-1970

	Concurrent	Highest Contagion Correlation After Lagging
Argentina*-Brazil	-.45	-.31 (1 Year)
Argentina-Chile	.77	.77
Brazil*-Peru	.48	.61 (2 Years)
Chile-Peru*	-.54	-.20 (2 Years)
Colombia*-Peru	.17	.35 (1 Year)
Colombia*-Venezuela	-.11	.13 (2 Years)

(*) Indicates lagging country.

Source: See Figure 1.

both concurrent and the highest contagion correlations.
We first paired the partners' budgets concurrently
(that is, 1960/1960, 1961/1961 . . . 1970/1970). But
since information (perhaps "intelligence" is the proper
term) about procurement plans and actual deliveries is
not necessarily instantly available, we lagged the
appropriations of each actor for one and then two
years (1960/1961, 1961/1962 . . . 1969/1970; 1960/1962,
1961/1963 . . . 1968/1970). The assumption underlying
the two-year maximum incubation period is that the
contagion virus would be communicated and symptoms
would appear by this time even in a relatively isolated

and robust partner. By reversing the lagging country, we sought to identify the "independent actor"--the partner who sets the trend for the other actor.

The relatively high negative correlations of two pairs, Argentina-Brazil and Chile-Peru, which are known as major historical and contemporary rivals and interventionists in each others domestic and foreign affairs, present a stiff rebuke to the contagion thesis. An explanation is suggested by the high con-tagion correlations of Argentina-Chile and Brazil-Peru. Because they are less wealthy and because they began their military modernization later than Argentina and Brazil, Chile and Peru during the 1960's may have purchased a few relatively sophisticated systems (such as supersonic jet fighters or modern naval vessels) that were seen by military planners in Argentina and Brazil as placing their own systems at a decided dis-advantage. The correlations indicate that Argentina and Brazil quickly countered their ultramontane rivals. Therefore, the Argentina-Brazil coefficient does not necessarily mean that no contagion effect exists between the two republics; rather, their military budgets were influenced during the 1960's by third parties.

Chile-Peru may also reflect the ramifications of delayed modernization. Chile spent freely in the

1950's; Peru began to acquire major weapons systems in the early 1960's. We see from Table 4 that a two-year lag does significantly reduce the disparity between them (albeit, still revealing a negative relationship). Now that each has achieved a relatively advanced level of military modernization, the budgetary patterns of Chile and Peru during the 1970's will be a more valid test of contagion.

The finding that Chile and Peru are independent actors vis-a-vis their neighbors and each other but that Brazil, Argentina and Colombia seem to follow their neighbors should be considered in light of the relatively low salience of reversing the lagging partner. Only in the case of Colombia-Peru did swapping the partner lagged produce a significant change from negative to positive coefficient. No republic is a dominant independent actor such that it constantly sets the pattern for its neighbors and ignores their budgetary behavior. It seems likely that a major new system or re-organization by one of the six republics would provoke, within two years, increasing appropriations by its rivals. This probably holds true for apparently noncontagious Argentina-Brazil and Chile-Peru.

That spending by one Latin country is a determining force rather than merely a statistical artifact deserves the closest consideration.[45]

The Political Economy of Military Rule

Most of the data used to test hypotheses about the consequences of military rule have been socio-economic indicators such as growth in GDP, expenditures for social welfare services and military appropriations. This political economy approach is altogether consonant with what seem to be conditions governing research in Latin America. Indigenous scholars, rather than North Americans, will be conducting more and more of whatever field and survey research is undertaken; military establishments will become less, not more, accessible to research; and research priorities will shift from identifying elites and examining socialization and interest aggregation and articulation patterns to issues of policy consequences and analyses of social and economic aspects of nutrition, agricultural development, import substitution, multinational corporations, political demobilization, and alternative forms of social welfare services. By concentrating on the patterns and forms of resource exchange and allocation associated with different types of regimes, scholars from outside the region will be able to test proposi-tions from social science inventories while also serving (and being served by) host societies in Latin America.

By concentrating on outputs and outcomes, analysts

are directed to considerations of what groups hold
resources, how governments extract resources and who
bears the costs of and who benefits from public policy.
While such an orientation may not contribute much to
our understanding of the range of liberties enjoyed by
citizens of civilian- as opposed to military-ruled
societies, this political economy approach can go a
long way to eliminating the conceptual and methodological
confusion and ambiguity which beclouds both case studies
and quantitative analyses of military rule.

Such an approach for analyzing military rule might
begin with the following operational premises. In
order to survive, every regime (be it democratic or
totalitarian, elected or imposed) must extract and
allocate resources.[46] The quantity and exact resource(s)
needed vary widely, both for a single regime over time
and between regimes; but resources are the means by
which the regime induces or coerces compliance in order
to implement its objectives for the polity while making
its payments to the society. The resources of the
regime (i.e., "public" resources) include economic
goods and services, authority (the right to speak and
act in the name of the State), status, information, and
coercion.

These public resources are extracted from the
resources which are held in the society, e.g., economic

goods and services, information, legitimacy, violence
(no violence) and threat.[47] For any regime at a
particular point in time there is a minimum number of
groups and institutions whose allegiance must be
retained in order for the regime to survive. Since
the style and content of demands upon it determine
what resources the regime must allocate in order to
avoid bankruptcy, the groups (or "sectors" in political
economy terms) which compose its core combination vary.
When coercion must be invested or spent ("clubs are
trump"), the armed forces rise to predominance in the
core combination. This predominance of the armed
forces may be converted into authority, the ability to
establish public policy, the condition--irrespective
of holding the formal offices of government--of
military rule.

Since this conceptualization of politics is
founded on the extraction and allocation of resources
by government, political economy seems to provide a
comprehensive means for comparing civilian and military
regimes, both in terms of efficiency and effectiveness
and the relative costs-benefits to various sectors.
By conceptualizing resources to include authority and
status, two productive and scarce commodities in every
society, we expand the analysis into areas only vaguely
touched by exclusive reliance on output and outcome data.

In sum, both case studies and aggregate data tend
to support the consequences of military rule hypothesized above. It is clear, however, that concepts such
as "middle class," "imperialism," "democracy" and
"arms race" require substantial refinement if
hypotheses which employ them are to be empirically
tested. Given prevailing conceptual and methodological
difficulties, and in light of apparently changing
research parameters in Latin America, alternative
approaches must be sought in order both to test
existing models and to generate new research hypotheses.
A political economy model employing a resource-exchange
conceptualization of politics is one approach worth
consideration.

FOOTNOTES

*I am indebted to James Malloy and Thomas Skidmore for making unpublished materials available to me and to Barbara DePaola for comments and suggestions on an earlier draft of this paper.

1. For a discussion of military populism in Peru, see Julio Cotler, "Political Crisis and Military Populism in Peru," Studies in Comparative International Development, 6:5 (1970-71), 95-113; James Petras and Nelson Rimensnyder, "The Military and Modernization in Peru," in James Petras, Politics and Social Structure in Latin America (New York: Monthly Review Press, 1970), 130-158; and Anibal Quijano, Nationalism and Capitalism in Peru (New York: Monthly Review Press, 1971).

2. Useful surveys of the major works of the 1950's and early 1960's are presented by Alain Rouquié, "Le Rôle Politique des Forces Armées en Amérique Latine," Revue Française de Science Politique, 19 (August 1969), 862-893; Lyle N. McAlister, "Recent Research and Writings on the Role of the Military in Latin America," Latin American Research Review, 2:1 (1967), 5-36.

3. Edwin Lieuwen, Generals vs. Presidents: Neomilitarism in Latin America (New York: Praeger, 1964), 112-113.

4. Ibid., 130.

5. Martin Needler, "Latin American Military," Journal of Inter-American Studies, 11:2 (April 1969), 243.

6. Irving Louis Horowitz, "The Military Elite," in Seymour Martin Lipset and Aldo Solari (eds.), Elites in Latin America (New York: Oxford University Press, 1967), 149. Cf. Theodore Wyckoff, "The Role of the Military in Contemporary Latin America," Western Political Quarterly, 13:2 (September 1960, ". . . under certain conditions the military--far from being a threat to democratic institutions--may serve as a force to uphold and safeguard them. 762.

7. John J. Johnson, The Military and Society in Latin America (Stanford: Stanford University Press, 1964, passim.

8. José Nun, "The Middle-Class Military Coup," in Claudio Veliz (ed.), The Politics of Conformity in Latin America (New York: Oxford University Press, 1967), 104.

112

9. Horowitz, "Military Elites," 167.

10. Harold A. Hovey, United States Military Assistance: A Study of Policies and Practices (New York: Praeger, 1965), 70.

11. Ibid.

12. Petras, Politics and Social Structure, 313.

13. Horowitz, "Military Elites," 157; also see Edwin Lieuwen, Arms and Politics in Latin America, revised edition (New York: Praeger, 1961), 147.

14. Lieuwen, Arms and Politics, 229. See John D. Powell, "Military Assistance and Militarism in Latin America," Western Political Quarterly, 18:2 (June 1965), 382-392.

15. For a discussion of the pre-1964 role of the Bolivian armed forces, see James M. Malloy, "Revolutionary Politics" in James M. Malloy and Richard S. Thorn (eds.), Beyond the Revolution: Bolivia Since 1952 (Pittsburgh: University of Pittsburgh Press, 1971), 137, 142-144.

16. U.S. Agency for International Development, Summary Economic and Social Indicators 18 Latin American Countries: 1960-1970 (Washington, D.C., April 1971), 43.

17. William H. Brill, Military Intervention in Bolivia: The Overthrow of Paz Estenssoro and the MNR (Washington, D.C.: ICOPS, 1967), 53.

18. U.S. aid fell sharply in 1965 but picked up in 1966. See Table 9 in Malloy and Thorn, Beyond the Revolution, 390-391.

19. Melvin Burke and James M. Malloy, "Del populismo nacional al corporativismo nacional (El Caso de Bolivia, 1952-1970," Aportes, 26 (Oct. 1972), 66-96.

20. Ibid. Also see Richard S. Thorn, "The Economic Transformation," in Malloy and Thorn, Beyond the Revolution, 199-207.

21. Thorn, "Economic Transformation," 201.

22. Burke and Malloy, "Del populismo," passim.

23. For an account of the pre-1964 situation, see John W. F. Dulles, Unrest in Brazil: Political Military Crises 1955-1964 (Austin: University of Texas Press, 1970).

114

24. The present discussion of economic conditions in the post-1964 period is based on Thomas E. Skidmore, "Politics and Economic Policy-making in Authoritarian Brazil," revision of a paper presented at the Brazil Workshop, Yale University, 23-24 April 1971.

25. Alfred Stepan, The Military in Politics : Changing Patterns in Brazil (Princeton: Princeton University Press, 1971), 125-126; also see Riordan Roett, The Politics of Foreign Aid in the Brazilian Northeast (Nashville : Vanderbilt University Press, 1972).

26. Comptroller General of the United States, Problems in Administration of the Military Assistance Training Program (Washington, D.C., 1971), 12-14. Also see Robert P. Case, "El entrenamiento de militares latinoamericanos en los Estados Unidos," Aportes, 6 (October 1967), 45-56.

27. Department of Defense, Military Assistance and Foreign Military Sales Facts (Washington, D.C., 1971), 11, 23.

28. The Brazilian generals apparently feel the armed forces have earned an even larger share of Brazil's prosperity. Reorganization of the Army and expanded domestic weapons production are planned for 1972. See "Brazil Army Shuns Economics, Concentrates on Modernization," Miami Herald 11 April 1972.

29. Ronald M. Schneider, The Political System of Brazil (New York: Columbia University Press, 1971).

30. Philippe C. Schmitter, "The Persecution of Political and Social Scientists in Brazil," P.S., 3 (Spring 1970), 123-128; Ralph della Cava, "Torture in Brazil," Commonweal, 92 :6 (24 April 1970), 135-141.

31. Philippe C. Schmitter, Interest Conflict and Political Change in Brazil (Stanford: Stanford University Press, 1971), 212.

32. For an analysis of the conflicting interests of the middle class during a military regime, see Jerry L. Weaver, "Political Style of the Guatemalan Military Elite," Studies in Comparative International Development, 5 :4 (1969-1970), 63-81.

33. E. G. Warren Dean, "Latin American Golpes and Economic Fluctuations, 1823-1966,' Social Science Quarterly, 51 (June 1970), 70-80; Alaor S. Passos, "Developmental Tension and Political Instability : Testing Some Hypotheses Concerning Latin America," Journal of Peace Research, 5 :1 (January 1968), 70-86; Egil Fossum, "Factors Influencing the Occurrence of

Military Coup d'Etat in Latin America" ibid., 3 (1967) 228-251; Thomas A. Brown, Statistical Indications of the Effects of Military Programs on Latin America: 1950-1965 (Santa Monica: RAND Corporation, P-4144, 1969).

34. Robert D. Putnam, "Toward Explaining Military Intervention in Latin American Politics," World Politics,20:1 (October 1967), 83-110.

35. Arthur S. Banks and Robert B. Textor, A Cross-Polity Survey (Cambridge: M.I.T. Press, 1964).

36. Putnam, Military Intervention," 99.

37. Eric A. Nordlinger, "Soldiers in Mufti: The Impact of Military Rule Upon Economic and Social Change in the Non-Western States," American Political Science Review, 64:4 (December 1970), 1131-1148.

38. Irma Adelman and Cynthia T. Morris, Society,Politics and Economic Development: A Quantitative Approach (Baltimore: The Johns Hopkins Press, 1967).

39. Phillipe C. Schmitter, "Military Intervention, Political Competitiveness and Public Policy in Latin America: 1950-1967," in Morris Janowitz and J. van Doorn (eds.), On Military Intervention (Rotterdam: Rotterdam University Press, 1971), 425-506.

40. Adelman and Morris state: "The first step in preparing the data for the definition of qualitative indicators was to examine a large number of recent country studies, published and unpublished, and to extract from them the information relevant to the characteristics in which we were interested. We then drew up a preliminary classification scheme for each of the indicators we wished to include. We used a priori reasoning to specify and rank the elements in each definitional scheme and we determined the number of categories and the category limits in the light of the distribution of country traits and the nature of the country data . . . it became evident that the basic information for a number of variables was sufficiently inadequate to warrant a sizable intake of expert opinion in order that the country classifications be complete and valid. We therefore circulated to about thirty country and regional experts a description of the classification schemes . . ." Society Politics and Economic Development, 13.

41. Ibid., 74-76.

42. Cf., Philippe C. Schmitter, "New Strategies for the Comparative Analysis of Latin American Politics," *Latin American Research Review*, 2:2 (Summer 1969), 83-110.

43. Jerry L. Weaver, "Bureaucracy during a Period of Social Change: The Guatemalan Case," in Clarence E. Thurber and Lawrence S. Graham (eds.), *Development Administration in Latin America* (Durham: Duke University Press, 1973).

44. See David Gold, "Some Problems in Generalizing Aggregate Associations," *American Behavioral Scientist*, 8 (December 1964), 16-18.

45. Cf., Geoffrey Kemp, *Some Relationships Between U. S. Military Training in Latin America and Weapons Acquisition Patterns: 1959-1969* (Cambridge: Arms Control Project, Center for International Studies, M.I.T., C/70-5, 1970); Joseph E. Loftus, *Latin American Defense Expenditures, 1938-1965* (Santa Monica: RAND Corporation, RM-5310-PR/ISA, 1968); House of Representatives, *Hearings Before the Subcommittee on National Security Policy and Scientific Development of the Committee on Foreign Affairs, 91 Congress, Second Session, October 6, 7, 8; December 8 and 15, 1970* (Washington, D.C., 1970).

46. Warren F. Ilchman and Norman T. Uphoff, *The Political Economy of Change* (Berkeley: University of California Press, 1971).

47. Cf., Michael Lipsky, "Protest as a Political Resource," *American Political Science Review*, 62 (December 1968), 1144-1158.

FOREIGN MILITARY ASSISTANCE, NATIONAL MILITARY SPENDING AND MILITARY RULE IN LATIN AMERICA

Philippe C. Schmitter

Are flows of military aid from the United States, changes in the level of domestic spending for defense purposes and the propensity for the armed forces to intervene directly in political life related to each other in contemporary Latin America? A lot of people seem to think so. Numerous Latin American intellectuals, interest group spokesmen and politicians are further-more convinced that they are <u>positively</u> associated--that U.S. training programs and the availability of abundant grants and easy term credits for weapons acquisition whets the appetite of the domestic military establishment for both more weapons and greater political control. Even some U.S. congressmen and senators seemed to agree with a similar line of reasoning when offered it by testifying U.S. academics.[1]

On the other hand, officials of the U.S. Defense and State Departments have insisted that external

military assistance (MAID) is <u>negatively</u> related to
domestic military spending (DMS) in that it both substitutes for expenditures which would otherwise be made
from scarce national budgetary resources, and discourages
Latin American military establishments from purchasing
"useless," expensive, highly-sophisticated equipment.
As for military rule, these apologists tend to vacilate
between claiming that no relation exists between the MAID
and its occurence, and asserting that it is important
to back the Latin American militaries as the last
political bulwark against Communism, Castroite subversion or just plain anarchy.[2]

Leaving aside the <u>a posteriori</u> "lessons" drawn
from self-serving cases or the special pleadings of
obviously vested interests, it does seem plausible
that these three facets of the contemporary "military
problem" in Latin America might be closely inter-
related--so closely as to make inferences about antecedent cause and subsequent effect very difficult to
make. What is not clear is the direction and magnitude
of such interconnections. For example, announced
changes in the impending availability of external
support for training or weapons purchases might engender
contingent cutbacks in spending at the national level,--
if only to demonstrate "need." Conversely, increases
in domestic military spending may spill-over into

additional requests for foreign assistance. In short, external assistance and internal spending may be linked "subtractively," "additively" or even "multiplicatively" and this through causal sequences and over time-periods of unclear specificity.

Similarly, shifts in the external and internal resources going to the armed forces might be expected to influence their propensity to intervene more directly in national political life, but the direction and magnitude of the relationship also remains (logically at least) ambiguous. Rapid increases might trigger the military's appetite for even more but not provoke intervention in order to obtain it. Or, such increases might contribute to building institutional cohesion and self-confidence which might enhance their perceived "right to rule." Stagnant expenditures may disguise relative deprivation and/or subtle resistance by civilian actors to an over-ambitious military. Declining spending may indicate a winddown after substantial increases, consensual shifts to a new more limited (and less expensive) professional role, or the sort of con-certed attempt by a civilian regime to reallocate societal resources which might provoke open military opposition. In summary, short-term trends in domestic military spending seem plausibly related to a bewilder-ing variety of political outcomes.

These confounded "logics" are the natural result of any attempt to generalize about a region as variegated as Latin America. All of them "depend" on some prior, historical or structural, specification of contexts and these contexts differ considerably within Latin America, especially with regard to anything as complicated as "national armed forces." Even more, this state of relational confusion is a reflection of a fundamental epistemological difficulty in the social sciences. Apparently identical outcomes can be produced by completely different or unrelated causal sequences; apparently identical but incompletely specified causal sequences can produce divergent outcomes. One purpose of an inductive empirical exploration such as this is, therefore, improved understanding through "specification." It will attempt to build upon relatively simple and often rival, competing bivariate hypotheses by specifying additional, precedent and/or intervening conditions which make a given outcome possible or more likely. In short, the following data manipulations are not offered as a definitive effort to prove the probabilistic fit and trend of interrelations between military aid, military spending and military rule in Latin America, but an attempt to use observed patterns of empirical data to rebuild or respecify existing theory, as well as to pull together presently disparate "hunches" into a single, improved understanding of the area's civil-military problem.

Let us briefly review some of these rival but equally plausible hunches or hypotheses:

FOREIGN MILITARY ASSISTANCE AND
NATIONAL MILITARY SPENDING

I.A. Foreign military aid (MAID) substitutes for domestic military spending (DMS) enabling the regime to shift its resources to other priority areas, such as economic and social development. In its simplest form this would imply that for each dollar of incoming MAID, DMS would drop by an equivalent amount.

I.B. Foreign military aid (MAID), especially in the form of training, visits and advice on strategic doctrine, encourages domestic military spending (DMS) indirectly by stimulating appetites for new, more advanced weaponry and directly by forcing the regime to expend counterpart funds to meet the immediate domestic costs of installing such new equipment and tasks. Eventually, it may force national militaries to expend additional resources to meet replacement needs and ancillary, often unanticipated, organizational costs.

I.C. Foreign military aid (MAID) has no effect on domestic military spending (DMS) since the former tends to be treated as a sort of costless, self-encapsulated and rather erratic windfall above and

beyond "normal" defense expenditures which remain consequently unaffected. Much of Latin American defense
budgets consists of salaries, pensions and property
maintenance in any case and that small proportion
allocated for "capital improvements" is largely determined by longer-term, fixed processes of amortization
and replacement.

FOREIGN MILITARY ASSISTANCE
AND MILITARY RULE

II.A. MAID has a positive impact on the likelihood of military rule (MRULE) by improving the organizational and ideational self-confidence of national
military establishments (especially under the aegis of
U.S.-encouraged National War Colleges), by hardening
attitudes toward the threat of radical, "communistic"
movements, and by exposing Latin American officers to
the U.S. experience where, at least until recently,
civilian politicians have passively approved vast and
virtually unlimited allocations of resources for
military purposes. The latter cannot help but generate
invidious comparison with Latin America in countries
where civilian political groups have been less com-
pliant, budgetarily speaking.

II.B. MAID has a negative impact on MRULE by
encouraging a more inward-oriented, professional
orientation on the part of military establishments, by
reinforcing constitutional norms of civilian control

as exemplified by the donor country and, simply, by keeping the Latin American armed forces relatively satisfied with the prevailing levels and quality of equipment and training.

II.C. MAID has no impact on MRULE, the latter being determined primarily, if not exclusively, by conflicts and opportunities generated by endogenous political forces.

DOMESTIC MILITARY SPENDING (DMS) AND MILITARY RULE (MRULE)

III.A. DMS levels are inversely related to military rule in that decreases which involve declines in relative salaries and/or perquisites, or in the quantity and/or quality of equipment provide a strong institutional motive for seizures of political power. On the other hand, increases in DMS tend to be associated with relative institutional satisfaction and, hence, confinement to functional, professional roles.

III.B. DMS tends to be conversely related to MRUL in that secular decreases in spending reflect a long-term change in the societal role of the armed forces as they are pacified and come to accept voluntarily the strategic fact that the region's objective defense needs are minimal. On the other hand, long-term upward trends in DMS reflect an expansion in military role capabilities which will eventually spill-over into a pretension to exercizing political hegemony.

III.C. DMS levels are indifferently related to MRULE in that their increases and decreases tend primarily to reflect variations in rather fixed processes such as replacement of out-dated equipment and readjustment of salaries and maintenance expenses to cost-of-living changes. As such, they are a relatively autonomous, self-regulating matter with little or no impact on the global propensity for the armed forces to intervene directly in political life.

All of these hypotheses have at least a superficial plausibility and for each it is certainly possible to point to individual "confirming" cases. Unfortunately, few systematic and concerted attempts have been made to convert these variables into comparable operational measures, to examine all relevant cases or some sample thereof, and to test for the direction and significance of relationships.

Those studies which have applied these elementary cannons of comparative inquiry have shed some light on various bivariate relationships, but there have been few deliberate replications and/or cumulative findings. For example, Geoffrey Kemp has concluded, based on a study of eleven cases, that U.S. military assistance (especially its training component) is positively linked to certain patterns of subsequent arms acquisition and presumably therefore to higher levels of domestic

defense spending.[3] My own cross-sectional and longitudinal analysis of public policy in postwar Latin
America disclosed a significant relationship between
types of military intromission in politics and defense
expenditures.[4] Charles Wolf, Jr.[5] and Thomas A. Brown[6]
have argued that U.S. military aid has no consistent
relation to military rule; John Duncan Powell has
advanced and documented the contrary argument.[7] Unfortunately, differing case bases and time periods, data
sources and operational indicators and the use of weak,
often misleading, techniques of statistical inference
have simply left the issue further confounded and
confused.

Parenthetically, this sort of logically confounded
and empirically confused inquiry into the impact of
foreign military assistance upon domestic military
spending and rule is striking similar to the vigorous
debate which has raged for years among economists on
the impact of foreign economic aid upon domestic
savings/investment and economic growth. Given differences in the specification of operative variables, in
the treatment of varying intervening constraints and in
the selection of cases and time-periods to be examined,
their findings have diverged widely--even radically.[8]
If this is the case for such obviously quantificable
issues when posed in the supposedly more scientific

idiom and discipline of economics, what are we to
expect from an analogous inquiry in political science
where operational definitions are much more difficult
to establish, quantitative techniques much less
routinely used (and understood), and intervening constraints much less obvious and (probably) much more
numerous?

METHODOLOGICAL CAVEATS

Purely quantitative analysis faces some serious
limitations in probing the degree of probabilistic or
stochastic association between military aid, military
spending and military rule. Although numerical
indicators of all three sets of variables are not
difficult to find in the primary record or to create
from secondary sources, these may not be relevant given
the nature of the relationship hypothesized by several
observers. What may be more important than the absolute
magnitude of foreign military assistance are such things
as: 1) the type of aid proferred (e.g. training, grants,
credit-assisted sales or surplus stocks); 2) its timing
(e.g. before, after or during a change of regime, in
time of penury or prosperity); 3) its distribution (e.g.
whether to army, navy, air force, state militia, even
cavalry, artillery or staff school); 4) its content
(e.g. the ideological thrust of training, the policy
implications of different strategic doctrines; or 5)

the sheer fact that any aid at all is given (e.g.,
indicating policy approval or symbolic moral support).
If these qualitative and/or micro-quantitative aspects
are so important, seeking to associate changes in spending or intervention with changes in the dollar magnitude of total military assistance will simply be "beside
the point."

A related difficulty is that the publicly available figures on MAID may seriously and purposively
distort its real magnitude and especially its distribution across units. Even if one, as we have done here,
includes credit-assisted sales along with grants for
training and equipment acquisition, the Military
Assistance Program (MAP) "obviously cannot contain data
related to military assistance which do not have
budgetary impact. Nor can it contain items included
under other budgetary lines."[9] For example, the total
(worldwide) FY-1970 program was valued at $409 million
plus $70 of military sales credits. Not counted were
$25 million in "Ship Loans" and $225 million of "Long
Supply and Excess" or surplus arms, vehicles and aircraft (including new parts) declared "excess" and simply
given away. Other items not included in MAP were $525
million in AID public safety programs, $570 million in
straight commercial sales, $770 in cash sales and
Export-Import bank loans, $160 million for the operation

of U.S. military missions (MAAG) abroad, and $100
million of Food for Peace funds (!) spent on "common
defense purposes." In short, $479 million for FY 1970
appears on the formal ledger, while $2,375 million of
what could unquestionably be considered defense-related
support to foreign regimes appears elsewhere--if at
all!! Since we do not know how much from these categories has been going to Latin America and since we
have little reason to believe that it is there distributed in proportions similar to MAP this introduces
a probable source of systematic bias as well as under-
reporting into our calculations.

Also unit pricing policies seem to differ considerably from one transaction to another and there is
some evidence which suggests the prevalence of "package
deals" whereby arms are given or sold on official
credit at very low prices in exchange for commercial
(often non-military) sales at going rates.[10] Needless
to say, all this dissimulation, deliberate or not, makes
our principle independent variable, total military
assistance (grants, loans, credit-assisted sales, additional grants from excess stocks plus "other military
assistance grants") dubious for comparative purposes--
across units, over time or both.

Another serious obstacle to quantitative analysis
concerns the drawing of causal or even simple diachronic

inferences from synchronic or cross-sectional observations. We propose to get around this (partially) by utilizing two different research techniques. First, we shall explore relationships across two different cross-sections in time: (1) the postwar, pre-Alliance for Progress period (1945-64) and (2) the Alliance period (1962-70) for nineteen of the Latin American republics (Cuba is excluded for lack of data and, in the case of U.S. military aid, lack of variance in the latter period). Then, we shall switch to longitudinal (year-by-year) data on six South American polities for the period 1950-1970. Argentina, Brazil, Chile, Colombia, Peru and Venezuela were selected because comprehensive, reliable data on their military expenditures has recently become available[11] and because Geoffrey Kemp's more detailed breakdowns on military training and arms acquisition are available for five of these same units.[12]

Correlation and regression will be the statistical techniques used herein, almost exclusively. Our purpose, however, is not simply to scour the data for "statistically significant" associations, but to plot variable values against each other--bivariately and multi-variately, simultaneously and serially, and to fit lines to the data by means of least squares regression estimates. Subsequently, we will analyze the residuals from these plots, i.e. the disparity between the predicted and observed values for each case. This will permit us the most complete display of all relevant information and the detailed analysis of both conforming and deviant cases.

PART I

A SYNCHRONIC PERSPECTIVE: 1945-1961, 1962-1970

With the advent of the Alliance for Progress in 1961-62, U.S. military assistance increased greatly in quantity. During the sixteen previous years, U.S. $408.4 million was funneled to Latin American military establishments. In eight subsequent years, they received U.S. $864.7 million. At the same time, the type of aid began increasingly to emphasize training over grants for arms acquisition,[13] and the content of strategic doctrine shifted from continental defense to internal security and counter-insurgency.[14] The correlation of all these quantitative and qualitative changes seems to justify using 1961-62 as both an important turning point in policy and cut-off point for data aggregation purposes.

However, despite these changes, the matrices of data interrelations for the two time periods are strikingly similar--at least when absolute magnitudes are considered. The index of military rule (MRULE) is insignificantly related to either total MAID, total

TABLE 1

THE RELATIONSHIP BETWEEN CUMULATIVE MILITARY RULE,[1]
CUMULATIVE TOTAL U.S. MILITARY ASSISTANCE,[2]
TOTAL GROSS DOMESTIC PRODUCT,[3] AND
CUMULATIVE TOTAL DOMESTIC MILITARY
SPENDING:[4] 1945-1961, 1962-1970

Variable	Time Period: 1945-1961			
X_1 MRULE	1.000			
X_2 MAID	- .209	1.000		
X_3 Total GDP (1950)	- .084	.523	1.000	
Y DMS	- .043	.669	.938 (N = 13)	1.000

Variable	Time Period: 1962-1970			
X_1 MRULE	1.000			
X_2 MAID	.325	1.000		
X_3 Total GDP (1960)	.128	.704	1.000	
Y DMS	.245	.890	.910 (N = 19)	1.000

[1]A cumulative index of military rule; 1 = no military intervention, 2 = veto power, 3 = intervention. This index is based on the Putnam Military Intervention Index reported in Robert D. Putnam, "Toward Explaining Military Intervention in Latin American Politics," World Politics, Vol. XX, No. L (Oct., 1967), p. 109. Putnam's index was revised and extended to the periods 1945-50 and 1965-70.

[2]Includes Credit Assistance, Grants, Additional Grants from Excess Stocks, Other Military Assistance Grants and Export-Import Bank Military Loans. U.S. Agency for International Development, U.S. Overseas Loans and Grants and Assistance from International Organizations, 1945-69. A Special Report Prepared for the House Foreign Affairs Committee; and Department of Defense, Military Assistance and Foreign Military Sales Facts, 1971.

[3]In U.S. $; for 1950, Egil Fossum, "Factors

Influencing the Occurrence of Military Coups d'Etat in Latin America," Journal of Peace Research, 1967, No. 3, p. 247 citing original source as Mimeo, CEPAL, Santiago de Chile, 1966. For 1960, OAS, IASI, América en Cifras, 1965.

[4]U.S. $ at 1960 prices and 1960 exchange-rates, does not include DMS for 1970 and DMS for 1969 are budgeted and at current prices and exchange rates. For 1950-69, SIPRI (Stockholm International Peace Research Institute) Yearbook of World Armaments and Disarmament 1969/70 (New York: Humanities Press, 1970), pp. 278-81. For 1945-49, Joseph Loftus, Latin American Defense Expenditures, 1938-1965, Memorandum RM-5310-PR/ISA (Santa Monica: Rand Corporation, 1968), p. 11.

GDP or total DMS for both periods, although the signs change from consistently negative in 1945-1961 to consistently positive in 1962-1970. This suggests that the overall political role of the military may not be as assuredly the product of higher financial subsidization as several analysts have intimated. We will, however, return to this issue in our analysis of residuals.

On the other hand, the total size of the country's domestic economy is a very good predictor of that country's total (cumulative) military spending--.938 in 1945-61 and .910 in 1962-70. In short and not at all surprisingly, overall resource availability, seems to set fairly constrictive parameters on resource allocation for defense purposes. Whatever effect military assistance may have, it is likely to influence marginal increases above and below the amount "predetermined" by total GDP.

The total magnitude of U.S. military assistance
(grants and credit-assisted sales) is itself also
positively correlated with total GDP--indicating that
the United States does seem to scale its aid effort in
this domain roughly to the economic size of the country.
This "relative scaling" has been getting more intense.
It climbed from .523 in 1945-1961 to .704 in 1962-70.
The fact, however, that for both periods total military
aid was more closely and positively correlated with
total military spending than total GDP is an indication
that the marginal effect of such aid has been to raise
national defense expenditures above the level predicted
by GDP alone. The multiple R reached by entering all
three independent variables (actually the index of
military rule contributes very little) was .964 in
1945-61 and .975 in 1962-70. This is a sizeable,
positive increase beyond the .938 and .910 bivariate
correlations between total GDP and total national
military spending for the same time periods. It is
also worth noting that military assistance during the
Alliance for Progress was associated with even greater
marginal increases in spending by the Latin American
armed forces of scarce national resources--in direct
contradiction to the stated objectives of the Charter
of del Este.

In Table 2, the data have been transformed (where

TABLE 2

THE RELATIONSHIP BETWEEN CUMULATIVE MILITARY RULE,
PER CAPITA TOTAL U.S. MILITARY ASSISTANCE,
PER CAPITA GROSS DOMESTIC PRODUCT, AND
PER CAPITA TOTAL DOMESTIC MILITARY
SPENDING: 1945-1961, 1962-1970

Variable	Time Period: 1945-1961			
X_1 MRULE	1.000			
X_2 MAID	-.180	1.000		
X_3 Total GDP (1950)	-.312	.275	1.000	
Y DMS	-.259	.527	.904	1.000
				(N = 13)
Variable	Time Period: 1962-1970			
X_1 MRULE	1.000			
X_2 MAID	.062	1.000		
X_3 Total GDP (1960)	.132	.363	1.000	
Y DMS	.174	.738	.742	1.000
				(N = 19)

Source: See Table 1.

appropriate) into per capita measures--dividing the
total U.S. magnitudes of Table 1 by the national population totals for 1952 and 1961. This control for the
possible effect of size does not drastically alter the
matrix of relationships already discussed, although it
does bring out one aspect only dimly discernable in
Table 1.

Again, MRULE contributes insignificantly and the

per capita GDP is still the single best predictor of
per capita DMS. What has changed are the correlations
with military assistance. First, in both periods, it
emerges as much less associated with the size of the
economy. Now, expressed as an indicator of relative
development rather than total size, GDP is not so
crucial a factor of "relative scaling." Military
assistance is fairly evenly dispersed among Latin
American countries of differing levels of development
(although the more developed do get more of it in
U$S per capita). Second and, much more suggestive, is
the fact that aid is more independently correlated with
per capita defense spending, especially during the
Alliance period when it is almost as good as predictor
as per capita GDP (.738 vs. .742). Total military
assistance per capita significantly and positively
raises the anticipated level of national defense
expenditures above that predicted by per capita GDP
alone. Multiple R increases from .904 to .950 in 1945–
1961 with the inclusion of the former and the index of
military rule only "improves" it to .952. In the more
contemporary (1962–1970) period, it jumps even more
significantly--from .742 to .896--as the result of the
inclusion of per capita MAID.

This first pass at the data permits us to make our
first inductive inference: U.S. military grants, credit-

assisted sales and surplus stocks (total U.S. military
assistance) generally have had the net marginal effect
of raising national defense expenditures above the
level anticipated from the total size or relative
level of the nation's economy. National economic
factors, however, still remain more significant correlates of such expenditures, but have declined in predictive importance from 1945-61 to 1962-70. In effect,
Alliance for Progress military assistance has permitted
or encouraged Latin American countries to spend higher
total sums and per capita amounts on defense, independent of their developmental level.

Let us now pass to a more detailed unit-by-unit
analysis to see if this observed trend holds up and to
spot possible deviant cases. In addition, we will
return to the issue of the impact of military rule,
although a really close analysis of this must await
our switch to diachronic monitors of yearly performance.

It will be recalled that, above, we have demonstrated a tight, highly significant relationship
between total and per capita GDP and total and per
capita domestic defense expenditures for both time
periods. We have taken these two regression equations,
fitted a line to the respective scatterplots and read
off the residuals, i.e. the absolute difference for
each unit between its "predicted" position on the

TABLE 3

RESIDUALS FROM THE REGRESSION OF TOTAL GDP ON TOTAL
CUMULATIVE DOMESTIC DEFENSE EXPENDITURES BY RANK
ORDER OF TOTAL U.S. MILITARY ASSISTANCE:
1945-1961, 1962-1970*

Time Period:1945-1961		Time Period: 1962-1970	
Countries Rank-Ordered by Total MAID	Residuals In U$S Million	Countries Rank-Ordered by Total MAID	Residuals In U$S Million
1. BRA	+ 605.9	1. BRA	+ 499.9
2. PER	n.d.	2. ARG	+ 344.8
3. CHI	+ 550.1	3. CHI	+ 126.9
4. COL	- 544.7	4. PER	+ 219.5
5. VEN	+ 425.2	5. VEN	+ 564.1
6. ECU	+ 88.6	6. COL	+ 125.4
7. UGY	n.d.	7. BOL	- 21.2
8. ARG	- 68.7	8. ECU	- 37.6
9. DOM	n.d.	9. UGY	- 105.2
10. HAI	- 18.8	10. DOM	+ 86.3
11. MEX	- 924.3	11. GUA	- 120.9
12. NIC	n.d.	12. PGY	- 37.1
13. GUA	- 32.8	13. NIC	- 51.0
14. HON	- 12.2	14. HON	- 67.7
15. BOL	- 74.4	15. MEX	-1226.4
16. PGY	n.d.	16. ELS	- 58.0
17. PAN	n.d.	17. PAN	- 108.6
18. ELS	+ 20.5	18. COS	- 70.8
19. COS	- 14.2	19. HAI	- 62.4

$Y = - 16.4 + .28X$ 1952 $Y = 46.3 + .20X$ 1962
r = .938 r = .910

Source: See Table 1.

    *In order to check for the possibility that a few
outlying high values, e.g. Brazil and Argentina, were
responsible for producing excessively high correlation
coefficients and/or a skewed pattern of residuals, the
regressions were re-run with logged values for both
total MAID and total DMS. The result was to raise
(rather than lower) the resultant correlation coefficients while the pattern of residuals remained approximately the same. The very large absolute residuals for
Brazil, Mexico and Venezuela were, however, proportionately reduced.

TABLE 4

RESIDUALS FROM THE REGRESSION OF PER CAPITA GDP ON
PER CAPITA CUMULATIVE DOMESTIC DEFENSE
EXPENDITURES BY RANK ORDER OF PER
CAPITA TOTAL U.S. DEFENSE
ASSISTANCE: 1945-1961, 1962-1970

Time Period: 1945-1961		Time Period: 1962-1970	
Countries Rank-Ordered by Per Cap MAID	Residuals In U$S Per Capita	Countries Rank-Ordered by Per Cap MAID	Residuals In U$S Per Capita
1. UGY	n.d.	1. CHI	+ 32.63
2. PER	n.d.	2. VEN	+ 78.30
3. ECU	+ 27.23	3. UGY	− 26.24
4. CHI	+ 57.54	4. BOL	+ 21.99
5. VEN	+ 13.08	5. PER	+ 21.66
6. COL	− 25.44	6. NIC	− 1.45
7. BRA	− 18.34	7. ARG	− 19.99
8. DOM	n.d.	8. ECU	+ 6.47
9. NIC	n.d.	9. PGY	+ 8.88
10. HAI	+ 21.03	10. DOM	+ 19.52
11. PGY	n.d.	11. COL	− 7.89
12. HON	+ 3.72	12. GUA	− 6.94
13. ARG	− 9.86	13. PAN	− 42.01
14. GUA	− 16.94	14. HON	− 8.18
15. BOL	+ 11.39	15. BRA	− 17.34
16. MEX	− 41.45	16. ELS	− 7.78
17. PAN	n.d.	17. COS	− 19.14
18. COS	− 19.88	18. HAI	+ 1.79
19. ELS	− 2.07	19. MEX	− 34.29

$Y = -.36.7 + .47X$
$r = .905$

$Y = -18.8 + .18X$
$r = .742$

Source: See Table 1.

regression line and its "observed" or actual score.
These "mis-estimates," positive and negative, are displayed in Tables 3 and 4.

For example, Brazil emerges as a consistently
big spender in absolute terms. Given its large total
GDP, the regression equation predicted that Brazil

"should have" spent U$S 2695 million from 1945-61 and U$S 2365 million from 1962-70. In the former period, however, Brazil actually spent $605.9 million more than expected and U$S 499.9 million more in the second. Mexico represents an opposite case. With a similar total GDP, it "should have spent" and amount almost equivalent to Brazil. Actually, it spent only U$S 798.8 million cumulatively from 1950-61, and U$S 1040.2 million from 1962-70. Or, that was U$S 924.3 million and U$S 1226.4 million less than anticipated.

Chile and Venezuela were consistent overspenders; Costa Rica, Honduras, Guatemala and Haiti consistent underspenders in absolute terms. Colombia and Argentina went from negative to positive residuals; Ecuador and El Salvador went the other way. No comparative observations can be made about Peru, Uruguay, Dominican Republic, Nicaragua, Paraguay and Panama for lack of data.

Table 4 with per capita figures shows a different pattern of over- and under-spenders on defense. Brazil, for example, has changed to consistently negative residuals, while Haiti moved to positive ones. As a rule the per capita residuals are more consistent across the two time periods.

On the vertical axis of both tables, the nineteen Latin American countries are rank-ordered according to

the total amount (Table 3) or the per capita amount
(Table 4) of U.S. military assistance. The patterns
displayed by all four columns of residuals make it
clear why the addition of information on either indicator of military assistance improves our ability to
predict defense spending. The greater the total or
the per capita amount of external aid, the greater the
probability of that unit's having a positive residual
in national military expenditures.

There are, of course, exceptions. Colombia in the
pre-Alliance period, was spending less and receiving
relative large amounts of assistance. The contrast with
Chile, whose GDP was roughly similar, is dramatic.
Chile did receive a bit more military aid than Colombia
(U$S 48.7 million vs. U$S 42.4 million), but spent over
twice as much at the national level on defense-related
matters. The only other exception in column one of
Table 3 is El Salvador which "overspent" by U$S 20.5
million when it spent a total of U$S 78.4 million. Its
future military opponent, Honduras, with a 1950 GDP
of comparable total size only spent U$S 49.9 million.

During the Alliance period, (1962-70) the effect
of foreign military aid on enhancing total national
military spending is very striking on a case-by-case
basis. Only one exception appears--the Dominican
Republic! Otherwise, the high positive residuals are

grouped at the top, the negative ones at the bottom of
the rank-ordering.

The per capita regressions displayed in Table 4
show, of course, a very different set of ranks and
residuals, since the control for size greatly affects
the scores of all units. Brazil, which was a "high-
roller" before, acquires a negative "low-roller" position in per capita terms and, concordantly, drops in
ranking as a per capita recipient of U.S. military
favors. Others sustain their earlier notoriety. Chile,
Venezuela, Peru and Ecuador still occupy the top of
both the residual pattern and list of aid recipients;
Mexico, Costa Rica, Panama, Honduras and El Salvador
the bottom of both.

The frequency of manifestly deviant cases in both
columns of Table 4 (especially for the earlier time
period) challenges our earlier conclusion, although the
general distribution is still confirmatory. Some very
low per capita military spenders (Bolivia: U$S 9.59;
Haiti: U$S 14.11; Honduras: U$S 26.2 for the whole
1950-61 period) get positive residuals because their
low GDP per capita predicts that they "should have had"
lower--even negative expenditures per capita! On the
other hand for the 1962-1970 period, several high
spenders, e.g., Uruguay and Argentina, get negative
residuals--especially embarassing with regard to our

working hypothesis in that both have received relatively high per capita levels of U.S. military support. At both extremes, in other words, more curvilinear relations seem to obtain. The linear projections of a regression equation result in excessively high and low estimates for such "extreme" outlying cases.

/Although space does not permit an extended treatment of the issue, it should be noted that direct military aid alone (grants for training and arms acquisition) does not have such a significant marginal association with national military spending. It barely raises the multiple R beyond that already attained by total or per capita GDP alone and, hence, its pattern of residuals is nowhere near as consistent as those based on total military assistance, i.e., that which includes credit-assisted sales and surplus stocks./

Now we return to the issue of military intromission in politics. Our attempt to introduce this factor by means of a quasi-continuous index of military rule or intervention, summed separately across the two time periods, yielded very little. Countries with a high score on it neither received more total or per capita military assistance, nor spent more on total or per capita national defense expenditures. Nor, of course, did they receive or spend less. Why this might be the case can be gleaned from Table 5.

TABLE 5

RESIDUALS FROM THE REGRESSION OF TOTAL GDP ON TOTAL
CUMULATIVE DOMESTIC DEFENSE EXPENDITURES
BY DEGREE OF MILITARY POLITICAL
INTERVENTION: 1945-1961, 1962-1970

Degree of Military Intervention	Residuals in 1945-1961 U$S Million		Residuals in 1962-1970 U$S Million	
I. "Non-Political" (1960,66)	CHI	+ 550.1	CHI	+ 126.1
	MEX	- 924.3	MEX	-1126.4
	COS	- 14.2	COS	- 70.8
	UGY	n.d.	UGY	- 105.2
	COL	- 544.7	COL	+ 125.4
	BOL	- 74.4	PAN	- 108.6
II. "Transitional" (1960)	VEN	+ 425.2	VEN	+ 564.1
"Constitutional Guardians" (1966)	GUA	- 32.8	GUA	- 120.9
	PER	n.d.	PER	+ 219.5
	ECU	+ 88.6	ECU	- 37.6
	BRA	+ 605.9	DOM	+ 86.3
	ARG	- 68.7		
III. "Dominant" "Military Regimes" (1966)	PGY	n.d.	PGY	- 37.1
	HON	- 12.2	HON	- 67.7
	NIC	n.d.	NIC	- 51.0
	ELS	- 20.3	ELS	- 58.0
	HAI	- 18.9	HAI	- 62.4
	PAN	n.d.	BRA	+ 500.0
	DOM	n.d.	ARG	+ 344.8
			BOL	- 21.2

Source: For degree of Military Intervention: 1945-61,
Edwin Lieuwen, Arms and Politics in Latin America (New
York: Prager, 1961), pp. 154-70; 1962-70, Edwin Lieuwen,
"The Latin American Military," Subcommittee on American
Republics Affairs, Committee on Foreign Relations, U.S.
Senate, 90th Congress, 1st Session, 1967, pp. 7-13.
Otherwise, see Table 1.

TABLE 6

PER CAPITA AND PER SOLDIER U.S. MILITARY ASSISTANCE BY DEGREE

OF MILITARY INTERVENTION: 1945-1961, 1962-1970

Degree of Military Intervention	Time Period: 1945-1961			Time Period: 1962-1970		
		U$S Per Capita	U$S Per Soldier		U$S Per Capita	U$S Per Soldier
I. "Non-Political" (1960,1966)	CHI	1187.80	6.17	CHI	1655.55	10.66
	MEX	65.45	.10	MEX	100.00	.14
	COS	83.33	.08	COS	n.d.	1.02
	UGY	3626.86	9.43	UGY	1569.23	7.15
	COL	1843.47	2.67	COL	1272.72	3.32
	BOL	52.33	.20	PAN	n.d.	2.83
II. "Transitional" (1960)	VEN	1365.21	4.13	VEN	1947.36	10.14
	GUA	178.57	.38	GUA	1872.22	3.17
	ARC	110.11	.52			
"Heavy Indirect Influence" (1966)	PER	1716.00	6.86	PER	1550.00	5.70
	ECU	1477.78	6.65	ECU	1723.53	4.81
	BRA	786.46	2.37	DOM	1077.78	4.46
III. "Dominant" (1960)	PGY	62.50	.63	PGY	807.79	4.54
	HON	297.29	.58	HON	1420.00	2.75
"Military Regimes" (1966)	NIC	422.22	1.31	NIC	1700.00	5.33
	ELS	14.70	.04	ELS	1050.00	1.83
	DOM	400.00	2.29	BRA	924.88	2.22
	HAI	610.16	.89	HAI	180.00	.18
	PAN	29.41	.09	ARG	831.25	4.92
				BOL	1872.22	6.83

Sources: See Tables I and V.

The residuals from the bivariate regression of total GDP on total cumulative defense expenditures, when grouped by the three "degrees of military intervention" suggested by Edward Lieuwen for 1960 and 1966 show a fairly clear pattern.[15] The "non-political" militaries tended to have less than expected levels of spending--with Chile a consistent exception. Those polities "dominated" by their respective armed forces also tend toward being underspenders--with the glaring exceptions of two more recent converts from "transitional" status: Brazil and Argentina. Peru has since joined this fold and it, too, has a very sizeable positive residual. Otherwise, it is the systems which have intermittently restive militaries, self-appointed "constitutional guardians," (or which have recent histories of such behavior) that are the "overspenders."[16] There are exceptions, of course. Guatemala is an especially puzzling one in that a very repressive military regime reigned in the first period and protracted guerrilla warfare prevailed in the second. Yet, it remained a consistent "underspender"--and a relatively heavy military aid recipient from 1961 to 1970. Argentina in 1945-1961 and Ecuador in 1962-1970 were also exceptions.

The military assistance-military rule relationship is by no means as clear. Analysis of residuals--

i.e. controlling for the effect of GDP Size or developmental level--is relatively meaningless since the
bivariate correlations are weak between such general
ecological conditions and the extent of subsidization
of Latin American military establishments. We are left
with a simple display of the raw data in U$S per capita
and U$S per soldier by the threefold classification of
types of military rule. Before the Alliance for Progress, the "dominant" military regimes definitely
tended to get less support--in toto et per capita.
Guatemala is perhaps a dubious exception in that after
the Castillo Armas' coup of 1954 it might better be
placed in the bottom category. Mexico and Costa Rica
do, however, stand out as both low spenders and low aid
recipients. So does Bolivia for the earlier period.
The "transitional" cases tended to receive the most
support, but Chile and Uruguay belied this--as did
Argentina in the opposite sense. The per soldier
receipts vary similarly.

With the Alliance for Progress, military assistance increased considerably and tended to even out
across regime-types. Particularly heavy raises went to
the "dominant" military establishments of Paraguay,
Honduras, Nicaragua and El Salvador. Bolivia which fell
all the way from "non political" to "dominant" status
in six years according to Lieuwen and also rose from

U$S 52.33 to U$S 1872.22 per soldier in foreign assistance. Other "decaying" regimes (Argentina and Brazil)
also saw their military assistance raised. Of course,
only a detailed time-series analysis will permit us to
observe what preceded what. On the other hand, the
Dominican Republic and Panama, which according to
Lieuwen succeeded in "civilianizing" their armed forces
during this period, were rewarded or encouraged to do
so with increased military aid during the Alliance
period. Panama's progress, however, was hardly sus-
tained. Nor can the Dominican military yet be described as safely confined to barracks.

Some Quasi-Conclusions

1. Higher absolute and per capita levels of MAID
are associated with a cross-sectional, cumulative
tendency toward higher absolute and per capita levels
of DMS. This relationship is especially apparent as a
marginal or residual effect raising DMS above levels
predicted by total size or relative degree of economic
development. This has become even more marked during
the Alliance for Progress period. Proposition I.A.,
the "subtractive or substitutive" hypothesis, is only
consistent with a few deviant cases (Colombia, 1945-
1961; Bolivia and Uruguay, 1962-1970). Proposition
I.C., the "indifference hypothesis," is plausibly valid
from the pattern of per capita residuals for 1962-1970,

although the predominate weight of evidence supports
I.B., the "additive hypothesis."

2. None of the hypotheses linking MAID and MRULE
are exclusively and significantly supported by the
cross-sectional data. Before 1962 "dominant" militaries definitely received less support, but afterwards
almost equivalent amounts of MAID went to all three
types of military regimes. Since several of the countries whose civil-military relations deteriorated also
were the recipients of large MAID increases, the II.A.,
"positive impact," hypothesis could help explain the
Argentine, Brazilian and Bolivian cases--while the per-
formances of Panama and the Dominican Republic until
1966 were consistent with II.B., i.e., the "civilianiza-
tion hypothesis" that increases in MAID decrease the
likelihood of direct MRULE. Otherwise, the bulk of the
evidence suggests "no impact" or Proposition II.C. as
being the most plausible hunch. Chile, Mexico, Costa
Rica, Colombia, Venezuela, Guatemala, Ecuador, Paraguay,
Honduras, Nicaragua and El Salvador maintained more-or-
less the same type of civil-military arrangement from
1945-1961 to 1962-1970 despite large increases in MAID.
Uruguay and Haiti saw their MAID go down without an
appreciable change in relative institutional status.

3. Domestic military spending and types of
military political hegemony would seem to be curvi-

linearly related. Spending at less than anticipated
levels was (1945-1961) fairly closely associated with
"entrenched" regimes--those consistently dominated
either by civilians or by the military. The exception,
Chile, could be rather nicely explained away by the
effect of massive MAID in both periods. Subsequently
in 1962-1970, however, the DMS-MRULE relation becomes
less obvious as deviant cases proliferate and residuals
increase in size. In any case, this relation well
illustrates how difficult it is even to speculate
inductively about causality without at least some ink-
ling of temporal priority. Perhaps, as we now shift
to the six case longitudinal or diachronic analysis we
will be able to shed some light on whether those high
relative DMS levels preceded or succeeded changes in
MRULE. Until then, both Propositions III.A. and III.B.,
remain plausible, if incompletely specified and possibly
reversible in causal terms, although III.C.--the "null
hypothesis"--is more or less excluded by the synchronic
evidence.

PART II

A DIACHRONIC PERSPECTIVE: 1950-1970

The list of virtues enjoyed by time series or
diachronic analysis over cross-sectional or synchronic
approaches is impressive,[17] especially with regard to
the drawing of causal inferences. Nevertheless, the

wider availability of "one-shot" surveys, the shallow-
ness and incompleteness of most data series, the
greater statistical simplicity and lack of even
speculative hunches about probable lead-and-lag relationships have confined most aggregate data analysts
to ahistorical, cross-unit comparisons. Those who
venture to analyze the covariance of historical trends
within and across units quickly lose that sense of
finality and security imparted by "highly significant"
cross-sectional correlations. Apparently singular
variables begin to appear as "bundles" of sub-processes
--each with a different lagged effect upon other social
and political processes. Most seriously, the strong
assumption of uniformity of relationship across all
polities and/or cultures is called dramatically into
question. Comparisons of serial correlations within
different units leads to the disclosure, not only of
different lead-and-lag times, but different. even
dramatically opposite, patterns of association. For
example, foreign military aid may be positively linked
to national defense spending in one country, negatively
in another! Seizures of power by the military may be
followed by sharp upturns of defense spending here and
downturns there! The "all-in-the-same-pot" approach of
cross-sectional analysis, especially where coupled with
"uniformly valid" indicators measured as cumulative

totals or moving averages will fail to catch this
diversity in process. This will be the outcome even
where such analyses are followed up by detailed treatment of cases deviant from the established trend.

Availability of Domestic Resources

In Part I of this essay, we found strong evidence
which suggests that the total economic resources of the
society are closely associated with its level of total
national or domestic defense spending in Latin America.
The serial regressions (1950-1970) presented in Table 7,
although they cover only six polities: Argentina,
Brazil, Chile, Peru, Colombia and Venezuela, instead of
the full regional sub-set (minus Cuba), confirm these
findings. Resource availability, measured as total GNP
in constant 1969 U$S correlates diachronically very
closely with total military spending in constant 1967
U$S. This relation is highest in Peru (.957), followed
by Venezuela (.912), Brazil (.891), Chile (.835) and
Colombia (.828). Only Argentina, which had by far the
most erratic pattern of DMS, challenges this observation.
There the correlation was only .464.

The slope of the regression, i.e. the proportional
increase in DMS for each unit increase in GNP, did, however vary. In Chile (.032), Peru (.029) and Brazil
(.024) it was steepest. In Venezuela (.016) and
Colombia (.011), despite persistent civil strife, each

TABLE 7

SERIAL REGRESSIONS OF DOMESTIC MILITARY SPENDING ON GROSS NATIONAL
PRODUCT: PATTERN OF STANDARDIZED RESIDUAL VALUES FOR SIX
SOUTH AMERICAN COUNTRIES

I. Brazil: 1950-70*

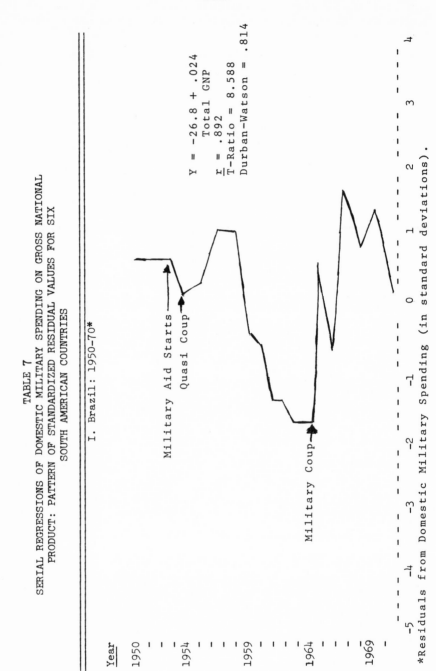

$Y = -26.8 + .024$ Total GNP
$\underline{r} = .892$
T-Ratio = 8.588
Durban-Watson = .814

*Residuals from Domestic Military Spending (in standard deviations).

TABLE 7 (Continued)

II. Argentina: 1950-70*

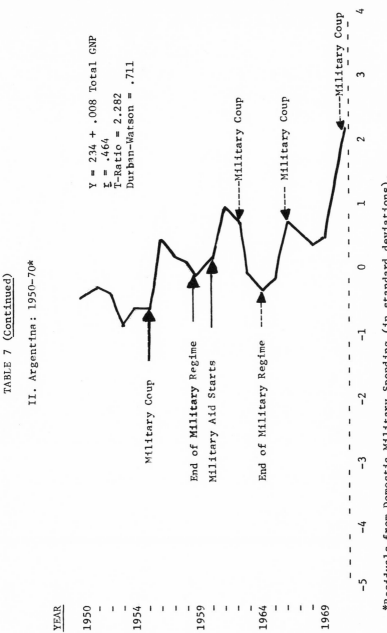

$Y = 234 + .008$ Total GNP
$\underline{r} = .464$
T-Ratio = 2.282
Durban-Watson = .711

YEAR

*Residuals from Domestic Military Spending (in standard deviations).

TABLE 7 (Continued)

III. Chile: 1950-70*

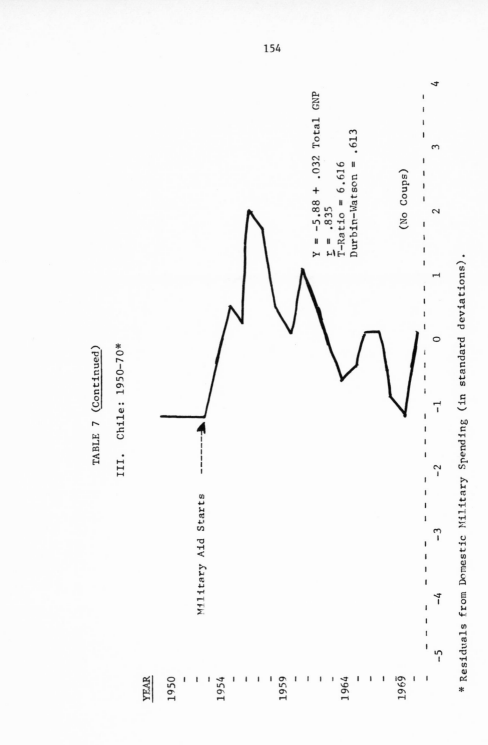

Military Aid Starts -------

YEAR

1950

1954

1959

1964

1969

Y = -5.88 + .032 Total GNP
r = .835
T-Ratio = 6.616
Durbin-Watson = .613

(No Coups)

-5   -4   -3   -2   -1   0   1   2   3   4

* Residuals from Domestic Military Spending (in standard deviations).

TABLE 7 (Continued)

IV. Peru: 1950-70*

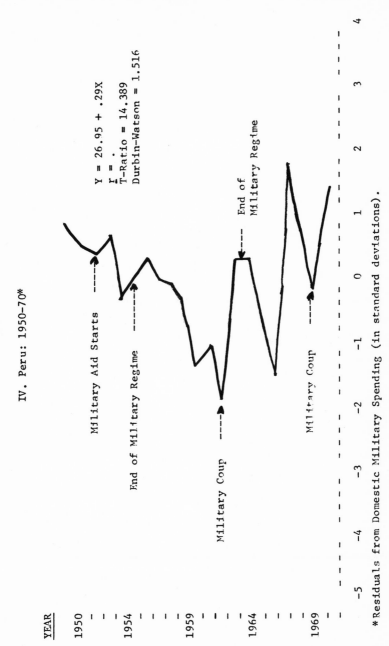

$Y = 26.95 + .29X$

$r = .$

T-Ratio = 14.389

Durbin-Watson = 1.516

*Residuals from Domestic Military Spending (in standard deviations).

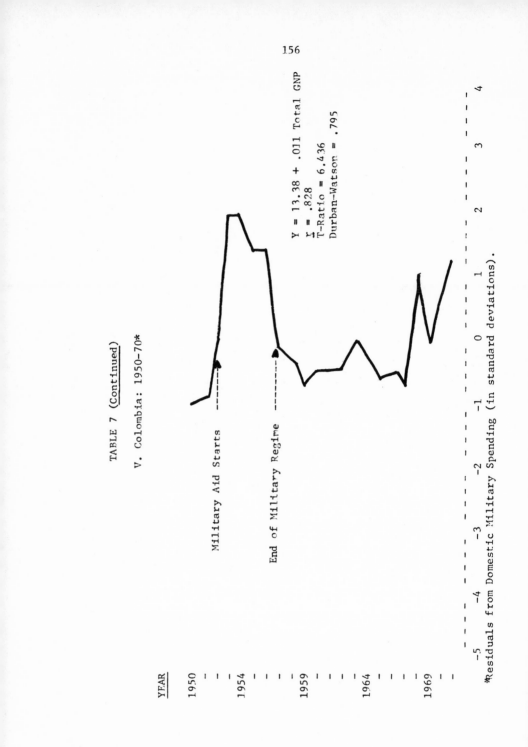

TABLE 7 (Continued)

V. Colombia: 1950-70*

*Residuals from Domestic Military Spending (in standard deviations).

157

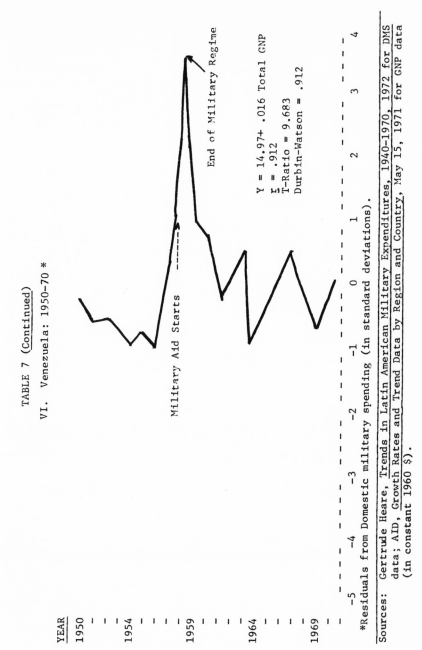

TABLE 7 (Continued)

VI. Venezuela: 1950-70 *

Military Aid Starts - - - - -

End of Military Regime

$Y = 14.97 + .016$ Total GNP
$\bar{r} = .912$
T-Ratio $= 9.683$
Durbin-Watson $= .912$

YEAR
1950
1954
1959
1964
1969

-5 -4 -3 -2 -1 0 1 2 3 4

*Residuals from Domestic military spending (in standard deviations).

Sources: Gertrude Heare, Trends in Latin American Military Expenditures, 1940-1970, 1972 for DMS
data; AID, Growth Rates and Trend Data by Region and Country, May 15, 1971 for GNP data
(in constant 1960 $).

additional dollar of gross national income "bought" slightly less military spending. In Argentina, where both GNP and DMS performed so erratically, there was virtually no upward slope at all (.008).

Put another way, the long-term propensity for individual Latin American countries to allocate a part of each GNP increment to defense "needs" varies. Cross-sectional regressions will produce a single value for this relationship, but that assumes a communality of process across all units which simply does not exist. So, Chile and Peru have spent approximately 3¢ of each $1 GNP increase on defense, Brazil 2.4¢, Venezuela 1.6¢ and Colombia only 1.1¢. Why the persistent and significant (except for Argentina) differences in the "decision rules" regarding military expenditures exist is, of course, not indicated by our data. Detailed comparative case studies, comparing the wage, pension, arms acquisition and training policies of, say, the Colombian and Peruvian militaries might draw out the reasons for such divergence.

Argentina remains a puzzle. Why is its military spending pattern so erratic? Qualitative information suggest several "hunches:" general budgetary instability, interservice rivalry, destruction of equipment due to internecine combat, deliberate diversification of weapons suppliers or just plain, poor planning and judgment. One important and unique fact is that until recently Argentina was the only Latin American country with a sizeable arms manufacturing capacity of its own.

The finding that total DMS and total GNP are strongly related seems rather obvious, although I know of no research which replicates it in other sub-sets. In general, discussion of military spending in developed countries has revolved around the issues of arms races between competing powers or the effects of the spiraling costs of weapons technology. In peripheral dependent countries, like the Latin American republics, which are relatively isolated from great power conflicts, which do not seem to be facing the prospects of an immediate armed international struggle and which are generally incapable of producing major weapons systems, the military perform different functions--more symbolic than real, more internally oriented than externally motivated. Hence, most of the elements which go into spending decisions are relatively unrelated to the classic functions of the armed forces, i.e. the defense of the nation from external attack or aggression in the cause of national agrandizement.

One suspects that, in such a setting, military policy-makers make a rough yearly calculus of prospective expenditures which incorporates the previous year's expenditures plus some increment. One likely

crude measure for arriving at this incremental estimate
is GNP growth--a less volatile and more predictable
standard of comparison than total governmental revenue.
Hence, military spending as a per cent of GNP has
remained constant or increased relatively steadily,
while military spending as a per cent of total governmental revenue has performed much more erratically.

Of course, the above is pure speculation. Whether
such a crude "decision-rule" exists or not, only
detailed in situo case studies will tell. We can, however, probe its possible existence with aggregate data.
Presumably, if this year's military spending is based
on the past year's plus some increment related to GNP
growth, then by lagging the values for total GNP by one
year, we should increase our capacity to predict DMS.

TABLE 8

MULTIPLE REGRESSIONS OF DOMESTIC MILITARY SPENDING
UPON SIMULTANEOUS GROSS NATIONAL PRODUCT AND GROSS
NATIONAL PRODUCT LAGGED BY ONE YEAR

	Independent Variables			
	Degree of Association (Bivariate r)		Test of Significance (T-Ratio)	
	GNP*	GNP_{t-1}	GNP	GNP_{t-1}
Argentina	.439	.770	+ 2.07	+ 5.24
Brazil	.883	.874	+ 8.00	+ 7.65
Chile	.815	.797	+ 5.98	+ 5.61
Peru	.957	.966	+14.08	+15.89
Colombia	.802	.796	+ 5.69	+ 5.59
Venezuela	.901	.903	+ 8.83	+ 8.91

*The bivariate correlations of DMS and GNP differ
slightly from those reported in Table 7 since by
lagging GNP by one year one observation was "lost" to
the analysis from each case.

Table 8 indicates that with one striking exception, this was not the case in Latin America from 1950
to 1970. As a rule, the capacity to predict DMS either
remains the same or declines very slightly. But for
Argentina, the increase is very impressive. Multiple
R leaps from a modest .439 to .770, almost as good as
that of the other five. Inference suggests that
especially in this country where total GNP has been so
erratic, military policy-makers do respond by raising
or lowering their expenditures with a one year lag.

So far our exploratory model of domestic military
spending has been structured in terms of internal
resource availability only. An alternative specification, more consistent with much of the quantitative
literature on North American policy-making would stress
bureaucratic inertia or incrementalism in which spending over time varies as a function of the previous
year's expenditure in a particular sector or agency
plus some standardized additional amount.[18] Rather than
be affected by the future anticipated or past observed
level of gross national product, DMS in a given year
could be predicted simply from the values of DMS for
the previous year (DMS_{T-1}) and so forth in a self-
sustaining, autoregressive sequence.

Because empirically there exists a high inter-
correlation (multicollinearity) between total GNP and

DMS_{T-1} for virtually all of our six cases, it is not statistically possible to partition the variance between these two rival models. In fact, for Colombia and Venezuela, the correlations of DMS with GNP and with DMS_{T-1} are virtually identical. For Brazil and Peru, there are only minor predictive improvements, but in opposite directions. In the former, DMS_{T-1} correlates .917 with DMS (compared to .892 for GNP and .874 for GNP_{T-1}); in the latter, GNP and GNP_{T-1} are both better predictors than DMS_{T-1} (.957 and .966 vs. .930). For Argentina and Chile, however, the "bureaucratic inertial" model is a marked improvement, especially in Argentina where the correlation increases from a quite modest .464 (GNP X DMS) to .739 (DMS_{T-1} X DMS). Nevertheless, for this case, it is GNP_{T-1} which is the single best environmental predictor (.770).

Given the impossibility of partitioning such interrelated variance and the confusion in predictive patterns, we will work consistently in this essay with developing further the model based on resource availability/constraints. The reader should be aware, however, that an initial and operative specification based on bureaucratic inertial assumptions might have generated different tentative findings with respect to the marginal relevance of other factors.

Regardless of the specific nature of the deci-

sional process involved, the task of further analysis
is rather clear. If our only object is to predict the
total level of DMS over time, the bulk of our work is
done. The task which remains is, however, much more
interesting and challenging. What is associated with
the scatter, the peaks and troughs or sinosoidal curves
about the general trendline which itself is so con-
vincingly related to total GNP? What other social or
political changes over time affect these deviations
from the spending norm? Why do spurts occur? Do any
expenditures occasionally decline secularly when GNP
continues to climb? To answer these "marginal" concerns, we must turn to the availability of external
resources (U.S. military assistance), the stimulus of
regional competition (defense spending in adjacent
countries), the imperatives of internal security
(levels of domestic political instability) and the
nature of political hegemony (military rule).

Availability of External Resources

The cross-sectional analysis suggested that
cumulative U.S. military assistance had a general, but
hardly uniform, tendency to raise domestic military
spending above levels predicted by gross national
product alone. The serial analyses summarized in
Table 9 weakly reconfirm the direction of that finding.
Annual MAID figures tend to be (with one major exception)

positively associated with higher annual DMS totals.
But these data manipulations considerably reduce its
magnitude, i.e. the statistical significance of its
already marginal impact.

TABLE 9

MULTIPLE REGRESSIONS OF DOMESTIC MILITARY SPENDING
BY GROSS NATIONAL PRODUCT AND U.S. MILITARY
ASSISTANCE COMBINED: 1950-1970

| | Independent Variables Upon DMS | | | | |
| | Degree of Association (Bivariate r and Multiple R) | | | Relative Significance in Multiple Regression of GNP and MAID (T-Ratios) | |
	GNP Alone	MAID Alone	GNP and MAID	GNP	MAID
Argentina	.464	.679	.726	+ 1.58	+ 3.44
Brazil	.892	.111	.894	+ 8.35	− .63
Chile	.835	.551	.856	+ 5.34	+ 1.01
Peru	.957	.182	.967	+15.65	− 2.20
Colombia	.828	.468	.828	+ 5.17	− .02
Venezuela	.912	.751	.944	+ 7.37	+ 3.16

For three countries, already singled out in
Part I as "overspenders" and high total cumulative
recipients of MAID, the addition of annual data on
inflows of U.S. military assistance significantly
improves our ability to predict annual DMS totals and
the effect is positive: Argentina, Venezuela and Chile.
For Brazil and Colombia--both also cited in Part I as
"evidence" for the positive residual impact of MAID--
the diachronic analysis reveals MAID to be of no

significant effect on a simultaneous year-to-year basis.
None of the scatter about the GNP-DMS trend line can
be "explained" by the U$S totals of MAID for these
units. Peru, also adduced as confirmatory positive
evidence in Part I, presents us with the really paradoxical finding. Here the inclusion of annual MAID
improves our predictive ability (multiple $\underline{R}$ increases
from .957 to .967), but the direction of that (infered)
impact is negative! As MAID goes up, Peruvian DMS dips
down below the regression line, suggesting substitution
of external for domestic resources, rather than addition.

Data analyses with values for MAID lagged by one
year failed to alter the general patterns discussed
above. Predictive accuracy for Brazil, Colombia and
Peru increased slightly; predictive accuracy decreased
a little for Chile and Venezuela, and a significant
amount for Argentina.

If one shifts from an external resource to a
bureaucratic inertial set of assumptions (as discussed,
infra p.161-2) and then examines the marginal effect of
MAID along with DMS_{T-1}, rather than GNP, upon DMS the
pattern is by no means as clear. Overall predictive-
ness increases slightly for Brazil and Chile, and
markedly for Argentina. It declines for Venezuela and
Peru and remains unaltered for Colombia. The direction

of the effect of MAID upon DMS does not change, but
its magnitude or significance (as measured by the T-
Ratio) does. For every case, MAID becomes a significantly weaker contributor to domestic military spending. The statistical reason for this is fairly obvious.
DMS_{T-1} is much more independently correlated with MAID
than is GNP, thereby, robbing it, so-to-speak, of its
strength of association. One inferential reason this
suggests is that the impact of MAID is in fact, spread
out over several years of military spending in some
distributed lag manner. Hence, introduction of this
previous value in the equation seeking to predict DMS
at the present moment masks the longer term relationship.

The plots of standardized residuals presented in
Table 7 also hint at some interesting relationships,
although the relatively shallow time perspectives makes
analysis tenuous. Both Brazil and Chile enter the plot
in 1950 to 1953 with regular, well-predicted levels of
DMS. As soon as military assistance starts, total
military expenditures immediately become more erratic--
increasing for Chile, decreasing for a short period,
then increasing thereafter for Brazil. For Peru,
already in a secular decline from 1950-53, military
assistance hardly affects that pattern which persists
until the coup of 1962. Colombia, on the contrary, was

in a phase of upward DMS and MAID did not seem to
affect this which continued until the coup of 1955
turned it downward. For Argentina and Venezuela, such
"interrupted, quasi-experiments" are more difficult to
perform since MAID did not begin until relatively late.

Stimulus of Regional Competition

Although scholarly inquiries have tended to down-
play their significance, an abundant journalistic
literature has decried the existence of rampant arms
races within Latin America. Certain sequentially
related purchases of new, "prestigeful" weapons systems:
aircraft carriers, tanks and supersonic jets have been
adduced as proof that these countries are exceedingly
sensitive to each other's defense posture. Nevertheless, since such purchases--no matter how visible--
constitute but a small portion of total defense expenditures, if only because payment for imported armaments
is often stretched out for a considerable period, they
are not likely to have a great impact on our calculations. Hence, we are dealing with the broader issue of
whether increases and decreases around the total
expenditure trend linked so closely to GNP are followed
in adjacent, competing countries. Even if such gross
shifts go "unaccompanied," this still leaves plenty of
room for symbolic-type arms races, of course.

Table 10 indicates that, by-and-large, such gross

TABLE 10

MULTIPLE REGRESSIONS OF DOMESTIC MILITARY SPENDING BY GROSS NATIONAL
PRODUCT, U.S. MILITARY ASSISTANCE AND DOMESTIC MILITARY SPENDING IN
ADJACENT COUNTRY: 1950-1970

	Degree of Association (Bivariate r and Multivariate R)			Relative Significance in Multiple Regression of GNP + MAID + DMS-ADJ (T-Ratios)		
	GNP Alone	GNP + MAID	GNP+MAID + DMS-ADJ	GNP	MAID	DMS-ADJ
Argentina	.464	.726	.820	+1.41	+2.24	+2.77
Brazil	.891	.895	.895	+5.03	− .63	+ .41
Chile	.835	.856	.870	+2.94	+1.44	-1.31
Peru	.957	.966	.967	+8.66	-1.60	− .35
Colombia	.828	.828	.881	+5.38	+ .39	-2.61
Venezuela	.912	.944	.945	+4.64	+2.45	− .50

shifts do go "unaccompanied." For Brazil, Peru and
Venezuela, our predictive capacity barely increases
when domestic military spending patterns in Argentina,
Chile and Colombia, respectively, are simultaneously
entered into the multiple regression along with our
two previous determinants: GNP and MAID. The T-ratios
for partial coefficients also show low levels of significance. Of course, all the DMS measures are highly
correlated with each other for the simple reason that
all are so closely linked to increasing GNPs and the
latter are serially correlated with each other throughout Latin America. The spuriousness of this evidence
for an "arms race" is clearly revealed when the relevant GNP indicators are simultaneously considered. The
independent effect of adjacent DMS "competition"
reduces to nothing.

Interestingly, those three countries whose military expenditures are apparently ignored by their
"competitors" seem to be attentive to those who are
ignoring them! In short, if arms races at the level of
total DMS do exist in Latin America, they seem to be
assymetric. Argentina, in particular, seems to keep a
positive eye on Brazil; its DMS goes up after Brazil's
does, other factors being considered at the same time.
For Chile and Colombia the linkage is inverted. As
the expenditures of their "potential enemy" (Peru and

Venezuela, respectively) increase, their DMS decreases!

Lagged values would seem to have a special relevance for such inter-country sensitivities, since military spending changes are not often simultaneously known. Hence, the effects observed above should be strengthened by entering into the predictive equation the previous year's DMS from "competing" countries.

TABLE 11

MULTIPLE REGRESSIONS OF DMS UPON GNP AND DMS IN
ADJACENT COUNTRY, AND GNP AND DMS IN ADJACENT
COUNTRY LAGGED BY ONE YEAR

	Degree of Association (Multiple$\underline{R}$)		Test of Significance in Multiple Regression with GNP (T-Ratios)	
	GNP + DMS-ADJ$_t$	GNP + DMS-ADJ$_{t-1}$	DMS-ADJ$_t$	DMS-ADJ$_{t-1}$
Argentina	.742	.768	+ 3.67	+ 4.06
Brazil	.885	.883	+ .37	− .03
Chile	.830	.854	− 1.16	− 2.00
Peru	.961	.962	− 1.14	− 1.38
Colombia	.871	.854	− 2.87	− 2.35
Venezuela	.921	.914	− 2.00	− 1.55

Table 11 generally supports that contention--and reveals some heretofore ignored relationships. In three cases, e.g. Argentine responsiveness to Brazilian DMS, Chilean to Peruvian DMS and Peruvian to Chilean DMS, the significance of one-year lagged values is greater than that of simultaneous ones. Brazil, however, remains "indifferent" to Argentine military expenditures. For the Colombia-Venezuela dyad, lagged values contribute slightly less than simultaneous cues.

However, Table 11 discloses a relationship which was disguised in Table 10. In Table 10, the effect of adjacent DMS was considered simultaneously with both GNP and MAID levels. In this multivariate context, it was largely "partialed out." When, however, MAID is not jointly introduced, stronger effects emerge. The interesting pattern is the significant <u>negative</u> responsiveness of two dyads: Chile-Peru and Colombia-Venezuela. In both cases with GNP simultaneously considered, the countries answer "perversely" to each other's changes in DMS. For example, as Chilean expenditures go up, Peruvian ones go down and vice-versa. Again, this would not appear on a bivariate plot since both DMS are so closely linked to increasing GNP in general trend terms. One possible explanation of this inversion (shared by Colombia and Venezuela) is that we are in fact observing a dyadic arms race, but one which is out of phase by five or more years. Only longer series and more qualitative breakdowns would permit us to prove that such a relationship exists.

Imperatives of Internal Security

Given the frequently made observation that the primary function of the Latin American military is "internal defense" or the control and repression of domestic political groups in the name of "law and order," it is reasonable to hypothesize that DMS will vary with the magnitude of the threat which such groups pose to the established regime. In short, some of the scatter about the upward-sloping trend-line may be associated with responses to political instability or civil strife. We have found some of that scatter linked to MAID and very little to DMS in competing countries, but a good deal remains "unexplained." Perhaps, domestic political instability can contribute some predicted variance.

The indicator (virtually the only one readily available) I have used to measure political instability is an index devised and compiled by Ivo and Rosalind Feierabend. This scored, on a yearly basis from 1948 to 1965, some 28 categories of events from North American news sources relating to political change and instability. Each event was weighted on a seven-point scale and totals were then calculated for each year.[19] In this analysis I have used the 1950 to 1965 series. The loss of the last five years in comparison to the earlier data manipulations affects the strength of the basic DMS-GNP relation, but not in any dramatic fashion.

A quick scanning of Table 12 both in terms of its impact on the degree of association and its independent relative significance reveals that internal political

TABLE 12

MULTIPLE REGRESSIONS OF DOMESTIC MILITARY SPENDING BY GROSS NATIONAL

PRODUCT AND INTERNAL POLITICAL INSTABILITY: 1950-1965

| | Independent Variables | | | | | | |
| | Degree of Association (Bivariate r and Multivariate R) | | | | Relative Significance in Multiple Regression with GNP (T-Ratios) | | |
Countries	GNP Alone*	GNP+ IPI_t	GNP+ IPI_{t-1}	GNP+ IPI_{t-2}	IPI_t	IPI_{t-1}	IPI_{t-2}
Argentina	.697	.707	.670	.682	+.60	+.43	+.61
Brazil	.730	.740	.763	.758	+.66	+1.78	+1.68
Chile	.788	.790	.717	.728	-.40	+.65	+.66
Peru	.942	.945	.943	.941	-.80	+.55	-.12
Colombia	.596	.597	.381	.436	-.09	-1.00	-1.30
Venezuela	.846	.855	.799	.851	+.84	-.01	-1.86

*The bivariate correlations of DMS and GNP differ slightly from those in Tables VII and VIII since by lagging IPI by two years, two initial observations were "lost to the analysis from each case.

Source: See Table VII for DMS and GNP; and Ivo K. Feierabend and Rosalind L. Feierabend, directors, Cross National Data Bank of Political Instability Events, Public Affairs Research Institute. San Diego State College, January, 1965.

instability (IPI) has little predictable effect on
domestic military spending. Based on the simultaneous
data set, i.e. all information from the same year,
three countries (Argentina, Brazil and Venezuela) show
a positive but not very significant effect; two countries (Chile and Peru) show a negative, but even less
significant effect and one country (Colombia) registers
complete indifference. One can hardly call that a
clear finding, although it is important to point out
that not only are the Feierabend data of dubious
reliability but the technique of summed totals for a
single year often results in identical scores for years
or units which hide quite different patterns of component events. One country will get, say, a "fifteen"
for six food riots and a couple of cabinet reshuffles;
another will receive the same for two general strikes
and an assasination; yet another will receive that
score while engaged in a protracted but sporadically
active guerrilla struggle. Intuitively, one suspects
that to the extent that military policy-makers are
sensitive to IPI, they would respond differently to such
identical scores.

The one and two year lagged values (IPI_{T-1} and
IPI_{T-2}) reveal even more confused partial associations.
In Brazil, IPI_{T-1} makes a rather significant contribution to higher predicted values, which continues on to

IPI_{T-2}. For Colombia, the inverse occurs--the longer
instability values are lagged, the better they become
as inverse indicators of DMS! For Venezuela, the
simultaneous data on instability have positive associations with military expenditures, the two-year lagged
data show the most significant negative pattern of
association!

One is tempted to dismiss these confusing findings as the product of unreliability and invalidity in
one's indicator of political instability. For example,
Colombia with its endemic violencia in which hundreds
of thousands of lives were lost gets an aggregate score
not far above that of Peru and far below that of
Argentina where relatively few people have been killed
as the result of political instability. Also as
mentioned, the twenty-eight categories of events,
despite weighting, tend to give relatively greater
importance to the sort of minor events which occur with
greater frequency in any polity: cabinet shuffles,
strikes, demonstrations, "turmoil", etc. Most seriously,
violence which becomes "routinized" and especially which
is perpetrated by authority groups tends to go under-
reported.[20] This certainly accounts for much of
Colombia's deceptively peaceful profile.

With these important reservations in mind, nevertheless, this inductive probe suggests that domestic

military spending was not related to internal political
instability in some common, law-like manner from 1950
to 1965. The burden of proof lies upon scholars who
can devise better diachronic indicators or who can
conduct more detailed case investigations to demonstrate the contrary.

Impact of Military Rule

From the sequence plots of residuals in Table 7
only two things are clear about the impact of successful military seizures of power or civilian regimes
restored after periods of military hegemony.
(1) Changes in the pattern of total domestic military
spending are associated with prior changes in the
nature of political regimes, (2) Changes in the pattern
of military spending also occur, however, in the
absence of shifts from military to civilian rule or
vice-versa.

The observation that military seizures of power
(and to a lesser extent, the restoration of civilian
rule) are associated with significant marginal changes
in total defense expenditures beyond the extent predicted by total resource availability says nothing
about the direction of such changes. The sequential
plots provide no clear and consistent answer to this
question. On five occasions (Brazil 1954/55, 1964;
Argentina 1955/56, Peru 1962/63, 1969), DMS rose

markedly the very year or within a year after power
was usurped; on three occasions (Argentina 1963, 1964;
Colombia 1954), they fell markedly. Restorations of
formal civilian hegemony twice resulted in substantial
upturns in military spending in Argentina(1959, 1964),
but downturns in Peru (1955, 1963) Colombia (1957),
Venezuela (1959)! In short, no policy response is
exclusively associated with regime change in one or the
other direction, although the probabilistic evidence
suggests that incumbent generals will raise total DMS
above levels predicted by GNP for that country and
incumbent civilians will do the opposite.

The sequential plot for Chile which experienced
no successful coups during the period clearly establishes the second point--that upturns and downturns
may also have nothing to do with change in regime-type
or even normal incumbencies. Perhaps, if one had
information on unsuccessful conspiracies, inter-service
rivalries and garrison pronunciamentos, one could
provide a plausible explanation for the peaks and
troughs which remain around the trend-line, even when
MAID, DMS in adjacent countries and IPI have been taken
into account along with total GNP. My hunch is that
even the most complete data on civil-military and
internal military relations would not yield very much
because a good deal of that scatter about the trend-

line has nothing to do with political conflict, social struggle or economic performance. At least for Brazil, Chile, Colombia and Venezuela, the scatter is crudely sinosoidal--or would be if the data series were extended. This movement, first climbing above the line, then falling across and below it, only to raise again above the line, may be related to periodic readjustments of salaries and maintenance costs to inflation and/or to cyclical processes of amortization and replacement of obsolete or used equipment. Many of these sharp up-turns and downturns may only be the result of officers seeking to maintain (and occasionally to advance) their economic well-being and social status and/or of the need to replace aged tanks, delapidated warplanes and rusting ships.[21] Once started in motion by the origi-nal equipment purchase, such sinosoidal demand curves for replacements are built into expenditures by the decay rate of the weapons system involved.

A third speculative generalization could be induced from the plots. While we have emphasized the effects of antecedent regime changes upon subsequent spending patterns, the direction of causality could be reversed. It appears from all cases (except Chile in 1958) that when DMS exceeds or even approaches two standard deviations above or below the level of expend-itures predicted by GNP, the chances of a military

coup ensuing are rather great. What we earlier interpreted as a significant upturn or downturn would often
be explained in terms of a regression effect or return
towards more normal or predictable levels of DMS after
exceptional decreases or increases.[22] Rather than
MRULE determining the level of military expenditures
(DMS) wide swings in the latter may provoke the former
which merely acts subsequently as a normalizing agent.

Whichever causal inference one wishes to draw,
Part II of this essay has well illustrated that, its
methodological merits to the contrary not withstanding,
diachronic analysis does not provide tidy and definitive answers to questions raised by synchronic approaches.
Instead, it is revealed to be a device for discarding
and/or whittling down ahistorical findings, for "un-
bundling" what appear to be unitary processes across
and within units, and for refocussing inquiry on previously neglected aspects of the problem.

Conclusion

The purpose of this exercise in inductive
empiricism has been twofold. On the one hand, I have
sought to display in a systematic comparative manner
descriptive material on the observed relationships
within a set of indicators. On the other hand, I have
attempted by means of speculative inferences to make
heuristic use of these data to advance a more general

form of understanding about the multiple components of
the"civil-military problem" in Latin America--and more
specifically about the determinants of domestic military spending.

Descriptively speaking, the "quasi-conclusions"
(see infra, pp. 147-9) drawn from the cross-sectional
manipulations of Part I hold up rather well under the
longitudinal scrutiny of Part II.

1) The primary factor associated with total
domestic spending for defense purposes is overall
domestic resource availability (operationalized here in
in terms of total GNP).

2) Increases in total U$S amounts of external
military assistance are temporally and positively
associated with higher than anticipated levels of
domestic military spending, although the relation is
weak for Brazil and Colombia and inverted (i.e. significantly negative) for Peru. In general, the diachronic observations are much less convincing than the
synchronic ones for this relationship.

3) Changes from civilian to military rule and
vice-versa definitely are followed by marked changes in
total defense spending, but the direction (up or down)
of these changes varies.

4) Substantial deviations in domestic military
spending above or below the trendline established by

TABLE 13

A SYNOPTIC TABLE OF GROSS NATIONAL PRODUCT, U.S. MILITARY ASSISTANCE, DOMESTIC
MILITARY SPENDING IN ADJACENT COUNTRIES AND INTERNAL POLITICAL
INSTABILITY AS PREDICTORS OF DOMESTIC MILITARY
SPENDING IN SIX LATIN AMERICAN
COUNTRIES: 1950-1970

	GNP Simultaneous	GNP Lagged	MAID Simultaneous	MAID Lagged	DMS-ADJ Simultaneous	DMS-ADJ Lagged	IPI Simultaneous	IPI Lagged
Argentina	++	+++	++	+	++	+++	0	0
Brazil	+++	+++	0	-	0	0	0	+
Chile	+++	+++	+	0	-	---	0	0
Peru	+++	+++	--	--	0	---	0	0
Colombia	+++	+++	0	0	--	---	0	-
Venezuela	+++	+++	++	0	0	---	0	0

Code : +++ Very significant positive association
        ++ Significant positive association
        + Positive association
        0 No association
        - Negative Association
        -- Significant negative association
        --- Very significant negative association

overall resource availability frequently occur <u>before</u>
military seizures of power or coups which return
civilians to office. In these cases, the effect of
regime change is generally to force a return to more
"normal" or predictable levels of defense spending.

5) Levels of domestic military spending in
adjacent "competing" countries have a relation with
DMS, but the nature of that relation varies from one
unit to another. Brazil is an exception in that its
DMS is indifferent, positively or negatively, to that
of Argentina.

6) Levels of internal political instability, at
least as operationalized by the Feierabends' event-
scored data, have no consistent simultaneous or lagged
relationship with DMS.

These descriptive findings from the dischronic
data are summarized in Table 13. Heuristically, they
suggest that it does make some sense to postulate a
more-or-less common policy process whereby South
American countries allocate resources to their respective military establishments. Inconsistencies in
the general pattern do exist and the explanation of
these demands further empirical and theoretical specification. The impact of foreign military aid varies
from highly significant and positive, to indifferent,
to highly significant and negative. A similarly wide

range of outcomes in domestic military spending is
associated with defense expenditures in neighboring
and competing countries. Also, while the GNP-DMS
correlation is strikingly constant, its slope is not.
Some Latin American armed forces regularly and consistently absorb a larger proportion of increased
national economic resources than others.

This preliminary exploration has succeeded in
raising several such contextual puzzles to the surface, but has contributed little to elucidating them.
More detailed breakdowns of aggregate data, for
example, of national defense expenditures into salaries,
pensions, maintenance replacement, and "capital
improvements," and of foreign military assistance into
training and arms acquisition, might improve our
inferential capacity, but essentially the function of
crude manipulations such as this one is to provide
parametric specifications within which detailed, focused,
case-specific inquiries can be conducted.

FOOTNOTES

1. Hearings before Subcommittee on Western Hemisphere
    Affairs, Committee on Foreign Relations, United
    States Senate, 91st Congress, 1st Session, United
    States Military Policies and Programs in Latin
    America (Washington: GPO, 1969), pp. 23-31.

2. Ibid.; also Hearings before the Subcommittee on
    Inter-American Affairs. Committee on Foreign
    Relations, United States House of Representatives,
    91st Congress, 1st Session, New Directions for the
    1970's: Toward a Strategy of Inter-American
    Development (Washington: GPO, 1969), pp. 498-539;
    The Rockefeller Report on the Americas (Chicago:
    Quadrangle Books, 1969), pp. 32-3; 59-65.

3. "Some Relationships between U.S. Military Training
    in Latin America and Weapons Acquisition Patterns:
    1959-1969," Arms Control Project, Center for
    International Studies, MIT, February, 1970. See
    also Jacob S. Refson's "U.S. Military Training and
    Advice. Implications for Arms Transfer Policies,"
    Arms Control Project, Center for International
    Studies, MIT, CL. 70-4 (February, 1970).
        Thomas Hovey in his United States Military
        Assistance (New York: Praeger, 1965) para-
        doxically concludes that prior to 1960
        when the magnitude of MAID was considerably
        less, "United States military missions
        probably aggravated the problem (the drive
        for increased military expenditures and
        military coups) instead of alleviating it"
        (p. 54), but with subsequent MAAG coordina-
        tion and the strategic shift to counter-
        insurgency and civic action, "it is clearly
        erroneous to assume that military aid has
        'caused' the high level of defense prepara-
        tions in Latin America or that these large
        expenditures are required solely to maintain
        equipment furnished by the United States"
        (p. 66). Also he states "it seems logical
        to conclude that the impact of the training
        portion of the military aid given to Latin
        American countries has not been to
        encourage military coups" (p. 69).

4. "Military Intervention, Political Competiveness and
    Public Policy in Latin America: 1950-1967," in M.
    Janowitz and J. vanDoorn (eds.), On Military
    Intervention (Rotterdam: Rotterdam University Press,
    1971), pp. 425-506.

5. "The Political Effects of Military Programs: Some
    Indications from Latin America," Orbis, VIII
    (Winter 1965), 871-893.

6. "Statistical Indications of the Effect of Military
    Programs in Latin America, 1950-1965," Rand
    Memorandum, No. P-4144, July, 1969.

7. "Military Assistance and Militarism in Latin
    America," Western Political Quarterly, XVIII
    (June, 1965). Also, Irving L. Horowitz, "The
    Military Elites," in S. M. Lipset and A. Solari
    (eds.), Elites in Latin America (New York: Oxford
    University Press, 1967), p. 173.

8. For a review and restatement of this literature,
    see G. F. Papanek, "Aid, Foreign Private Investment,
    Savings and Growth in Less Developed Countries,"
    Economic Development Report,No. 195, Development
    Advisory Service, The Center for International
    Affairs, Harvard University, 1971.

9. General Robert Jefferson Wood, "Military Assistance
    and the Nixon Doctrine," Orbis, XV (Spring, 1971)
    p. 263. The figures cited below come from the same
    source. pp. 264-65.

10. For an example, see Geoffrey Kemp, "Rearmament in
    Latin America," The World Today, XXIII (September,
    1967), 376.

11. Gertrude E. Heare, "Trends in Latin American
    Military Expenditures, 1940-1970," Office of
    External Research, Bureau of Intelligence and
    Research, U.S. Department of State, December, 1971.

12. "Some Relationships," op. cit.

13. For an account of the changing rationale in support
    of military assistance, see Michael J. Francis,
    "Military Aid to Latin America in the U.S. Congress,"
    Journal of Inter-American Studies, VI (1964), 389-
    404. For a critical study of this new emphasis on
    training, consult John Saxe-Fernandez, "U.S.
    Politico-Military Activities in Latin America,"
    paper presented at the Conference on Canada, Latin
    America, and United States Foreign Policy, North-
    western University, February 17-20, 1972.

14. See Willard F. Barker and C. Neale Ronning,
     Internal Security and Military Power: Counter-
     Insurgency and Civic Action in Latin America
     (Columbus: Ohio: Ohio State University, 1966).
     Also, see Thomas Hovey, op. cit., passim.

15. Arms and Politics in Latin America, Rev. ed.
     (New York: Praeger, 1961), pp. 154-170; Subcom-
     mittee on American Republics Affairs, Committee
     on Foreign Relations, United States Senate, 90th
     Congress, 1st Session, The Latin American Military
     (Washington, D.C.: GPO, 1967), pp. 7-13.

16. This constitutes a replication of my earlier study
     on public policy which used different indicators
     and time periods, "Military Intervention, Political
     Competitiveness and Public Policy in Latin America:
     1950-1967," pp. 441; 446; 455-6; 484.

17. See Robert Burrowes, "Multiple Time Series Analysis
     of Nation-Level Data, Comparative Political Studies,
     II, No. 4 (January, 1970), 465ff.

18. The locus classicus for this incrementatist
     argument is Aaron Wildavsky, The Politics of the
     Budgetary Process (Boston: Little, Brown, 1964).
     For a recent theoretical review and summary of
     empirical evidence, see Ira Sharkansky, The
     Routines of Politics (New York: Van Nostrand,
     1970).

19. For a discussion of the scoring system devised by
     Ivo K. and Rosalind L. Feierabend, see Betty
     Nesvold, "Scalogram Analysis of Political Violence,"
     in J.V. Gillespie and B. A. Nesvold (eds.), Macro-
     Quantitative Analysis (Beverly Hills, California:
     Sage Publications, 1971), pp. 167-186. For a sub-
     stantive article which utilizes these data,   see Ivo
     K. and Rosalind L. Feierabend, "The Relationship
     of Systemic Freustration, Political Coercion, and
     Political Instability: A Cross-National Analysis,"
     in ibid., pp. 417-440. The yearly data used in
     this study were taken from a computer printout
     made available by the Inter-University Consortium
     for Political Research.

20. For an analysis which reveals very substantial and
     systematically biased distortion in the Feierabend
     data for Caribbean countries, see Charles F. Doran,
     Robert E. Pendley and Georges E. Antunes, "A Test
     of Data Reliability: Global versus Regional Sources,"
     Unpublished manuscript, Rice University, Oct., 1971.

21. This interpretation is strongly, if summarily, stressed in Gertrude Heare, _Trends_, pp. 6-8.

22. For a general discussion of such "regression effects," consult D. T. Cambell and H.L. Ross, "The Connecticut Crackdown on Spending: Time Series Data in Quasi-Experimental Analysis," in E. Tufte (ed.), _The Quantitative Analysis of Social Problems_ (Reading, Mass.: Addison-Wesley, 1970), pp. 1141-15.

III

FUTURE PERSPECTIVES FOR ARMS CONTROL

AND MILITARY RULE

THE PROSPECTS FOR ARMS CONTROL IN LATIN AMERICA: THE STRATEGIC DIMENSIONS

Geoffrey Kemp

The purpose of this paper is simple. It is to draw attention to the complexities and confusions that surround most discussions about strategy, arms control and the role of force in Latin America. In the view of this author the realities of the military, as distinct from the purely political, factors in many Third World areas, especially Latin America, have been under-researched by the academic scholars. They have often argued that since Latin American countries have no genuine military requirement for sophisticated armaments, they should spend their scarce resources on schools rather than weapons. However, the justifications for these opinions are seldom articulated in a very profound manner. One purpose of this paper is to suggest a method of analyzing some of the more general strategic aspects of these problems.

It is taken for granted that the political success

of any arms control negotiations between the United
States and the Soviet Union on nuclear weapons limitations necessitates the most detailed understanding of
strategic issues. However, in contrast to the sophistication of the SALT debates, arguments regarding the
military balance of power in many Third World areas
seldom reflect analytical strategic judgments.

At present Latin America does not display the
volatile ingredients for international conflict that
exist in areas such as the Middle East. However, at a
time when the political future of Latin America is
uncertain and the political will of the United States
to pursue a "forward" foreign policy in doubt, it would
be foolish to presume that Latin America will forever
remain a backwater under the military hegemony of the
United States, an externally-enforced "security com-
munity."

By discussing some of the basic strategic problems
of Latin America, it is hoped that a new and heretofore
ignored perspective will be introduced into any discussion of arms control alternatives. It is possible
to make analytical judgments whether or not certain
military force structures provide greater capabilities
for certain types of military missions than other force
structures that require an equal amount of resources
to procure, maintain and operate. Conversely, it is

possible to suggest how alternative weapons procurement policies can influence military capabilities.

The paper will first outline some of the most important ingredients that influence the strategic environment in Latin America. The next section will consider the types of military forces that can be associated with alternative types of military capabilities. The final section will examine alternative arms transfer and arms control options, given the prior discussion on alternative force requirements.

THE STRATEGIC ENVIRONMENT

The primary influences that have determined the precise defense budgets, force levels, and weapons inventories in most Latin American countries have been based upon domestic political calculations. To understand fully the complexities of the role of the military in Latin America requires attention to sociological and bureaucratic factors. Nevertheless, there is some utility in approaching the issues of military power from an essentially apolitical and purely strategic perspective.

One reason for such an approach is that many of the constraints on Latin American military force requirements and capabilities display a degree of rigidity that cannot be changed in the short-run, no matter what domestic or external political factors are at work. First, most Latin American countries are, by accepted standards, less developed and thereby lack the technical and economic infrastructure required to support large, modern military forces. Second, the geography of many regions of Latin America presents major military logistics problems for certain military operations that are not found in, say, the Middle East or Southern Africa. Third, the relative physical and political isolation of Latin America from the main foci of international conflict has meant that none of the external powers, apart from the United States, have invested heavily in military base facilities in the area since 1945 and none, apart from the U.S., maintain forces capable of quick military intervention in Latin countries. It can be argued that this last trend may be changing, but as yet the Soviet Union has virtually no capacity to exercise military power in the region, apart from its limited presence in Cuba.

Although there has only been one interstate conventional war (El Salvador-Honduras, 1969) in Latin America since 1945, there have been many instances of internal conflict, some being extremely violent. There remain enough sources of conflict in the sub-continent to suggest that the present decade, like its predecessor, is unlikely to be blessed with peace and tranquility. Border and territorial disputes currently exist between Ecuador and Peru, Argentina and Bolivia, Bolivia and Chile, Argentina and Chile, Argentina and Britain (the Falkland Islands), Brazil and Paraguay, Venezuela and Guyuana, Venezuela and Colombia, Guatemala and Honduras, Costa Rica and Panama, and Honduras and Nicaragua. Internal conflict, including guerrilla activity, persists in many Latin American countries but especially in Argentina, Brazil, Colombia, Guatemala, and Uruguay. Furthermore, while instances of Cuban intervention in Central and South America show little sign of increasing, the political developments in Chile and Uruguay, paralleled by a more virulent sense of anti-U.S. nationalism in many other Latin American countries suggest that the area may become the focus of more international political competition than it has during the past twenty-five years of U.S. hegemony.

Because our ability to predict the political future of Latin America is fraught with uncertainties, it is especially important to stress those elements of the Latin American infrastructure that are not likely to change dramatically, no matter what revolutions and counterrevolutions occur over the next decade. For a long time to come most Latin American countries will remain very dependent upon external powers for many of their basic military force requirements, but this dependence will vary from one country to another. The

194

willingness of external powers to become embroiled in
the affairs of the hemisphere is also likely to vary.

To demonstrate this dependency and its implications, some very general discussion on the strategic
resources of Latin America is presented.[1] This, in
turn, will be followed by an analysis of the role of
strategic geography in influencing the military environment in South America.

Latin American Economic and
Industrial Resources and the
Procurement of Weapons

1. Indigenous Macro-Economic Indicators. For
many purposes the size of a country's GNP is the most
useful macro-indicator of its potential military
strength. High GNPs tend to correlate with large
industrial capacity, which in turn indicates a large
pool of skilled manpower that can be used to produce
and operate military hardware. Per capita GNP is
another useful macro-indicator. High per capita GNP
usually correlates with high levels of education and
industrial skills, both of which are essential for the
maintenance and operation of "sophisticated" weapons
systems.

It is often necessary to go beyond general overall data on GNPs and per capita GNPs. One important
refinement would be to focus upon the percentages of the
GNP and the labor force that are attributable to the

manufacturing and industrial sectors of the economy,
excluding construction, mining and oil extraction and
refining. Since a significant factor determining the
ability of a country to operate modern military forces
is the technical skills of the armed forces, a country
that has a large GNP and/or high per capita GNP that
is primarily attributable to its agricultural base and/
or mining base is less likely to have a pool of trained
technicians who can be used in the armed forces than a
nation whose GNP is partly attributable to a large
manufacturing and industrial sector.

Tables 1 and 2 summarize some very general data
on these points from a selected group of the most
important Latin American countries.

It will be seen that of the major Latin American
countries Brazil, Mexico, and Argentina stand out as
large, fairly industrialized countries, in theory
capable of maintaining higher levels of sophisticated
armed forces than their neighbors. The next group,
what one might call the "medium" Latin American powers
--Colombia, Chile, Peru, Venezuela, and Ecuador--also
have consistently greater industrial capacity than the
remainder of the countries in the hemisphere, including those not listed in the tables.

These indicators are, however, extremely general.
To be more precise in relating potential military

TABLE 1

TOTAL LABOR FORCE AND PROPORTION IN MANUFACTURING
FOR SELECTED LATIN AMERICAN COUNTRIES

	Total Labor Force (millions)		Total Manu-facturing (millions)	Labor Force in Manufactur-ing (Per Cent)
Argentina	7.4	(1960)	1.9	25
Bolivia	1.9	(1967)	0.11	6
Brazil	34.0	(1970)	3.1	9
Chile	3.1	(1969)	0.74	24*
Colombia	5.1	(1964)	0.77	13
Ecuador	2.2	(1965)	0.30	14
El Salvador	9.9	(1964)	0.11	13
Guatemala	1.3	(1964)	0.14	11
Honduras	0.8	(1968)	0.08	10*
Mexico	16.1	(1969)	2.9	18
Peru	4.1	(1969)	0.57	14
Venezuela	3.0	(1969)	0.51	17

*Includes construction.

Source: AID Economic Data Book, Latin America. Agency
for International Development, Washington, D.C.,
July 1971.

capacity to existing military capacity, it is neces-

sary to examine defense budgets and expenditures.

2. Defense Budgets in Latin America. A com-

parison of the national defense budgets over time pro-

vides one indicator of the level of national resources

that have been devoted to national security. Although

the bizarre nature of industrial accounting methods in

some countries make specific national comparisons a

risky business, generally speaking the budgetary figures

can be used to indicate broad patterns and trends in the

defense effort over time. In particular, the gross

size of defense budgets over time gives some indication of the types of defense efforts these countries
can make.[2]

The following table suggests this. Although the
table does not cover all Third World countries, it does
include most of those that have been engaged in full-
scale armed conflict over the past decade. Apart from
Cuba, the Latin American proportions fall considerably
below the mean and somewhat below the median figure.

If trends in Latin American defense expenditures
are examined solely within the context of the hemisphere, several specific issues need to be addressed.
A new study sponsored by the U.S. State Department on
Latin American military expenditures, 1940-1970, provides us with the most recent analysis on the subject.[3]
The conclusions of the report, though not startling,
are illuminating. Military spending in 1970 in the six
largest Latin American nations (Argentina, Brazil,
Chile, Colombia, Peru, and Venezuela) accounted for
about 70 per cent of all appropriations in the hemisphere. The total size of their regular military manpower accounted for about 75 per cent of the hemispheric total.[4] Although the total expenditure in 1970
for these six countries was 4 1/2 times the total for
1940, the proportion of the GDP spent on defense was
about the same, and the proportion of central government

TABLE 2

DEFENSE EXPENDITURE AS PERCENTAGE OF GNP: SELECTED

THIRD WORLD COUNTRIES

Middle East and North Africa	1966		1969	
	Per Cent	Rank	Per Cent	Rank
Algeria	3.9	(16)	5.8	(13)
Iran	3.6	(17)	6.6	(10)
Iraq	10.5	(7)	10.0	(8)
Israel	12.2	(3)	25.1	(1)
Jordan	12.2	(3)	18.0	(4)
Libya	1.4	(30)	1.9	(29)
Morocco	4.0	(15)	2.4	(27)
Saudi Arabia	6.8	(10)	8.8	(9)
Sudan	3.1	(19)	5.0	(14)
Syria	11.1	(5)	14.4	(5)
U.A.R.	11.1	(5)	13.3	(7)
Asia				
India	3.6	(17)	3.5	(17)
Indonesia	4.8	(11)	2.3	(23)
Korea N.	15.4	(2)	24.9	(2)
Korea S.	4.4	(13)	4.0	(15)
Malaysia	4.1	(14)	3.6	(16)
Pakistan	4.5	(12)	3.3	(18)
Philippines	1.3	(31)	1.5	(31)
Vietnam N.(1967)	22.5	(1)	21.3	(3)
Vietnam S.	7.7	(9)	13.6	(6)
Africa South of Sahara				
Ethiopia	2.8	(21)	2.2	(24)
Nigeria	1.5	(28)	5.9	(12)
Rhodesia	1.6	(27)	2.0	(25)
South Africa	2.9	(20)	2.4	(22)
Latin America				
Argentina	1.5	(28)	2.6	(20)
Brazil	2.2	(23)	2.6	(20)
Chile	1.9	(26)	1.7	(30)
Colombia	2.0	(25)	2.0	(25)
Cuba	7.0	(8)	6.1	(11)
Mexico (1968)	0.7	(32)	0.7	(32)
Peru	2.6	(22)	3.2	(19)
Venezuela (1968)	2.2	(23)	2.1	(28)
Median =	3.6		Median = 3.5	

Source: The Military Balance 1970-71 (London, Institute for Strategic Studies, September 1971), pp. 110-111.

expenditure somewhat smaller. In terms of inter-service (Army, Navy, Air Force) expenditure, the growth of air force appropriations has been most spectacular since in 1940, when most Latin American air forces were exceedingly small in comparison to armies and navies.[5]

The study contains also an interesting discussion of the relationship between personnel, organizational, and procurement costs. It is pointed out that increasing personnel and organizational costs are absorbing larger proportions of defense appropriations, thus confirming the trends that have been readily apparent in Western Europe and North America for several years.[6] In general terms, this means that for a given level of defense appropriations, relatively less funds have become available for the maintenance, operation, and replacement of military equipment. Thus, within the "weapons" budgets, trade-offs have to be made between maintaining existing equipment and procuring new equipment. Unless supplementary appropriations for additional weapons can be found, a new squadron of jet fighters or a new destroyer will compete with existing weapons for increasingly scarce operation and maintenance funds. The strategic implication of this trend in defense expenditure will be examined later.

3. Defense Material: The Supply of Arms for

<u>Latin American Countries</u>. Defense budgets give some
indications as to the magnitude and patterns of the
defense effort over time. However, budgets alone do
not indicate the extent of the dependence upon the
external powers. This section focuses upon one particular defense resources--arms.[7]

Modern arms may not be essential for the successful or protracted use of military force in many less
developed country environments including Latin America.
For example, the mass killings in Ruanda-Burundi in
1962, and the Indonesian Civil War of 1965, and the
killings in the Colombia "Violencia," were primarily
accomplished by <u>hand weapons</u>. Equally, the unsuccessful use of heavy firepower weapons by Egypt against the
Yemeni Royalists in the 1962-67 Yemen War and by Iraqi
forces against the Kurds during the 1960-70 war suggests that unless force structures and the capabilities
of technical personnel are related to the military and
physical environment in which they are to be used,
modern arms may not be as advantageous as might be
believed.

Nevertheless, modern arms (automatic small arms,
mortars, artillery, armored vehicles, aircraft,
missiles, and warships) are of great value in many
strategic environments and, what is more, are usually
<u>perceived</u> to be essential for the maintenance of an

efficient, well-disciplined modern army, navy, or air
force. It is quite clear that the supply of arms has
been one of the key factors in determining the nature
and cost of military planning programs in Latin
America. There are basically two ways a country can
obtain arms. It can produce them itself, or buy them
from, or be given them by external countries.

A. Indigenous Supply. Table 3 summarizes the
ability of Latin American countries to manufacture and
assemble various classes of weapons in year 1950. It
can be assumed that any country that does not appear on
the list had no meaningful weapons supply capabilities
at all in 1950. Only Argentina, Brazil, and Mexico had
any substantial ability to manufacture and assemble
heavy motor vehicles. Only Argentina and Brazil could
have been considered competent in a very limited sense
in the field of aircraft assembly. Certainly only
Argentina and Brazil had any appreciable ship-building
capabilities in 1950.

Table 4 summarizes the estimated capabilities of
Latin American countries ten years later. The total
number of countries who could manufacture and assemble
small arms fell from five to four owing to the shutting
down of installations in Chile that were specifically
geared to allied requirements for World War II. As
regards aircraft production, by 1960 Argentina and

Brazil had the ability to assemble light piston-engined trainer aircraft; these countries also had some capability in the light piston-engined transport field; and had the ability to assemble under license subsonic jet combat aircraft or subsonic armed jet trainers.

TABLE 3

MANUFACTURING AND ASSEMBLING CAPABILITIES

OF LATIN AMERICAN COUNTRIES IN 1950

	Small Arms and Ordnance	Heavy Trucks	Artillery	Tanks	Aircraft	War-ships
Argentina	X	X	–	–	X	X
Brazil	X	X	–	–	X	X
Chile	X	–	–	–	–	–
Dominican Republic	X	–	–	–	–	–
Mexico	X	X	–	–	–	–

TABLE 4

MANUFACTURING AND ASSEMBLING CAPABILITIES IN 1960

	Small Arms and Ordnance	Heavy Trucks	Artillery	Tanks	Warships
Argentina	X	X	–	–	X
Brazil	X	X	–	–	X
Dominican Republic	X	–	–	–	–
Mexico	X	X	–	–	–

	Aircraft		
	Light Trainer A/C	Light Transports	Jet Combat Mach 1.0
Argentina	X	X	X
Brazil	X	X	X

Sources: (for Tables 4-6): Various editions of the Military Balance the SIPRI Yearbooks on Armaments and Disarmament 1968/69, 1969/70; and the SIPRI study, Arms Trade with the Third World; the M.I.T. Studies on Arms Transfers to Less Developed Countries, in particular John H. Hoagland and Priscilla Clapp, Notes on Small Arms: Janes All the World Aircraft (various editions); Janes Fighting Ships (various editions).

Table 5 estimates the weapons production capabilities of Latin American countries as of January,
1972. Whereas the total number of countries who can
manufacture and assemble small arms has not risen, there
have been some improvements in other weapons categories
for selected countries.

TABLE 5

MANUFACTURING AND ASSEMBLING CAPABILITIES IN 1972

	Small Arms and Ordnance	Heavy Trucks	Artillery	Tanks, Armored Vehicles	War- ships	Missiles Rockets
Argentina	X	X	–	X	X	–
Brazil	X	X	–	X	X	X
Chile	–	–	–	–	X	–
Dominican Republic	X	–	–	–	–	–
Mexico	X	X	–	–	–	–
El Salvador	X	–	–	–	–	–

	Aircraft		
	Light Trainer	Light Transports	Mach 1.0
Argentina	X	X	X
Brazil	X	X	X
Chile	X	–	–

It can be seen that the military requirements for
Latin American armed forces cannot be based upon the
ability of the domestic industry to supply arms unless
requirements are very limited. If "rational" standards
of military planning exist, military requirements are
usually believed to be based upon assessments of potential or existing adversary force levels, capabilities,
and perceived intentions. These factors may be changed

very quickly if the supply curve of arms is elastic.
That is to say, if external powers can provide large
quantities of arms and training to one adversary in a
short time frame, the other adversary or adversaries
will probably feel it necessary to seek external supplies
themselves to redress "the arms balance" or will have to
rely upon their own resources to compensate for any
weakening in their own military position. These, of
course, are the classic ingredients for a competitive
"arms race." Since the external supply curve for most
weapons is much more elastic than the domestic supply
curve, the rate of change of Latin American weapons
inventories is perhaps more volatile than that for
"self-supplied" areas.

Table 6 shows the approximate proportions of the
weapons inventories of Latin American countries that
can be supplied from local sources. Although the
measures used to identify the "proportions" are very
crude and employ an ordinal rather than an interval
scale, they highlight the point that, despite the growing capabilities of some Latin American countries to
manufacture certain types of weapons, overall dependence
on external industrial countries for most advanced
weapons systems remained extremely strong as of
January 1972.

B. External Arms Supplies. Since several studies

appeared recently that discuss in great detail the
patterns of external arms transfer to Latin America, I
will only highlight some of the most significant features
of this process.[8]

As with the case of comparative levels of defense
expenditure, the absolute level of weapons transferred
to Latin America has been relatively very low. It was
not until Peru purchased the French Mach 2.0 Mirage V
in 1968 (against U.S. wishes) that a sale or grant for
super-sonic aircraft on the sub-continent had been
concluded, apart from earlier Soviet transfer of
Mig.-21's to Cuba. Given the considerable absolute
wealth of several Latin American countries by the
standards of lesser developed countries, the reluctance
to procure sophisticated weapons, especially prestigious
aircraft, needs some explanation. The reasons are
complex and can only be assumed. Among the more
important would seem to be the following:

1. The absence of major conflict between well-
   armed adversaries. The only Latin American
   country to have faced an adversary armed
   with advanced aircraft in the 1960s (the
   U.S.) was Cuba. Cuba did procure Mach 2.0
   aircraft.

2. The efforts on the part of the U.S. to
   build up Latin American naval capabilities
   in the period 1947-60 and Latin American
   internal security capabilities in the
   1960s resulted in the transfer of either
   second-hand warships or relatively
   unsophisticated counter-insurgency
   systems.

TABLE 6

PROPORTION OF 1972 INVENTORIES ATTRIBUTABLE TO
DOMESTIC ASSEMBLY AND PRODUCTION

	Small Arms. and Ordnance	Heavy Trucks	Artillery	Tanks	Transport A/C	Combat A/C	Warships	Missiles/ Rockets
Argentina	M	S	-	S	S	-	S	-
Brazil	M	M	-	-	S	-	S	S
Chile	S	S	-	-	-	-	-	-
Cuba	S	-	-	-	-	-	-	-
Dominican Republic	S	-	-	-	-	-	-	-
El Salvador	S	-	-	-	-	-	-	-
Mexico	M	S	-	-	-	-	-	-

M = Most

H = Half and Half

S = Small

- = None

3. The general effort of the U.S. executive and legislature to prevent the transfer of super-sonic aircraft and large missile systems to the sub-continent.

4. The existence of a fairly close-knit security relationship between the United States and its Latin American allies and the concomitant ability of the United States to intervene in local conflicts.

5. The inability, or unwillingness, of the Soviet Union to provide major military assistance to all Latin American countries, apart from Cuba.

6. The lack of purchasing power, especially foreign exchange, on the part of many small Latin American countries, thereby denying themselves the ability to buy arms on the commercial European market.

However, it could be argued that many of these constraints have been eroded. As the United States Congress become increasingly reluctant to appropriate funds for military and economic aid to Latin American countries, the U.S. will have less influence over the procurement patterns of the local countries. In which case, given constant or growing demand for certain types of arms, one can expect an increasing number of supplier nations to become interested in the market. In this context the West Europeans have already demonstrated their willingness to sell advanced arms and the possibility of Soviet transfers to countries other than Cuba may become a reality. Given the current situation, Chile might seem a likely target for Soviet sales or aid efforts.

C. The Geographical and Man-Made Milieu in
South America.* The use of military force is very sensitive to the physical and man-made milieu in which it
operates. It is therefore important to be aware of some
of the major constraints that these milieus may impose
upon hypothetical military activities by Latin American
countries. Since the purpose here is to suggest a
method of analysis rather than provide a detailed study,
our focus will be upon the most important South
American countries.

Geographically, South America may be divided into
three major physical elements--the stable eastern
shields or highlands, the rugged western fold mountains,
and the broad intervening trough. These three elements
may be further subdivided into a series of regions:
1) the eastern shields include the Guyana Shield, the
Brazilian Shield and plateau, and the Patagonian Highlands; 2) the Western Andes mountain chain (some 5,580
miles long) includes a series of distinct ranges or
cordilleras in Venezuela, Colombia, Ecuador, Peru,
Bolivia, Chile, and Argentina; and 3) the intervening
lowlands include the Orinoco, Amazon, and Parana river-
basins, and a number of rift valleys in eastern Brazil.

---

*I am indebeted to my research assistant, Mr.
Charles Perry of the Fletcher School of Law and Diplomacy,
for his help in drafting this section.

With regard to climatic conditions in these regions, the continent's great range of latitude (approximately 30° N to 50° S) and many changes in altitude result in extreme variations in temperature and rainfall, and general climatic conditions. Vegetation ranges from dense, humid rain forest to arid coastal desert.

However, these general features tell us relatively little about the conditions of specific areas. In postulating certain strategic situations, calculations concerning the ease with which military forces can traverse terrain are easier to make at the regional or local level. Within particular regions, population centers and lines of communications between neighboring countries are better integrated, and the availability of specific access points (border passes) and alternate routes of approach are easily identified.

Brazil's strategic position (long Atlantic coastline, massive navigable river system, and boundaries with ten of the twelve South American countries) has both great advantages and great disadvantages. Throughout much of its territory, Brazil offers a few target areas and little hospitable sanctuary area for either conventional invaders or guerrilla forces. Population-commercial-industrial centers are concentrated along the northeast and southeast coastlines, and the good lines of communication are located in these areas.

Brazilian forces, therefore, have less territory to
defend against large scale, conventional attack, and
may arrange their defenses on the most strategic points
of access to these regions. To this end, most present
Brazilian forces are deployed in the northeastern states
(closest to European and African coasts) and along the
Parana and Uruguay rivers in the southeast (Frontier
Elements Group).

Yet, because of the very concentration of strategic centers along the coast in the Sao Paulo-Rio area,
Brazil might be vulnerable to some form of naval attack,
particularly from Argentina. Also there are a number
of Argentine airfields in the "Mesopotamia area" between
the Parana and Uruguay rivers (northeast districts of
Corrientes and Misiones) which could be upgraded to
serve as military bases. An Argentine air assault from
this area might be combined with a naval assault. Large
scale military operations in the other districts of
Brazil are improbable, and in the south Brazilian
forces share many of the advantages of Argentine forces.
There are a number of suitable airfields in Brazil's
Rio Grande Do Sul State; and the distances from here
to Argentine centers in Entre Rios and Buenos Aires
districts are shorter than the distances from the
Argentine Mesopotamia to Sao Paulo and Rio. In the
Sao Paulo-Rio area itself, modern transport facilities

and alternate route systems provide a mobile, flexible
line of defense for Brazilian ground forces. Finally,
in the interior regions of Brazil, the Guyana Highlands,
Amazon Basin, and Central Highlands discourage large-
scale movement on the surface and along many tributaries; and while this area isolates the coastal centers
from the rest of South America, the scattered interior
airfields (Porto Velho, Manaus) could provide Brazilian
aircraft with takeoff points toward western and northern
countries.

Argentine defenses in the north and northeast are
vulnerable to both naval and air assaults by Brazilian
forces or any combination of Brazilian, Paraguayan, and
Uruguayan forces. Most land routes and waterways from
southern Paraguay and Brazil, and the flatlands of
Uruguay converge south on the Rosario-Buenos Aires-La
Plata axis. If intervening forces penetrated the
Buenos Aires-La Pampa districts, they would find easy
road and rail passages into population-commercial
centers. Penetration west and south would be more
difficult thanks to the Sierras de Cordoba and limited
lines of communication. The desert areas of Patagonia
in the south, however, might be conducive to mech-
anized operations if the logistics problem could be
overcome. This area offers at least two possible routes
through the low Andes to Southern Chile.

This particular area becomes more significant in the context of Argentine-Chilean hostilities. Here the geography between Argentina and Chile works in two directions. On the one hand, the close proximity of Santiago and Valparaiso to Argentinian airfields in the Mendoza district have clear strategic disadvantages for Chile. What is more, Chilean naval facilities along the coast are vulnerable to Argentinian air strikes whereas major Argentinian naval bases are far removed from Chile. However, the Andean range provides Chile with a natural and formidable barrier against any Argentinian land attach with armor. In order to move armor up from Mendoza through the passes and into Chile would require an extraordinarily good logistics operation that would be very vulnerable to defensive tactics. Furthermore, the center of Argentinian power and resources in Buenos Aires is hundreds of miles away.

In the context of maritime power, the advantages probably lie with Argentina. If Argentina wished to, it could almost certainly occupy the relatively defense-less southern area of Chile including Tierra del Fuego and thereby control the Magellan Straits. This could then bring about Chile's traditional fear, namely that Argentina might become a Pacific naval power.

The geography of Chile is therefore not con-ducive to easy security against air attack, but does provide for good defenses against a land attack in the Central Santiago region. If the necessary force structure was available, Chile's best defense against Argentina would seem to be a strong air defense combined with a pre-emptive air strike capability against any Argentine air bases along the border and against the Buenos Aires-La Plata axis (but this latter capability would be virtually impossible due to long air distance over Argentine territory).

Thanks to the narrowness of the terrain, the higher cordillera, and the limited number of approach routes, northern Chile is less vulnerable to attack from Peru, Bolivia, or Argentina. There are no direct railroad links between Peru and Chile (indirect route via Bolivia), and the only adequate surface road is the Pan-American Highway, running from Peruvian coastal valleys and intermontane basins to the Chilean coast road at Arica. Chilean ground forces could easily block access through the single border pass; and while Peruvian strategic centers near Lima are within striking range from Chilean airfields in the north (Arica, Iquique, Antofagasta), central Chile is isolated from the closest Peruvian airfields by some 835 miles of rugged terrain. The only other possible Peruvian move against Chile might be some form of amphibious landing near an exposed coastal link to the central lines of communications.

Bolivia would, also, be at a disadvantage against Chile. There are only two railroad links (no roads) through the Andes to Chile (La Paz-Arica line and Uyuni-Antofagasta line) and the population-commercial centers of La Paz-Cochabamba-Sucre-Santa Cruz are vulnerable to air attack from northern Chile. On the other hand, Bolivian centers are protected from Chilean ground forces by the western and central cordillera, and the high altitudes of the Andean Altiplano and the rugged ridges surrounding the La Paz-Cochabamba axis discourage easy or accurate air attack. With regard to possible Peruvian-Bolivian hostilities, neither country appears to maintain a substantial advantage over the other. Opposing forces could make use of the road between La Paz and Puno, Peru, and Lake Titicaca, but neither possibility is likely. Once again the key would be air power, but, owing to the high altitudes of Bolivia and the hanging fog in Peruvian coastal vallyes, its effectiveness would be questionable.

The lowlands of both Bolivia and Peru, however, could be open to unconventional warfare sponsored by local insurgents or by Brazil. There is no reason why Brazil presently might wish to sponsor such conflict in either country, but it has some routes of access and supply from western outposts (Porto Velho) along Amazon tributaries. However, both lowland areas are relatively isolated from food supplies, and population in these areas is small and scattered.

While there has been some tension around the Peru-Ecuador border, communication via the Pan American Highway and the Chira River is difficult. Air strikes from Peru would run up against the problem of heavy cloud cover over the populated paranas and sierra regions of Ecuador (Quito, Riobamba, Cuenca). The primary rail and road ways follow a common path from Tulcan south to Quito, Riobamba and Guayaquil and could be disrupted with interdiction bombing from either Colombia or Peru. Such tactics would, however, immobilize attacking forces as well as isolate defending forces. Naval or amphibious incursions from Peru would probably center on the Santa Elena Peninsula and Gulf of Guayaquil regions. Yet again, topography creates mobility problems. Throughout the rainy season (December to April), the tropical lower basin areas are largely flooded and the few roads become impassable. Finally, some Amazon tributaries running from Ecuador to Peru may be navigable (Napo, Pastaza rivers), but they generally terminate in the unpopulated Peruvian lowlands.

In the northeast corner of South America, lines of communication between Colombia and Venezuela are limited but well developed. The Cucuta-San Cristobal border axis serves as a gathering point for roads running northeast from Bogota and Bucaramanga, and southwest from Caracas, Barquisimeto, and Tachira. As long as the border pass and the Liberator Bridge remain intact, surface transport routes are available; and, in the context of Colombia-Venezuelan hostilities, the advantages of air power and ground defense would lay with the forces in control of the Cucuta-San Cristobal regions. Other strategic areas in Colombia and Venezuela would include the Magdalena Delta and Valley, which serve as entrance points to Colombia's south to north transport routes, and the Gulf of Venezuela-Lake Maracaibo areas, which open onto the major west-east routes in Venezuela. The Pacific coast of Colombia is isolated from Venezuela by sheer distance and the western cordillera, and there are few population clusters or transport routes in the eastern lowlands. In Venezuela, most of the Orinoco tributaries do not run close to any possible Colombian staging areas (with the important exception of Puerto Carreno).

In sum, there are relatively few areas in South America where major inter-state conflict involving large-scale movements of ground forces is probable or even possible; the principal regions are located in northeast and southeast Brazil, the Parana River-Plate Estuary zones of Paraguay, Uruguay, and Argentina, the border regions of central Chile and Argentina, and the

northeast regions of Colombia (western Venezuela).
However, the very restraints of the land milieu may
increase the attractiveness of air and sea power as a
means of competing with adversaries or potential
adversaries.

MILITARY MISSIONS AND FORCE REQUIREMENTS

It was stated at the beginning of this paper that
arms control issues should not be decoupled from the
train of strategic thought. It makes little sense to
attempt to increase, maintain, or slacken controls on
arms transfers unless some notion of the possible
effects of such actions are examined. In this section
some of the points addressed earlier are drawn together
in an effort to provide a conceptual setting for discussing some military implications of alternative arms
transfer and control options. In particular, the
relationship between resources, the milieu, military
missions, and military requirements will be considered.

The following paragraphs are meant to suggest
some ways of looking at "preferred" force structures
for different military missions, in different environments over different general types of terrain.

First, a few words should be said concerning the
bias, perspective, and terminology of this approach.
A primary assumption is that "Western" standards of
rationality for defense planning represent a preferred

mode for designing force structures. That is to say,
it is <u>assumed</u> that the governments of Latin American
countries have an interest in maximizing the potential
effectiveness of their military forces for any given
military budget and that the measures of effectiveness
used would be clearly defined military ones. In reality
such clear cut objectives never obtain, not even in the
governments of the advanced Western powers. In many
Latin American countries the division of the defense
budget would rarely seem to have been made with the
potential efficiency of the <u>overall</u> military force
structure to fulfill certain military missions upper-
most in the minds of the political and military elites.
Weapons have been purchased for reasons of national
prestige, to sustain the political power-base of one
particular branch of the armed services, to pay off
political favors to external and domestic pressure
groups, and many other reasons. Nevertheless, the
utility of the "rational" approach is that it does provide some base from which to make judgments about
"irrational" force allocations.

Another important bias of this section is that
the focus of the analysis is basically directed towards
the <u>established government</u> and not upon irregular
political units who may operate in or out of a particular country and who may use force as a means of

working towards political goals. The suggested rational
designs for force-structures are therefore made with
the regular armed forces in mind. Furthermore, no
attempt is made to discuss police forces, and para-
military units, which often play an extremely important
role in internal security missions.

With regard to the other definitions used,
"attack" missions refer to those military activities
that involve the use of force against a variety of
enemy targets. Included in this composite category
might be search and destroy missions by ground forces,
and interdiction and close support missions by air and
naval forces. "Defend" missons refer to those that
are primarily static and are reactions to enemy initiatives. It should be pointed out that "attack" missions
are not necessarily synonymous with "offensive" missions,
neither are "defend" missions necessarily equated with
"defensive" missions. It is quite possible to argue
that many "defend" missions serve to provide cover for
"attack" missions and many "offensive" missions (for
instance against enemy air bases) are designed to protect, i.e., defend one's air force from enemy "attack."

"Permissive" environments refer to those strategic
environments where the enemy is assumed to have no
major force units and no weapons above small arms.
"Friendly" communication areas and bases are secure.

"Hostile" environments assume that the enemy has major force units that are equipped with high firepower weapons. "Open terrain" refers to flat, or gently undulating ground with good roads and with no major obstacles such as wide rivers. "Moderate terrain" refers to undulating ground with some major obstacles and some good roads. "Difficult terrain" refers to mountains, marshes, jungles, soft desert, and many major obstacles and few roads.

"Preferred" Force Structures for "Attack" and "Defend" Missions over Varied Terrain

"Permissive" Environments. For attack and defend missions in a permissive environment over open and moderate terrain, the preferred marginal characteristics for ground forces would be mobility; firepower is considered less important. Although alternative types of ground forces (e.g., infantry, armor or air cavalry forces) have the ability to provide both mobility and firepower in differing degrees, in the case of air support systems there are some clear cut alternative choices. For instance, a choice would have to be made between procuring for the same cost one unarmed transport aircraft to assist with mobility or one strike aircraft to provide firepower. In this environment, if a marginal choice has to be made, transport aircraft or helicopters might be preferred over strike aircraft.

Similarly, the kinds of naval craft (patrol boats) that
are best suited to provide mobility and density (e.g.,
to cover a large shore-line in depth) are not necessarily the best systems for providing firepower support
(destroyers).

For the attack and defend mission in the permissive environment over <u>difficult</u> terrain, many of the
same considerations apply as for the open and moderate
terrain environments, except that even greater emphasis
would need to be placed upon mobility and therefore
rather less emphasis on firepower. This would indicate that for a country planning to operate in very
difficult terrain against a poorly armed enemy, it
would be important to ensure that the force has good
mobility, that is to say, helicopter and short take-off
and landing (STOL), fixed wing support aircraft, light
trucks, and possibly a few tracked or air cushion
vehicles. It should also be noted that the types of
systems that can increase mobility in this environment
vary from $1 million helicopters to pack mules,
bicycles, and good footwear for the soldiers.

Thus, the emphasis on mobility at the expense of
firepower for all the permissive environments would
suggest that the most rational expenditure by armed
forces preparing for these contingencies would be,
<u>given severe budgetary constraints</u>, emphasis on heli-

copters, trucks, transport aircraft, tracked vehicles
and other mobile vehicles, medium guns, and small arms.
This rational standard should enable one to say whether
or not a particular country, whose military problems
are known or can be assumed, has optimized its resources
for these particular military purposes. Clearly, the
appearance of aircraft carriers, Mach 2.0 aircraft,
SAMs, and tanks in a country that presently only faced
a permissive enemy would suggest either that a dramatic
change in military contingencies and the military
environment were being planned for, or were thought
probable, or that an irrational allocation of military
resources had been made, if based on criteria of military effectiveness.

Hostile Environments. In a "hostile" environment
the preferred marginal characteristic for ground forces
for both attack and defense missions with open-to-
moderate terrain is firepower.

Since firepower is the preferred characteristic
for both attack and defense, one would expect priority
for air support to go to those systems that are preferred for the strike role in the hostile environment.
This would suggest a system such as the U.S.A.-4 Skyhawk.
Naval forces could also contribute firepower to these
missions if the action were along coastlines. Missile-
firing P.T. boats, and gunboats all have an offensive

ship-to-shore capability.

It should, however, be emphasized that though the additional increments of firepower provided by strike aircraft and naval systems have been mentioned, in many cases it may be cheaper and more effective to buy extra firepower by procuring more howitzers and field artillery. Air and naval firepower support is an extremely expensive way to deliver ordnance, especially for defense missions, when the crucial advantages of long range air support do not apply so markedly. For the defense role it is suggested that firepower (i.e., tanks, artillery, and strike aircraft) is also the preferred characteristic.

In a hostile environment (open to moderate terrain) the purchase of Mach 2.0 prestige jets or tanks, or destroyers and carriers, may not be so damaging to the overall military capabilities of the force provided these prestige systems can be kept serviceable and provided one is aware of the military opportunity costs of such procurement.

For the hostile environment with difficult terrain, mobility would probably once more take preference over firepower for the attack role, while for the defense role mobility and firepower can be considered as equally important. Strike aircraft could be used to supplement firepower, though if the choice had to be made between

transport and strike aircraft, one assumes again that
transport aircraft might be preferred.

For the defense mission, firepower assumes a high
priority, so it might be expected that heavy armor
would be preferred provided the difficult terrain
allowed it to be used. If terrain was so difficult as
to rule out the use of armor and heavy guns, priority
might be placed on strike aircraft with a good payload.

For many reasons, including simplicity, the two
environments, permissive and hostile, have been considered separately; no attempt has been made to discuss
preferred forces for a mixed environment. However, it
is important to consider some of the changes in the
suggested optimum design of forces that might occur if
a dynamic environmental situation prevailed. How might
force designs change over time, given either that the
military environment changes or that decisions have to
be taken in advance to prepare for a new military
environment? How and to what extent should the planner
attempt to insure against possible future contingencies
and at the same time retain a maximized effectiveness
for present contingencies?

If the threat perception changed to the point
where adversary forces were thought to be achieving
more effective capability, one would expect more
emphasis to be placed on procuring additional marginal

increments of firepower.[9] In terms of systems, the
trade-off would be between additional troop-carrying
trucks, armored personnel carriers, and transport aircraft and naval systems on the one hand and artillery,
howitzers, tanks, strike aircraft, and heavy firepower
warships on the other hand. In addition, a greater
proportion of resources would be devoted to protection,
e.g., SAMs, interceptors, anti-tank missiles, armored
cars and tanks.

These predicted changes may appear to be obvious
when discussed in overall terms; but if attention is
given to marginal increments rather than overall changes
the expected pattern may appear to be more complicated.
For instance, one general conclusion of this analysis
is that it is difficult to separate out those ground
and naval systems that are preferred for attack or
defense, but that for air systems the difference is
more rigid and obvious. Thus, a small country that
faced an increasingly hostile environment and chose to
invest heavily in single-purpose air defense systems
(interceptors, SAMs, and the associated radar) would,
according to this analysis, sacrifice some "attack"
capability for "defense" capability.

Nevertheless, given the extremely high costs of
air defense systems, it would be reasonable to assume
that is a small country with limited resources invested

heavily in Mach 2.0 interceptors with little or no ground attack capability, the opportunity costs in terms of alternative military systems would be huge. This would not necessarily mean that the capability of the recipient for offensive action had been downgraded, but rather that the potential for procuring forces to further increase offensive capabilities had not been maximized.

Although the offense-defense actions and reactions are very complicated--the purchase of air defense systems may increase the protection for offensive strike aircraft or ground systems--air defense systems with little or no ground attack capability can be regarded as among the least "offensive" major systems a small, less developed country can purchase.

For many less developed countries one could carry the argument a stage further and say that any major allocation of resources in supersonic Mach 1.5-2.0 jet aircraft of any category will not usually contribute toward a maximization of the country's overall military capabilities. Though jet aircraft are preferred for the hostile environment, there are many subsonic jet air-craft that have the most preferred characteristics unless a very high premium is placed on an air defense capability.

Thus it is suggested that the country that spends

$15 million on several squadrons of A-4s or A-37s will buy more offensive capability than the country that opts for a few Mach 2.0 aircraft such as Mirage IIIs or Vs. To repeat, it is usually the latter systems that have received all the publicity when transferred to Latin America on the assumption that the transfer of these systems are primarily responsible for escalating an arms race. Few critics of arms transfer policies seem as concerned about the transfer of subsonic jets, armored cars and trucks. <u>Yet this analysis suggests that when a less developed country re-equips or increases its inventory with these latter systems, it will probably be procuring a greater offensive capability, especially if the technical constraints endemic in most less developed countries are present</u>.

These assumptions are based upon rational decisions to maximize the military utility of different military forces for different environments and missions. Because normal procurement decisions are rarely so simple, it would be misleading to use these kinds of guidelines as a paradigm for suggesting ways inventories will change from environment to environment. However, the guidelines may enable more accurate assessments to be made about the manner in which actual procurement patterns differ from the rational standards based only upon military utility.

For instance, a country facing an internal
insurgency against a poorly armed enemy may very well
have procured or procure systems not designed to
optimize its counter-insurgency capabilities. For
many reasons--political bargaining, lead-time requirements, weapons availability, existing inventories--
"least preferred" systems may be bought and success-
fully employed in combat because those operating the
systems are extremely competent. But in certain circumstances, one could assume that a country facing a
certain military enviornment will attempt to maximize
its military potential within defined parameters. To
what extent the country will be able to take the kinds
of rational decisions that will lead to an optimization
of forces within a particular time-frame will depend
upon its monetary resources, the generosity of its
friends, the availability of weapons systems, the ease
with which it can modify its forces to cope with new
systems, domestic political and technical constraints,
etc.[10]

Qualitative assessments of the preferred characteristics of systems for different environments can be
used to suggest ways of refining one's thinking about
the nature and meaning of weapons procurement between
countries. For instance, many popular descriptions of
arms races assume that the aim of the "race" is to out-

number, or equal, an opponent in terms of the quantity
and quality of weapons in active inventories: Country
A purchases two squadrons of MIG-21s, therefore Country
Y purchases three squadrons of F-4s, etc. This numbers
game may be a reliable indication of those kinds of
arms races described by a colleague as "imitative," but
it may not be representative of an arms race based on
careful strategic calculations.[11]

A more sophisticated way of examining the procurement pattern of adversaries would be first to analyze
the characteristics of the opponent's forces and then
proceed to calculate which of these characteristics
have changed, and by what amount, as a result of a new
input of systems and how these changes affect mission
capabilities. Did the mobility, firepower or protection
capability of Country X increase, remain constant or
decrease when two squadrons of A-4s were added to the
inventory? What were the opportunity costs of particular procurement decisions? What does this change mean
for Country Y's capabilities? These calculations can
only be made by reference to the particular geography,
military environment, and technical capabilities of the
recipients.

FORCE STRUCTURES AND SOME ALTERNATIVE ARMS
TRANSFER POLICY OPTIONS

No matter what the particular objectives of a
major donor country who transfers arms to Latin America,

or anywhere else, an appreciation of the relationship between arms transfers and their <u>military utility</u> to the recipient is essential if alternative donor options are to be fully explored. That is to say, even if the primary objectives of the donor are political and only indirectly related to strategic considerations, it is still useful to examine the military variables in order to assess the possible political effects of arms transfers.

On certain occasions the major donors of arms may not wish to maximize the military capabilities of recipients but may be more concerned with achieving political influence. In the case of Soviet transfers to Indonesia in the 1950s and 1960s, this was achieved by providing highly visible, prestigious and sophisticated weapons systems to an extremely poor, technically backward country. In the case of U.S. transfers to Latin America, recent U.S. objectives would appear to have been to maximize <u>certain</u> military capabilities of recipients (e.g., counter-insurgency in a "permissive" environment), but dampen others (e.g., sophisticated air defense).

Put more formally, it can be argued that arms transfers (and training) policies are a function of a donor's strategic, economic and political interests, which can be assessed on both a long-run and short-run

basis. However, it is not always the case that all
branches of the donor's government will agree on optimum transfer policies.

In theory there are endless ways the complex
and often conflicting objectives of arms transfers can
be weighed. With regard to a potential recipient, it
might be assumed that a donor will want to calculate in
very general terms which of its various policy goals it
wishes to maximize as a result of a transfer, what
effect this policy will have on other goals, and how
these goals are to be reconciled with the policies and
bargaining power of the recipient. The combinations of
policy alternatives are numerous, since the donor could
wish to improve, sustain, or weaken certain economic,
political, or strategic capabilities of the recipient
and weaken, improve, or sustain certain others in both
the long and the short run.

To those whose pragmatic experience leads them
to dismiss such a structure for decision-making, some of
these alternative policies seem very unrealistic. But
it would seem reasonable to say that _some_ of these
alternatives are considered by a major donor. For
instance there is no reason why a donor should not
attempt to improve certain of its own interests in an
arms transfer by trying to _weaken_ certain of the capabilities of the recipient.

Country A Requests Weapons
System X from the United States

1. What are current U.S. arms transfer policies
toward Country A? To improve or sustain or weaken
certain of A's military/political/economic capabilities?
To avoid any military aid programs? To sell arms to
help domestic industry? What policy goals pertain in
this particular case?

2. Why does Country A want Weapons System X?:
(a) Political Factors: (i) A's relations with immediate
neighbors; (ii) A's relations within regional framework;
(iii) A's relations within Alliance and International
Organization framework; (iv) Bureaucratic and Party
rivalry (e.g., interservice competition); (v) National
Prestige. (b) Military Factors: (I) "Peace" time
situations: (i) What are immediate neighbors' military
capabilities? (ii) What is the regional military environment (are most countries well armed or poorly armed?);
(iii) What military allies does Country A have? (iv)
What military allies do potential adversaries have?
(v) What is present status of Country A's forces? How
many weapons serviceable? State of readiness? Morale
of forces, etc." (vi) What is the internal security
situation?

(II) "War" time situations: (i) Is conflict
external or internal? (ii) Is military environment
"permissive" or "hostile." (iii) Over what terrain

is conflict mainly taking place? (iv) How effective
have armed forces and weapons systems proved in conflict so far?

    3. <u>What is likely to happen if the United States
agrees to supply Weapons System X</u>?: (a) <u>Economic Costs</u>:
(i) Who pays, i.e., sale or aid? (ii) When and under
what terms? (iii) How much will sale earn, or how much
will assistance cost? How much technical assistance
required, etc?" (b) <u>Effect of transfer on U.S. political
and military options</u>: (i) Will transfer be precursor
for additional requests? From Country A? From Country
A's neighbors? From other countries? (ii) Will transfer tie United States to closer political and military
involvement with Country A? (iii) Will transfer antag-
onize or strengthen U.S. political and military relations
with Country A's neighbors?

    4. <u>Suppose the United States does not supply
Weapons System X</u>?: (a) <u>Constraints on the United States</u>:
(i) Political (current domestic policy on arms transfers); (ii) Own military requirements; (iii) Economic
cost; (iv) Transfer may lead other local countries to
request assistance or sales from the United States, or
U.S.'s allies, or U.S.'s enemies. (See also 3 [<u>c</u>])
(b) <u>United States offers to supply Weapons System Y
instead</u>: (I) Country A accepts Weapons System Y; (i)
<u>What is likely to happen if U.S. agrees to supply</u>

Weapons System Y instead of Weapons System X? This
would need a repeat analysis of paragraph 3); II) Suppose
A rejects offer of Weapons System Y: Relevant questions
for the United States: a) what happens if no one supplies
A? (i) Refer to analysis in paragraph2: (a) and (b);
(ii) what is A's indigenous weapons production capacity"?
(iii) Would refusal to supply arms encourage A to expand
indigenous weapons production option? What might be
effect of this? In the short-run? In the long-run?
b) Who else can supply Weapons System X or Y? (i) How
many countries? Who are they? (ii) Political, strategic, and economic relationship of other potential
suppliers with A; (iii) What would other suppliers stand
to gain by supply of System X or Y in the short-run and
in the long-run? (a) Economic advantages; (b) Political
advantages; (c) Military advantages; (iv) How important
is it for the United States to prevent other suppliers
from gaining advantages?

If this set of questions is representative of the
types of considerations that may be made by rational
donors who can indulge in the luxury of systematic
analysis, it can be seen that they go far beyond the
narrow confines of expected outcomes based solely upon
criteria of military efficiency. Many nuances of
policy have to be considered, especially the inter-
actions of one major donor's interests with those of

another.   Nevertheless, the military criteria are an
important, indeed central, feature of the analysis.

The Arms Control Perspective

Donor countries can restrict the supply of certain
arms to less developed countries engaged in conflict.
In those cases where one donor has a virtual monopoly
over the supply of arms to a particular recipient, arms
control objectives that involve major adjustments in
the flow of weapons can more readily be achieved than
in those cases where there are alternative suppliers
who are willing and able to compete for political
influence with recipients.

For instance, during the late 1960s, U.S. legislation placed stress upon the need to embargo the transfer of jet aircraft, missiles and other "sophisticated"
weapons to most countries in the Third World including
Latin America.   However, one problem with the policies
that call for embargoes upon the transfer of advanced
weapons is that the number of systems over which the
major suppliers (the United States, Soviet Union,
Britain and France) still have a monopoly are few in
number and are eroding--aircraft carriers, cruisers,
jet bombers, certain types of very sophisticated
tactical aircraft, and major missile systems.   Since
it can be argued that many of these systems are "least
preferred" from a military standpoint in many Latin

American military environments, the effects of embargoing or drastically rationing these transfers could be significant. For example, it might·persuade those recipients to whom the weapons are "least preferred" to focus their procurement on simpler, but more "preferred" systems such as light tanks and tracked vehicles, howitzers, Mach 0.5-0.9 aircraft, combat support aircraft, helicopters, patrol boats and small arms which are currently (1972) produced by at least ten suppliers and are also available in the second hand market. This could have the result of increasing the overall capabilities of some countries to conduct large-scale military operations which are against the arms control interests of the major donors. One conclusion would therefore be that transfer restrictions imposed by the major donors on those weapons that are only produced by a few major countries could result in a shift of demand from advanced to less advanced systems and with it an overall increase in the effective military capabilities of the recipients.

On the other hand, it can be argued that, if the donors wish to minimize the ability of recipients to conduct protracted acts of military aggression against neighbors, they do not necessarily do so by refusing to supply Mach 2.0 aircraft and aircraft carriers. The enormous opportunity costs of providing air defense systems or a carrier force to a relatively poor country may so drain it monetary and technical reserves that it has nothing left to spend on systems such as Mach 0.9 strike aircraft, light tanks, and trucks. Therefore, in those areas where a primary goal of supplies is not to minimize the defense burden of the recipient, the transfer of certain types of advanced systems may realistically serve certain arms control interests more than the supply of less advanced systems.

In the case of most Latin American countries, donors will not be able to work on the assumption that "rational" military planning is the most significant determinant of policy. In those areas where the suppliers wish to improve certain strategic capabilities of the recipient and are concerned lest the recipient's defense budget rise at the expense of economic development, but cannot ignore the need to provide some prestige weapons, an intelligent arms control policy might be to provide those prestige systems that have the most military utility commensurate with the requirements and capabilities of the recipient. In this way, political "add-on-costs" would be minimized. In Latin America there is a comparative advantage in terms of costs for labor-intensive ground forces and a comparative disadvantage in terms of capital intensive sea and air forces. Emphasis by the supplier on building up elite,

prestigious ground forces, such as Special Forces or
small units of Air Mobile Cavalry, would probably have
far more military utility than emphasis on warships or
supersonic jets and could, if presented properly, cover
the prestige requirement.

However, it is difficult to generalize on this
point since each situation will have its own particular
nuances; those countries that already have prestigious
air forces or navies will be extremely reluctant to
abandon them for elite ground forces. Also, the other
political "costs" of creating elite ground forces have
to be borne in mind. It is often these forces that are
most capable of staging a coup d'etat against the
civilian government and installing a military dictatorship, as recent experiences in the hemisphere and Africa
have amply demonstrated.

A major conclusion of this paper is that it is
often very difficult to distinguish between "preferred"
weapons systems for external use and internal use. For
instance, given the geography of several Latin American
countries and some in Central America, such as El
Salvador and Honduras, it can be argued that if these
countries improve some of their military capabilities
to fight internal war, they also improve some of their
capabilities for fighting external war. Thus, Chile and
Argentina might actually improve their respective

capabilities to fight a <u>border war,</u> as a result of
donor pressure, they focused on procuring forces for
major internal security contingencies and abandoned
some of the more prestigious items in their navies.
<u>An implication would be that a long-term cost of</u>
<u>assisting certain countries to build up their forces</u>
<u>for major internal security operations may be to</u>
<u>enhance their capacity for waging effective external</u>
<u>war more so than the provision of certain systems, such</u>
<u>as warships, usually associated with external opera-</u>
<u>tions</u>.

Not <u>all</u> attempts by the major suppliers to
restrict the transfer of arms to Latin America will
have adverse long-term consequences. There are some
countries in Latin America where, on the face of it,
both the long- and short-term interests of some
suppliers would seem best served by reaching some
agreement to restrict the transfer of certain classes
of weapons. The difficulty, of course, is that the
recipients will not always perceive supplied interests
converging with their own. If the case for denying a
recipient an arms request seems overwhelming, then few
can doubt that donors' interests will determine their
actions. It would be equally naive to assume that the
recipient will accept these decisions and forego
indefinitely weapons it considers vital to its security.

However, there is a great difference between
embargoing the supply of all arms and rationing the
types and number of systems supplied. Insofar as
qualitative restrictions may occasionally serve supplier interests, it is worth repeating that generalizations about the types of systems that would fall into
a "most restrictable" class are difficult to make.

The tasks involved in weighing all these various
policy implications are difficult and diffuse and cannot be disassociated from the overall strategic posture
of the supplier countries themselves. The paradox for
those interested in more restrictive arms control
policies remains difficult to resolve. If a primary
objective of supplier arms transfer policy is to regulate the flow of weapons that are most likely to improve
the military capabilities of the recipient, the chances
are these systems will be in plentiful supply elsewhere.
How, for instance, can suppliers agree to embargo,
proscribe, or regulate the flow of vital military equipment such as three-ton-trucks when the supply of these
items is so profuse?

The problem is compounded if the political, rather
than military utility, of weapons systems is included,
as it must be, in the analysis. Many weapons systems
that have a low military utility in certain Latin
American environments have, nevertheless, a high

political utility, e.g., those that look impressive on
national parade days--surface-to-surface missiles,
supersonic jet aircraft, etc.

Thus, although demand based on military utility
may be low for these systems, it may be high when based
on political utility. It probable that high prestige
systems will be in demand in Latin America for as long
as prestige factors influence decision-making. If all
prestige systems had universal low military utility,
the strategic--as opposed to economic--implications of
their transfer could be discounted. However, some
prestige systems have a higher military utility than
others and some countries that presently cannot operate
these systems effectively may one day learn how to do
so.

Thus the transfer of prestige system to some
countries will have an effect on both the military and
political perceptions of cautious planners in neighboring states. It may be that those responsible for
defense allocation and force design in the neighboring
state are not subject to these same political constraints. In which case, the forces procured by the
"rational" state will not necessarily be the same as
those procured by the "irrational" state, but may well
reflect a more useful military capability. Therefore,
it should not be thought that prestige acquisitions

have an irrelevant or minimal effect on the overall

arms build-up in a conflict region. On occasion the

reverse may be true.

FOOTNOTES

1. There is not space to embark upon a detailed analysis
   of the determinants of military power in modern and
   less developed societies. For a good treatment of
   this general subject see Raymond Aron, Peace and War:
   A Theory of International Relations (Praeger, 1968),
   Chapter II. See also Klaus Knorr's excellent book,
   Military Power and Potential (Heath, 1970).

2. A more accurate indicator of the defense efforts
   would be an examination of the functional components
   of annual defense expenditures. Unfortunately the
   quality and availability of data on functional
   defense allocations by the majority of less developed
   countries is very restricted.

3. Gertrude E. Heare, Trends in Latin American Military
   Expenditures 1940-1970: Argentina, Brazil, Chile,
   Colombia, Peru, and Venezuela. A report prepared
   under contract for the U.S. Department of State,
   Office of External Research. Department of State
   Publication 8618, December 1971.

4. Ibid., p. 3.

5. Ibid., p. 1

6. Ibid., p. 7.

7. For reasons of space it is not possible to examine
   all the other resources that combine to provide for
   the national security of a country, e.g., numbers of
   trained scientists, trained military manpower, etc.

8. See, in particular, Amelia Leiss with Geoffrey Kemp,
   et al., Arms Transfer to Less Developed Countries,
   (M.I.T. Center for International Studies Publication
   No. C70/1, Cambridge, Mass., 1970); Amelia Leiss,
   Past Patterns in Arms Transfers (M.I.T. Center for
   International Studies Publication No. C70/2, Cambridge,
   Mass., 1970); The Arms Trade with the Third World,
   Stockholm International Peace Research Institute
   (Humanities Press, New York, 1971).

9. It is important to stress that the significant changes would need to be measured at the margin rather than in gross or absolute terms. In an environment changing from permissive to hostile, major overall increases in both firepower and mobility would be expected.

10. Although it is usually easier to change from complicated to less complicated equipment than vice-versa, there will still be a period of learning to adjust to new equipment of any time.

11. Amelia C. Leiss, "The Elements of an Arms Race," unpublished memorandum, June 1968.

12. A similar, but more detailed discussion of these points is to be found in Geoffrey Kemp, Classification of Weapons Systems and Force Designs in Less Developed Country Environments: Implications for Arms Transfer Policies (M.I.T. Center for International Studies, Publication No. C70/3, 1970).

UNITED STATES FOREIGN POLICY AND
LATIN AMERICAN MILITARY RULE

James R. Kurth

The relationships between unequal states are uneasy ones. Uneasy too are the political scientists that have to analyze them, for they have no good terms at hand. The terms of officials--collective security, Alliance for Progress, Partners in Development--are cant; the terms of radicals--imperialism, neocolonialism, neoimperialism--are coarse. It is therefore not surprising that use of the terms center-periphery and external dependency should have expanded in the last few years from Latin Americans to North Americans and from economists to political scientists.[1] Nor is it surprising that, as currently used, these terms are often as vacuous, ambiguous, or dubious as the ones they have displaced. For the problems with the terms for unequal relations derive from more basic problems with the theories about them.

This paper will examine two basic sets of

problems that arise in the analysis of relations between unequal states: (1) problems in analyzing the causes of the large state's foreign policies toward the small, and (2) problems in analyzing the consequences of the large state's foreign policies for the small. The focus will be on the relations between the United States and Latin America, that oldest, largest, and, in many ways, most institutionalized system of unequal states in the world today.

THE UNITED STATES AND LATIN AMERICA: TWO PROBLEMS IN EXPLANATION

How can the major U.S. policies toward Latin America be explained? Why, for example, did the United States undertake a massive military intervention in the Dominican Republic in 1965 rather than a lesser form of intervention or no intervention at all? Why did it undertake sizeable counterinsurgency programs with military aid and military advisors in many Latin American states in the 1960's? Why did it undertake economic pressures but little more against the Allende regime in Chile in 1970-1972? And what are the prospects for similar U.S. interventions, involvements, or pressures in the future?

The problem with questions about the causes of a foreign policy is not that there are no answers but that there are too many answers. Around the Dominican intervention, or around the counterinsurgency programs,

or now around the Chilean nonintervention, or more
generally around nearly every major U.S. policy toward
Latin America, there has grown up a cluster of competing explanations, a thicket of theories, which prevents
us from having a clear view of the making of that
policy. For example, did the Dominican intervention
result only from the emotional fears of one man,
Lyndon Johnson, or from distorted information from
parochial bureaucrats, or from an administration's
efforts to avoid the political costs of a "second
Cuba," or from corporate pressures to preserve economic
interests, or, after all is said and done, from
rational calculations about communist threats to
international stability, or from some combination of
these factors? Even today, men debate each other over
such competing explanations of the Latin American
policies of the United States.

How to explain major U.S. policies toward Latin
America is one problem. What these major U. S.
policies explain about Latin America is another. And
here there is a second debate.

For some, there is an obvious answer: U. S.
policies are the major explanation for Latin America's
economic underdevelopment, or social disorder, or
political authoritarianism, or for all of these. For
others, such answers are not obvious at all: rather,

U.S. policies make virtually no difference because these
economic, social, and political debilities result from
the internal characteristics of Latin American countries
and not from their external relations. And of course
for still others, mostly U.S. officials, the impact of
U.S. policies is positive.

Of course, in such debates about explaining the
foreign policies of great powers or the national debilities of small ones, some men would quickly prune away
some explanations as obviously being mere brambles on a
thicket of theories. They might say of the effect of a
hypothetical cause what Robert Dahl has said of the
power of a hypothetical act:

> Suppose I stand on a street corner and say to
> myself, "I command all automobile drivers on
> the street to drive on the right side of the
> road;" suppose further that all the drivers
> actually do as I "command" them to do; still
> most people will regard me as mentally ill if
> I insist that I have power over automobile
> drivers to compel them to use the right side
> of the road.[2]

But when we turn from traffic to politics, as we
know from Dahl's own efforts to analyze power, the difference between madmen or mad theories and rules of the
road or rules of political behavior is no longer so
obvious to so many objective observers.

THE OVERDETERMINATION OF U.S. FOREIGN POLICIES

In regard to the first problem in explanation,
that of the causes of a large state's foreign policies
toward small ones, we can distinguish six major,

competing, general explanations of the making of
foreign policy and especially of U.S. foreign policies;
the strategic, the psychological, the bureaucratic,
the democratic, the economic, and the stylistic.

1. The strategic explanation. This perspective emphasizes the international system and a state's
security and status within it as the determinant of
foreign policy. The strategic theorist abstracts from
his consideration the domestic influences on foreign
policy and instead collapses the nation and all its
groups and individuals into a unitary policymaker, e.g.,
"the statesman" or "the state." He then argues that
the statesman or state rationally calculate (or at
least should rationally calculate) foreign policy only
with regard to those strategic interests determined by
the nature of the international system. Great powers
in similar international situations act in similar ways.
Until recently, the strategic perspective probably was
the most common among scholars; balance of power theory,
game theory, bargaining theory, and the new theory of
collective goods are strategic approaches. Leading
strategic theorists are Hans Morgenthau, with his
theory of the balance of power and the national
interest, and Thomas Schelling, with his theory of
bargaining.[3] And, of course, U.S. officials usually

justify U.S. policies toward Latin America in strategic terms.

2.   The psychological explanation.   This perspective emphasizes the psychological structures or cognitive processes of leading policymakers, for example what in the Johnson administration was called "the awesome foursome." Psychological explanations were long limited to a primitive form of Freudianism, but recent works on cognitive processes have made important theoretical contributions.[4] Leading psychological theorists of general U.S. foreign policy are Charles Osgood, Joseph de Rivera, and Robert Jervis. Journalists' accounts of U.S. policies toward Latin America often emphasize the personal characteristics of U.S. policymakers.[5] Thus, Lyndon Johnson, Thomas Mann, a major policymaker for Latin America in the Johnson administration, and John Connally, Secretary of the Treasury in the Nixon administration, had in common a background in Texan politics and experiences with Mexican-Americans. It can be argued that their Texas past shaped their perceptions of Latin America and in particular the policies of Johnson and Mann toward the Panamanian riots in 1964, the Dominican rebellion in 1965, and the policies of Connally toward the Allende regime in Chile in 1970-1972.

3.   The bureaucratic explanation.   This approach

sees foreign policy as the outcome of competition among the bureaucracies and the policymaker's advisors. As such, it is a form of interest group theory with a shift in locus from Congress to the executive and a shift in content from "low politics" to "high politics."[6] Leading bureaucratic theorists of general U.S. foreign policy are Richard Neustadt and Roger Hilsman. The accounts by Arthur Schlesinger and Theodore Sorensen of the Kennedy administration's policies toward Latin America, including the abortive Bay of Pigs intervention, and the account by Abraham Lowenthal of the Dominican intervention take such an approach.[7] Closely related to the explanation from bureaucratic politics is the explanation from bureaucratic process; this explanation sees foreign policy as the output of processes and standard operating procedure within bureaucracies. Graham Allison's work on the Cuban missile crisis is an example of the bureaucratic or organizational process explanation as well as the bureaucratic politics explanation.[8]

4. The democratic explanation. This approach emphasizes the political system as the determinant of foreign policy, for example, the role of the separation of power and of Presidential and Congressional elections. Leading democratic theorists of general U.S. foreign policy are Kenneth Waltz, Theodore Lowi, and

Stanley Hofmann, in some of their arguments.[9] And it
is a familiar argument that Lyndon Johnson undertook
military intervention in the Dominican Republic because
he feared the political costs of a "second Cuba."[10]

    5. <u>The economic explanation.</u> This approach
emphasizes the economic system as the determinant of
foreign policy, for example, the role of industrialism,
capitalism, and the great corporations. Leading
economic theorists of general U.S. foreign policy are
William Appleman Williams, Gabriel Kolko, and Harry
Magdoff.[11] Leading economic theorists of U.S. policy
toward Latin America are James Petras and Andre Gunder
Frank.[12] The economic explanation of U.S. policy
toward Latin America probably is the one most widely
held by Latin Americans themselves.

    6. <u>The stylistic explanation.</u> This perspective
emphasizes the national style, the national character,
the history, or the ideology of a country as the determinants of foreign policy. "Our past, our principles,
and our pragmatism," as Stanley Hoffmann has put it.
Other stylistic theorists of general U.S. foreign
policy are Louis Hartz on "the liberal tradition" and
George Kennan on "moralism-legalism."[13] Stylistic
explanations have commonly been applied to those
occasions when the U.S. has refused to grant diplomatic

recognition to a Latin American military or revolutionary regime.

Let us imagine men who find fault with U.S. foreign policy and who hope to contribute to its correction. For them, each of the six major explanations has a different prescriptive implication.

1. The strategic explanation: individual reasoning with the leading policymakers or, alternatively, general repose, because for nearly every policy there can be constructed a rationalization in terms of strategic values.

2. The psychological explanation: personnel replacement.

3. The bureaucratic explanation: bureaucratic reorganization.

4. The democratic explanation: electoral or constitutional reform.

5. The economic explanation: industrial reorganization or even social revolution.

6. The stylistic explanation: millennial revolution which creates a new human being, literally a Great Cultural Revolution, or the opposite extreme, complete and cosmic repose in the face of inevitability.

In general, the prescriptive implications become successively more radical.

Given this array of competing explanations and the corresponding array of correcting prescriptions, how should we choose among them? Immediately, we confront a serious difficulty, what we can call the problem of alternative causes or the problem of a posteriori overdetermination.[14]

For nearly any event of interest in the analysis of foreign policy, we can discover or invent, a posteriori, several alternative explanations and sometimes even all of the explanations above, each of which is logically and plausibly a sufficient explanation for the event, is an exhaustive and therefore will seem an exclusive explanation for the event.

It is especially the case that nearly any foreign policy event can be explained or rationalized in terms of the international system, in strategic terms. Further, not only can most events be internationalized, but most can also be psychologized, bureaucratized, democratized, economized, and even stylized. But even this is not all. For the bureaucratic theory and the economic theory really are variations on a theme of rational policymaking, of "the strategy of conflict," with the locus of the rationality shifted from the level of the unitary, rational actor within the international system to the level of the unitary bureau within the bureaucratic system or the unitary corporation within the economic system. Theories of rational interest can be attacked at these lower levels just as theories of a rational or national interest can be attacked at the highest level. Thus, the bureaucratic and the economic theories can themselves be bureaucratized and economized and so on downward throughout the bureaucratic or corporate hierarchies ad infinitum.

In brief, a posteriori, the foreign policy event is overdetermined by several alternative and analytically coequal explanations. The logical dynamic of the process of discovering or inventing alternative causes is to equalize explanations, to destroy degrees of validity among them, while not destroying the explanations themselves. We are left with a violation of the principle of Occam's Razor, left entangled within a thicket of theories.

This condition of overdetermination with several alternative and analytically coequal explanations characterizes, for example, each of the most important U.S. foreign policies toward Latin America or related events of the 1960's and 1970's: the abortive Bay of Pigs intervention, the evolution of the Alliance for Progress, the Cuban missile crisis, the Dominican intervention, the counterinsurgency programs with military aid and military advisors in many other Latin American states, and the economic pressure but otherwise nonintervention against the Allende regime in Chile in 1970-1972.

At first glance, the obvious solution to the problem of selection of explanations is simply to look at the evidence, and the traditional sources of evidence are memoirs, newspapers, Congressional hearings and votes and, in some circumstances, certain banks of statistics such as aggregate economic data or public opinion surveys. But the very choice to look at certain sources of evidence contains biases toward certain theories.

Thus, Presidential memoirs usually will yield a strategic or a psychological approach, advisor's memoirs and newspaper leaks a bureaucratic one, Congressional records an approach emphasizing the separation of powers or economic interest groups, aggregate economic data an economic approach, and public opinion surveys a stylistic one.

In regard to the memoirs and accounts by the President or leading policymaker himself, he will obviously have a bias toward giving "good reasons" for a policy, even if these are reasons only after the fact and were not the real reasons at the time, and he will usually have a bias toward giving good reasons in terms of strategic and international values. Of course, the memoirist sometimes will appear to be candid or will neglect to remain alert, and he might refer to this or that bureaucratic, political, or economic pressure as decisive in his policy. But these cases are rare, as the Truman, Eisenhower, and Johnson memoirs illustrate.

The memoirs and accounts by the advisors will have a bias also, but a quite different one. Their

memories are of fierce and frantic struggles with
peers and near-peers for the attention and approval of
the President or policymaker. It is not surprising
that they should see all foreign policies as the outcome of an often chaotic clash of bureaucratic
interests.

Relatedly, political scientists in their studies
usually focus on those institutions and sources of
evidence which are unlikely to yield an economic theory
of foreign policy--and unlikely to yield a radical
prescription. It is not surprising that of all the
contemporary books and professional articles which
offer a radical analysis of U.S. foreign policy, only
a half dozen are by professional political scientists;
among these few, the works of James Petras stand out.[15]
In general, however, radical academic analyses of
foreign policy have been the work of economists and
historians.

A second obvious answer to the problem of
selection of explanations is to test a particular
explanation not with just one foreign policy event but
with many of them. Some explanations can be applied
to only a few events (e.g., psychological explanations
focusing on personal characteristics); others can be
applied to many events over many years and even over
many countries (e.g., strategic explanations focusing

on personal characteristics); others can be applied to
many events over many years and even over many countries
(e.g., strategic explanations focusing on the balance
of power, economic explanations focusing on capitalism).
Explanations which can be generalized to cover many
outcomes are, ceteris paribus, superior to those which
cannot. One should not make too much of the virtue of
generalization, however; the mere fact that a condition
is present in many outcomes does not necessarily mean
that it is important in any one of them.

Further, explanations which enjoy the virtue of
generalization are prone to suffer the vice of over-
prediction. Some explanations would have predicted
events which have never occurred. For example, most
economic theories of American imperialism would have
predicted American military interventions against communist revolutionary movements in China sometime in
1948-1949, in North Vietnam (Tonkin) in 1953-1954, in
Cuba in 1960-1962, perhaps in Laos in 1961-1962, perhaps
against the communist-supported coup in Iraq in 1958,
and perhaps against the Marxist government of Chile in
1970-1971. Indeed, they would have mispredicted as
many or more military interventions which did not occur,
as they would have correctly predicted military interventions which did occur (South Korea in 1950, Lebanon
in 1958 which they might not have predicted, the

Dominican Republic in 1965, South Vietnam since 1965 and the associated interventions in Laos since 1965 and in Cambodia since 1970). From this perspective, the most interesting question about the proxy intervention at the Bay of Pigs would be not why did it occur but why was it not followed by a full, and successful, military intervention.

Despite these cautions, generalizable explanations have an obvious attractiveness. In sections IV and V of this paper, we will consider the two most general explanations of great power foreign policies--the strategic and the economic--in more detail. But first, there is a second problem of overdetermination to be considered.[16]

THE OVERDETERMINATION OF LATIN AMERICAN POLITICS

The analysis of the causes of a great power's foreign policies toward weak states might be burdened with the problem of overdetermination, but surely, it might be said, the analysis of the consequences of these foreign policies for the weak states suffers no such difficulty. Take, for example, the impact of the United States upon Latin America or upon underdeveloped countries generally. The arguments about the consequences are familiar and can be summarized as follows:

The United States in Latin America (and in the Middle East and in Southeast Asia as well) has helped modernize the society and the economy. American export markets, direct investment, and economic aid have contributed to the commercialization of agriculture, the creation of infra-structure, and the establishment of manufactures. These, in turn, have contributed to rapid urbanization and less rapid industrialization in these regions. But although the United States has helped modernize the society and the economy, it has not helped modernize the polity. Rather, the effect of the U.S. has been to inhibit political modernization or political development as defined by Samuel Huntington, Lucian Pye, and others.[17]

The United States, it has been argued, has instead encouraged military rule--authoritarianism or praetorianism or both--in the internal politics of underdeveloped countries.[18] It has encouraged authoritarianism by giving aid to privileged and conservative groups, to what have been called the "clientele classes:"[19] the military, the police, the bureaucracies, the compradors, and the manufacturers dependent upon multinational corporations. It has also encouraged authoritarianism and sometimes praetorianism insofar as it has encouraged military coups (Guatemala 1954, Brazil 1964, perhaps Bolivia 1971, Iran 1953) or has undertaken military interventions itself (Dominican Republic 1965, South Vietnam and Laos since 1965 and

Cambodia since 1970, although Lebanon 1958 is a possible counterexample) or has undertaken interventions with military advisors (Guatemala, Peru, and Bolivia in the 1960's).

The United States, it is conceded by some, has occasionally encouraged a pluralism of sorts by giving aid also to some mass organizations: particular political parties, labor unions, and peasant groups. But in many underdeveloped countries, including many in Latin America, there is little political institutionalization, and pluralism decays quickly into praetorianism followed by authoritarianism.

The usual result of U.S. policies is thus a political system which features authoritarianism or praetorianism in its operation and conservatism or corporatism in its direction; the system operates by corruption, coercion, and coups, and it operates for bureaucrats, landlords, compradors, and a few manufacturers dependent upon multinational corporations. And where this political system has been threatened by social revolution, U.S. influence has deepened into U.S. intervention, and has aborted not only the revolution but the social justice, economic development, political order, and national independence which presumably would have ensued.

Such arguments about the consequences of U.S.

policies for the internal politics of underdeveloped
countries seem demonstrable; in fact, however, they are
merely debatable.

It is true that for the countries of Latin
America (and also for those of the Middle East and of
Southeast Asia), persuasive arguments can be made that
military rule, authoritarian regimes, and praetorian
actions result from U.S. policies. It is equally true,
however, that persuasive arguments can be and have been
made that such politics results from internal determinants. And, indeed, results from any one of several
different internal determinants: from the pattern of
political culture, from the residue of historical
conflicts, from the level of economic development, from
the degree of political organization, or from something
else. Without much effort, each of these factors can
be fashioned into an apparently sufficient explanation
for a country's authoritarianism or praetorianism. In
Latin America (and in the Middle East and in Southeast
Asis), authoritarianism and praetorianism are overdetermined outcomes: the same "consequence" seems to
issue from any one of several different "causes."
Accordingly, it is very difficult to demonstrate that
the absence of U.S. involvement would have resulted in
the absence of even the attenuation of military rule,
authoritarian regimes, or praetorian actions; another

factor would take its place and do the job.

More generally, we may again distinguish six major, competing, general theories or explanations, this time explanations of a weak nation's politics and different from those of a great power's policies, but giving us a second logical structure similar to our first: the international, the organization, the constitutional, the developmental, the historical, and the cultural.[20]

1.   The international explanation.   This perspective emphasizes the international system and the nation's position within it as the determinant of national politics.   Theories of imperialism, neo-colonialism, uneven development, and external dependency are all variations on the international theme.   Representative international theorists have been Paul Baran, Andre Gunder Frank, and James Petras; their intellectual ancestor is Lenin in his book, Imperialism.[21]

2.   The organizational explanation.   This approach emphasizes the degree of political organization as the determinant of national politics.   The gap between political participation and political institutionalization, the political struggle among parties, bureaucracies, and the military, and the relative institutionalization of these contenders are

all central variables in the organizational theory. Its major theorist is Samuel Huntington; his intellectual ancestor is the Lenin of What Is To Be Done?[22]

3. The constitutional explanation. This approach emphasizes constitutional forms and electoral laws as the determinant of national politics. The differences between unitary and federal states, between presidential and parliamentary systems, and between proportional representation and single-member districts, are examples of the concerns of constitutional explanations. Generally unused in the study of comparative politics today, constitutional explanations were widely employed a generation ago, although of course they have never been of much interest to Latin Americanists. A contemporary theorist is Douglas Rae.[23]

4. The developmental explanation. This approach emphasizes the levels and rates of social modernization and economic development, of commercialization, urbanization, industrialization, and communication, as the determinant of national politics. Early developmental theorists, such as Karl Deutsch, with his concepts of social communication and social mobilization, and Seymour Martin Lipset, with his work on the "social prerequisites of democracy," have been followed by a host of statistical and cross-sectional studies.[24]

5. The historical explanation. This perspective
emphasizes the great events in a nation's past, usually
world wars, civil wars, and social revolutions, as
having set the character of a nation's politics for
years thereafter. Accordingly, much of the work of
this sort has dealt with Europe, Russia, China, or the
United States, rather than with Latin America, Africa,
the Middle East, or Southeast Asia, or has dealt with
individual countries in these underdeveloped regions,
such as Mexico and Turkey. Representative historical
theorists are Stein Rokkan and Seymour Martin Lipset,
in their joint work, and Barrington Moore, whose work
also links with developmental theory.[25]

6. The cultural explanation. This perspective
emphasizes the political culture, the national
character, or the religious values of a country as the
determinant of its politics. Representative cultural
theorists are Gabriel Almond and Sidney Verba, in their
work on "the civic culture," Edward Banfield, with his
concepts of "amoral familism" and "class culture," and
Lucian Pye.[26] The cultural theory, of course, is
especially familiar to Latin Americanists. Numerous
writers have stressed the authoritarian consequences
of Roman Catholicism, Hispanic traditions, patron-
client patterns, etc.

Thus, given a political phenomenon which we wish

to explain, such as military rule, authoritarianism, or praetorianism, and given this array of competing explanations, we are again confronted with a problem of overdetermination.

Perhaps we can escape from the problem of over-determination if we turn from general political phenomena, such as paretorianism, to particular political events, such as the U.S. intervention in the Dominican Republic in 1965. After all, if there is one thing on which officials, liberals, and radicals in the United States are all agreed, it is that U.S. interventions make a difference. Officials say they prevent good consequences, but they all say that interventions have consequences. No one could argue that U.S. military intervention in the Dominican Republic in 1965, in South Korea in 1950, and in South Vietnam and Laos since 1965 did not make a difference in the outcome. Probably the same is true of the military intervention in Lebanon in 1958. But the case for U.S. advisory and proxy interventions is not so clear.

Let us consider the U.S. advisory and proxy interventions for the period since the Second World War. For some of the U.S. advisory interventions, it can be plausibly argued that the client regime would have suppressed the revolutionary movement even without U.S. military advisors (Guatemala, Peru, and Bolivia in the

1960's). This is true, <u>a fortiori</u>, about less intensive forms of intervention (U.S. police advisors in Latin America, U.S. support of the Central American Defense Council (CONDECA),[27] U.S. Military aid with arms and training in Latin America and in other under-developed countries). Conversely, the most extensive interventions with U.S. military advisors either failed and were abandoned (China in the 1940's) or failed and were escalated into full military inter-vention (South Vietnam and Laos in the 1960's). For Greece in the 1940's, however, the case is strong that U.S. military advisors and military aid changed the outcome.

There have also been several cases of U.S. proxy interventions, either acknowledged (Guatemala 1954, Cuba 1961, in a sense British Guiana 1963, Iran 1953) or alleged (Brazil 1964, Bolivia 1971). For some of these cases, it again can be plausibly argued that a coup would have occurred even without U.S. encouragement (Brazil 1964, Bolivia 1971, perhaps Iran 1953). And, of course, the biggest proxy intervention of all, Cuba 1961, was a resounding failure. For Guatemala in 1954 and British Guiana in 1964, however, the case is strong that U.S. support changed the outcome. But four military interventions, one advisory intervention, and two proxy interventions make for a rather small lumberyard from which to construct a theory of the political consequences of U.S. policies, no matter how large the pieces or how ugly the wood.

Some might argue that the threat of U.S. military intervention has deterred revolutionary movements in Latin America which would have otherwise occurred. But for the past half-decade, and after the Vietnamese experience, it has been rather implausible that the U.S. would intervene militarily in another guerrilla war. The threat has considerably declined, but revolutionary movements in Latin America have not generally increased.

In the next two sections of this paper, we will consider in more detail the two most general explanations of great power foreign policies--the strategic and the economic. In the concluding two sections, we will do the same for the two explanations of Latin American politics which are their closest counterparts --the international and the developmental.

INTERNATIONAL POLITICS AND U.S. FOREIGN POLICIES

Have there been other international systems composed of states of unequal power or societies of unequal development and comparable to the international system formed by the United States and Latin America? For the contemporary period, I would argue that there are three good candidates for comparison: the United

States in Southeast Asia, the Soviet Union in East
Europe, and France in Subsahara Africa. There are also
the developing system of the Soviet Union in the Middle
East and the declining system of the United States in
the same region. And, as we shall see below, there
have also been several comparable systems in the past.

More formally, there have been a number of international systems which, like the United States and
Latin America, have been characterized by each of the
following six features; we shall call such systems
hegemonial systems.

1. Resource inequality. The system is composed
of one great power and several small but formally
independent states. The ratio of the material
resources (such as GNP) of the great power to those
of the next strongest state is at least two to one.

2. Formal treaty. There are formal multilateral
treaties or agreements among the great power and the
small states or at least several bilateral treaties or
agreements between the great power and each of the
small states. These treaties and agreements in effect
define the membership of the system. In some cases,
the formal definition of relations reaches the point
of the establishment of a formal international organization which includes most of the states within the
system. (One of the best examples is the Organization

of American States; others are SEATO, the Warsaw Treaty
Organization, and Comecon.)

3. <u>Military alliance</u>. There is a military
alliance among the great powers and the small states
(e.g., the Rio Treaty, the Warsaw Treaty, the French
agreements with several African states). Often, it is
this military alliance which is the subject of the
treaties, agreements, and organizations mentioned in
feature (2). Often, too, military assistance or protection extends beyond mere alliance to include
military aid, military advisors, or military bases.

4. <u>Economic dependency</u>. The economic relations
--trade, investments, economic aid, or economic
advisors--of most small states in the treaty system
with the great power are much more intensive than their
economic relations with any other great power. Often,
certain important economic ratios reach the level of
20-25% or more (e.g., the small state's exports to the
great power as a percentage of the small state's total
exports; The great power's investment in the small
state as a percentage of the small state's total
investment or of its GNP; the great power's grants and
loans to the small state as a percentage of the small
state's total government budget).

5. <u>Foreign intervention</u>. The great power has
undertaken foreign intervention--military, advisory,

or proxy--in several small states in the treaty system.
Often, there is a general expectation, among elites and
counterelites in the states of the system, that there
are certain diplomatic and political limits to a small
state's behavior, the transgressing of which will
provoke the great power to undertake intervention
within the offending state. One such transgression is
the imminent defection of the small state to a competing
great power. Another, relatedly, is the imminent dis-
placement of a friendly regime within the small state
by an unfriendly one, along with signs that the new
regime will move internally toward ideological and
institutional forms which are similar to those of a
competing great power, increasing the probability of
defection of the small state to that power. In some
cases, the great power uses the international organization to legitimize its intervention (e.g., the O.A.S.
for Guatemala in 1954 and for the Dominican Republic
in 1965, the Warsaw Treaty Organization for
Czechoslovakia in 1968).

6. <u>System stability</u>. The system has shown a
capacity for stability, in the sense that war between
great powers has not been necessary for the maintenance
of the system, and for durability, in the sense that
the system has endured or probably could have endured
for at least a generation or some twenty years.

Such international systems have often been called by historians and political analysts regions of hegemony or "spheres of influence," and the small states have been called "client states" or "protectorates."

Since the Peace of Westphalia of 1648, which ended the Thirty Years War and established the legal grounds for a multitude of small but formally independent states within <u>Mitteleuropa</u>, there have been a number of hegemonial systems or close approximations. Defined within rather generous geographical and temporal limits, they are the following. Several have already been mentioned above.

1. France in the Rhineland (1648-1713).

2. Austria in Germany (1815-1866).

3. Austria in Italy (1815-1859). By a strict definition, the economic component of an hegemonial system was absent in the two Austrian systems.

4. Germany in Southeast Europe (1934-1941).

5. Britain in the Middle East (1932-1952).

6. The United States in Latin America (since 1945 and in Central America and the Caribbean since 1898).

7. The United States in East Asia, including Southeast Asia (since 1945).

8. The Soviet Union in East Europe (since 1945).

9. France in Subsahara Africa (since 1960).

> 10. Britain in the Indian States (1858-1947).
> This system was a limiting case between an
> hegemonial system and a colonial one, an
> extreme form of the indirect rule which
> Britain often employed elsewhere in the
> empire.[28]

These systems, of course, differ greatly from each other, and the same system may vary greatly within itself or over time. From the perspective of the citizen of a smaller state, it is the difference between being a Dominican in 1965 and a Chilean in 1970, or between being a Japanese in 1950 and a Japanese in 1970. By 1970, Chile and Japan could hardly be considered any longer to be client states of the United States in their respective regional systems.

There have been several more remote approximations to an hegemonial system. One has been the United States in West Europe since 1945, with a military alliance institutionalized in NATO and with an economic presence felt first through the Marshall Plan and later through the multinational corporations. Three others have been in the Middle East: (1) the United States in a few states since 1947 for brief periods; (2) the Soviet Union, which has been gradually establishing an hegemonial system since 1967; (3) The Ottoman Empire, which can be excluded because the system was generally one of states which were actually independent or even allied to enemies of the Ottomans but which were formally under Ottoman suzerainty. As such it is an excellent case of, to coin a word, a "suzeraintal" system, which is the inverse of an hegemonial one: in an hegemonial system, the states are actually dependent but formally independent; in a suzeraintal system, the states are actually independent but formally dependent. Another remote approximation was Britain in some parts of Latin American during the nineteenth century, with occasional military interventions or economic influence. There have also been abortive hegemonial systems, such as Japan in East Asia (1931-1941), Italy in Southeast Europe (1924-1941), and, some might argue but rather implausibly, China in East Asia (1960-1966).

Thus, every great power since the Peace of Utrecht (1713) has undertaken at some time some sort of hegemonial system, be it actual, approximate, or abortive. This might suggest that hegemonial systems are merely a predictable result of great power status. Such a view might stress the many similarities among them and especially the similarities with the hegemonial system of the United States in Latin America: there have been, for example, the Austrians in Germany, with their use of international organization (the German Confederation) for collective legitimation of political intervention; the Austrians in Italy, with their use of military intervention against revolutionary movements and in support of client regimes; and the Germans in Southeast Europe with their use of their large market for foreign goods as a powerful bargaining tool with underdeveloped countries. The United States in Latin America in its methods and perhaps in its aims is an heir to these three systems of Mitteleuropa. The Austrian and German hegemonial systems, in turn and in their way, were each heir to the Holy Roman Empire and to dreams that reach back more than a thousand years.

Such similarities among great powers in their relations with small states have interesting theoretical consequences. The similarities of course cast doubt on the validity of the official argument that the United States is uniquely non-imperialist. This is plausible if one focuses only on formal imperialism; but if one focuses also on "neo-imperialism," the U.S. is very much like many other historical and current great powers. Conversely, they cast doubt on the validity of the radical argument that the United States is uniquely neo-imperialist. More importantly, they cast doubt on theories of the domestic determinants of foreign policy. For if despite great differences in domestic structures, all great powers pursue similar policies toward many small states when they are placed in similar conditions in the international system, then domestic factors may be only marginal as determinants of a great power's foreign policies. Rather, the main determinants of foreign policies would be international factors, and the best explanations would be strategic ones.

Strategic explanations of U.S. hegemonial behavior in Latin America and elsewhere are familiar enough: they have been the official rationales of U.S. policy-makers for the undertaking of interventions in Guatemala, the Bay of Pigs, the Dominican Republic, and in other underdeveloped countries, and for the under-writing of military alliances, military aid, and counterinsurgency programs in Latin America and else-where. The explanations are summarized and symbolized by such words as "collective security," "containment," "credibility," and "the domino theory."

These terms may have been coined by Americans about their own policies, but the phenomena they des-cribe are among the most familiar in the history of international politics. For all the values which great powers have gained from their relations with small countries, the most common and most fundamental has been simply the negative one of strategic denial, preventing competing great powers from achieving control over the small country and from exploiting its resources for their own strategic purposes. Contain-ment is not merely an American policy but has been

historically the normal policy of every great power
against every other. The conclusions of game theory
are similar to those of diplomatic history: the safest
"minimax" strategy for a player over the long run is
the firm defense of his existing assets.[29] Consequently, strategic denial is one plausible explanation
for a great power's hegemonial policies, for the
hegemonial system, and specifically for foreign interventions, military alliances, military aid, and military
advisors. More than any other explanation for
hegemonial behavior in the literature of foreign policy
analysis, the strategic denial explanation succeeds on
the test of generality: strategic denial can be applied
to many hegemonial systems and to many events within
each system. Consequently, there is a heavy burden of
proof upon an advocate of an alternative explanation--
such as an economic one. He has a responsibility not
only to argue for his own alternative explanation but
also to argue against the strategic one.

It is true that in the early 1970's a strategic
explanation for U.S. policies toward Latin America
lacks a certain plausibility. Neither the Soviet Union
nor China pose an obvious or direct threat to U.S.
security interests in Latin America. For earlier
periods, however, a strategic explanation is more
convincing. In the late 1940's, when the Rio Treaty

and the O.A.S. were established, the strategic importance
of a Latin America free from enemy bases and of U.S.
access to Latin American raw materials in wartime had
been demonstrated in the recent world war and was highly
salient to U.S. policymakers. The perception of the
strategic importance of Latin American raw materials
was reinforced by the experience of the Korean War.
Given these recent memories and given also the bipolar
shape of the international politics of the time, the
U.S. proxy intervention in Guatemala in 1954 and the
conventional military aid programs of the 1950's are
readily explained. In the early 1960's, with the movement of Cuba into an alliance with the Soviet Union
which culminated in the Cuban missile crisis, it is not
surprising that the U.S. undertook counterinsurgency
programs with military aid and military advisors in
Latin America and finally military intervention in the
Dominican Republic in 1965 in order to prevent "a second
Cuba." But, a strategic theorist could continue, as
both the basic caution of post-1962 Soviet policy toward
Latin America and the basic weakness of communist
revolutionary movements in Latin America became clear
to U.S. policymakers, the U.S. military involvement in
Latin America declined and a "low posture" policy was
pursued. Thus, a strategic theorist would not have
been surprised when the U.S. did not attempt any mili-

tary intervention against the Allende regime in Chile upon its election in 1970. In any event, with Chile located as it was at the far end of the South American continent behind a desert and the Andes, few nations in the world were more remote from the Soviet Union or posed less of a threat to their neighbors. As for the future, the strategic explanation would predict that if the Soviet Union (or China) should come to sharply expand its presence or influence in Latin America, then the U.S. would renew its military involvement in various forms. But it would also predict that until that time the U.S. low posture will be maintained.

The strategic explanation, then, has the virtues of generality and plausibility. It also has its weaknesses, however. As noted earlier, the mere fact that a condition is present in many cases does not necessarily imply that it is important in any one of them. Moreover, the strategic argument suffers from a certain vagueness--"national security is an ambiguous symbol."[30] There have been situations where nearly any policy could have been justified by strategic reasons. For example, at the time of the Bay of Pigs failure, strategic reasons were given to go ahead with a full military intervention; conversely, a year and a half later, at the time of the Cuban missile crisis, strategic reasons were given to accept the Soviet missiles in

Cuba. In such cases, where strategic calculations are ambiguous or ambivalent, the balance toward one policy or toward another is tipped not by the strategic factor but by another--and we must therefore look beyond the strategic explanation to other theories.

SOCIAL MODERNIZATION AND U.S. FOREIGN POLICY

In the literature of foreign policy analysis, there is one other explanation for hegemonial behavior which does well on the test of generality, in the sense that it can be applied to several hegemonial systems. This is the economic explanation, focusing on the role of capitalism and the great corporations.

Existing formulations of economic explanations are subject to several major difficulties. First, there is the classical critique: theories which argue that imperialist policies are explained by capitalist economies generally neglect to explain why pre-capi-talist or mercantilist economies have also pursued imperalist policies, be they the early colonial empires of Spain and Portugal or the hegemonial systems of seventeenth-century France or nineteenth-century Austria.[31] There is also the modern variant: the theories generally neglect to explain why a post-capitalist or socialist economy, i.e., the Soviet Union, has also pursued imperialist policies, especially in East Europe where it has undertaken military inter-

vention, permanent occupation, and economic exploita-
tion. Economic explanations which focus on capitalism
are vulnerable to the argument of opposite causes (i.e.,
the same "consequence" seems to issue not only from a
"cause" but from its opposite), and they are vulnerable
both to the Right and to the Left. In contrast, strategic explanations which focus on strategic denial are
able to encompass most of the colonial and hegemonial
examples raised by both the classical and the modern
critiques.[32]

It is possible, however, to construct a more
general economic explanation--one that is indeed almost
as general as the strategic one--around a different
economic variable: the level of economic development
and more broadly the level of social modernization
rather than the type of economic system.

Among its analysts, social modernization is
usually defined in terms of such variables as commercialization, industrialization, urbanization, mass
communication, mass education, and social mobilization.[33]
There is the common classification of societies along
a continuum of social modernization and into three
basic categories: (1) traditional society, (2) transitional or modernizing society, and (3) modern society.
The trichotomy is, of course, somewhat simplified. The
different variables which define social modernization

do not always vary together; for example, in many
developing countries in the last decade, urbanization
has outpaced industrialization. Further, many writers
have pointed out "the modernity of tradition" or conversely the traditionalism in modern societies.[34]
Finally, the concept of modernization is limited too
much to a particular time. Imagine a society that is
commercial, urban, and marked by high political con-
sciousness and participation. Is this a modern society?
Hardly, for we have imagined ancient Athens or Rome.
Modernization seems to be much like "ancientization."
Despite these conceptual difficulties with the trichotomy, however, it can still be used for some broad
purposes.

Similarly, we can consider various patterns of
international relations between great powers and small
countries since the Peace of Westphalia (1648) and can
classify these patterns into three basic categories:
(1) suzeraintal systems (ceremonial subordination of
the small countries coupled with normal nonintervention
within them), (2) colonial systems (formal annexation
and direct administration of the small countries), and
(3) hegemonial systems (formal independence of the
small countries but foreign interventions, alliances,
aid, or advisors). (Additional patterns, such as
neutralization or simple nonintervention, have had

relatively few historical examples.)

We can then order the major suzeraintal, colonial, and hegemonial systems (including approximate hegemonial ones) since Westphalia, according to the levels of social modernization of the great powers and of the small countries. The results can be presented in a matrix (see Figure 1).

In most of the colonial and hegemonial systems, the great power has been at a more advanced state of economic development and social modernization than the small countries. This observation does not inspire surprise. The very definition of a great power implies that the country is among the most developed economies and probably among the most modernized societies in the international system of the time, and uneven development has often been seen as a sufficient condition for the domination of one country by another.[35]

Of more interest than mere uneven development and the domination associated with it, might be the different kinds of unevenness and the associated different kinds of domination. Uneven development normally may be sufficient to explain domination, but in itself it does not explain the form domination will take; there are different kinds of gaps with different implications for foreign policies. In particular, the different policies of a great power toward small countries cor-

relate roughly with the different levels of modernization of the great power in the following ways.

   Traditional powers and suzeraintal policies.   In
a traditional great power, rulers normally found a
policy of suzerainty more attractive than the alternative of colonial empire or sovereignty. With an
agrarian economy, the interests of a feudal aristocracy
or a patrimonial bureaucracy were dominant;[36] mercantile
and industrial interests were subordinate or nonexistent.
The economic interest of the aristocracy was in land;
that of the bureaucracy was in taxes. The political
interest of each, and a crucial element in its legitimacy, was in the ceremonial subordination of lesser
lords and lands but not necessarily in the direct
administration of them. With such interests dominant,
military values (force, honor, glory, conquest) might
be favored, but military methods (mobilization, organization, weapons, operations) were primitive. Thus, the
demand for foreign conquests might be high, but the
capability for sizable and flexible military operations
often was low, making difficult military intervention
within a country or military assistance to it. Further,
with an agrarian economy, the demand for foreign goods,
markets, and investment opportunities was low, and
political influence in a small country brought few
economic rewards. The net effect of these factors was

FIGURE 1

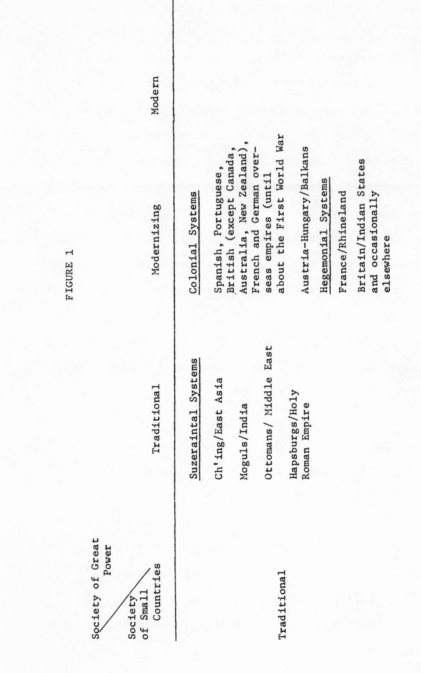

	Traditional	Modernizing	Modern
Modernizing		Colonial Systems France/North Africa and Indochina (1930s–1950s) Portugal/Sub sahara Africa (1960s–1970s) Hegemonial Systems Austria/Germany Austria/Italy	Colonial Systems Britain/Asia and Sub-sahara Africa (20th century) Hegemonial Systems Germany/Southeast Europe Britain/Middle East US/Latin American US/East Asia US/Middle East USSR/East Europe USSR/Middle East France/Subsahara Africa
Modern			Hegemonial Systems US/West Europe

complex. Economic and military interests pushed rulers toward annexation, but economic and military capabilities pushed them toward nonintervention. The best way to bridge these two extremes, and one which satisfied political interests also, was a highly viable mix: ceremonial annexation and normal nonintervention, that is, suzerainty.

Modernizing powers and colonial policies. In a modernizing great power, policymakers normally found a policy of sovereignty, colonial empire, somewhat more attractive than the alternative of hegemony and clearly superior to the alternative of suzerainty or nonintervention more generally. The modernizing economy included considerable mercantile elements and initial industrial ones. The demand for foreign raw materials and primary commodities, markets, and investment opportunities was high, and political influence in a small country brought considerable economic rewards. These economic considerations pushed policymakers toward sovereignty or hegemony. Strong and confident mercantile and industrial groups, however, saw full and formal control as a needless expense and preferred hegemony. John Gallagher and Ronald Robinson have termed this policy "the imperialism of free trade" and characterized it as "trade with informal control if possible; trade with rule when necessary."[37] As for

military values, they were challenged by bourgeois ones,
but they remained influential and were even intensified
in reaction, while military methods were greatly improved.
The military demand for foreign conquests remained high,
while the military capability for sizable and flexible
operations became high. These military considerations
pushed policymakers toward annexation and colonization,
sovereignty. The contrasting pressures from different
elites for different policies are summed up in two
quotes, each from a nineteenth-century Englishman speaking on English policy toward India. Thomas Macaulay in
1833 stated before Parliament the argument of modern,
bourgeois elites about the advantages of "the imperalism
of free trade:"

> It would be, on the most selfish view of
> the case, far better for us that the people
> of India were well governed and independent
> of us, than ill-governed and subject to us;
> that they were ruled by their own kings, but
> wearing our broadcloth, and working with our
> cutlery, than that they were performing their
> salaams to English collectors and English
> magistrates, but were too ignorant to value,
> or too poor to buy, English manufactures. To
> trade with civilized men is infinitely more
> profitable than to govern savages.[38]

James Mill at about the same time pointed out the
interest of traditional, landed elites when he criti-
cized the Empire as "a vast system of outdoor relief
for the upper classes."[39] Again, the effect of these
factors was complex. Economic interests and capabilities
pushed policymakers merely toward protection and inter-

vention, and military interests and capabilities pushed them beyond toward annexation and colonization. The normal way to resolve these differences was a simple one: to stop at the point where the pushing stopped, that is, sovereignty.[40]

Modern powers and hegemonial policies. In a modern great power, policymakers normally find a policy of hegemony to be superior to the alternatives of sovereignty or suzerainty. The modern economy includes considerable industrial elements. As in modernizing societies, the demand for foreign raw materials, other products, markets, and investment opportunities is high, and political influence in a small country can bring considerable economic rewards. However, it can be argued, in modern societies there is an optimal limit to the extent of influence or, more precisely, integration. The smooth functioning of industrial economies requires a high degree of social mobility and social integration which in turn requires a high degree of social homogeneity. If so, multinational empires combine poorly with modern societies. These economic considerations push policymakers away from sovereignty and toward hegemony. Military values are usually reduced to one influence among several, military mobilization becomes somewhat more difficult because of increasing anti-military values, but military organiza-

tion, weapons, and operations continue to develop.
The military demand for foreign conquest is low, and
the military capability for sizable and flexible
operations is somewhat more complicated than it is in
a modernizing society, but it remains high. These
military considerations also push policymakers away
from sovereignty and toward hegemony.

Let us make briefly a reciprocal argument about
the level of modernization of the small country.

Traditional societies in small countries generally
have been unable to withstand the strain of an hegemonial relationship; the legitimacy of the traditional
rulers and the viability of the agrarian economy have
usually disintegrated to the point that a great power
has stepped in and established direct control or a
colonial relationship. Conversely, modernizing
societies in small countries have been resistant to a
colonial relationship but usually have been receptive
to an hegemonial one; modernization generates nationalism, which can be focused against direct foreign
control and overt foreign presence but which cannot
find a tangible target in indirect foreign influence.

We can combine these considerations about the
levels of modernization of great powers and small
countries: the most stable and most probable combination for a suzeraintal relationship is a traditional

great power and a traditional small country; that for
a colonial relationship is a modernizing great power
and a traditional small country; and that for an hegemonial relationship is a modern great power and a
modernizing small country.

The relation between modern societies and hegemonial policies is best illustrated by the United
States. In contrast with all other great powers, the
United States was "born equal," "born modern,"[41] and
born anti-colonial; in consequence of them all it was
born to become hegemonial once it became a great power.[42]
The United States, not uniquely but especially, has a
propensity for hegemony.

Of all the hegemonial systems, the United States
in Latin America comes closest to being an ideal type.
Its decline may have been signaled with the advent of
the Allende regime in Chile, but much of it has endured
longer than any other hegemonial system (if we leave
aside the marginal system of Britain in the Indian
States). It has been a model, or at least an excuse,
for nearly every other hegemonial system in the twentieth century. And it has been among the most for-
malized, routinized, and institutionalized. Within
the framework and under the legitimation of the
Organization of American States, the U.S. has carried
out counterrevolutionary interventions, defense agree-

ments, and the Alliance for Progress; the constitution
of United States/Latin America, like the Constitution
of the United States of America, is an order among
states to "insure domestic tranquility, provide for the
common defense (and) promote the general welfare."
Hegemony, then, has been "the American way" of foreign
policy.

Post-modern societies and transnational organizations. But now some analysts have argued that a post-
modern or post-industrial society began to emerge in
the United States in the 1960's.[43] That proposition
is debatable, but given some speculations on the
character of post-modern society, it seems plausible
that in a post-modern great power antimilitary values
will increase and the use of military intervention as
an instrument of foreign policy will decline. (In
this sense, the Vietnamese War can be seen as only
accentuating and accelerating a pre-existing trend.)
At the same time, given the character of modern society,
modern small countries are unlikely to require advisory
interventions or to be vulnerable to proxy ones. If
so, it seems plausible that the combination of a post-
modern great power and a modern small country would be
a good one for the absence of military, advisory, or
proxy intervention within the political process of the
small country and for merely a relationship of military

protection against foreign attack and economic involvement through trade and investment. The most salient
elements of the relationship would be multinational
corporations. Such a relationship might be called,
following the work of Joseph Nye and Robert Keohane, a
transnational system.[44] The major example is the United
States in West Europe in the 1960's and 1970's; the
prototype is the United States in Canada.

These and other related observations about social
modernization and foreign policies are schematically
presented in the following diagram (see Figure 2). I
shall comment on it only briefly in this paper.

The three patterns of uneven development
(colonial, hegemonial, and transnational--represented
by diagonal lines) might be called the "normal"
patterns of relations between countries of unequal
power. Conversely, the patterns of even development
(vertical lines) might generally be called "abnormal."

Of the patterns of uneven development, the modern/
modernizing one is illustrated by most of the hegemonial
systems listed in the matrix on page 284. Seven clearly
fit the pattern: Germany/Southeast Europe, Britain/
Middle East, United States/Latin America, United States/
East Asia, United States/Middle East, France/Subsahara
Africa and the emerging Soviet Union/Middle East.
Three more approximate it: United States/West Europe,

in Portugal, Spain, and Greece; Soviet Union/East
Europe, in so far as the Soviet Union has been modern
and East Germany and Czechoslovakia are ignored; and
Britain/Indian States, in the twentieth century.

Similarly, the modernizing/traditional pattern
is illustrated by most of the colonial systems that have
existed since the seventeenth century.

Most of the patterns of even development are
illustrated by unusual or "abnormal" systems. Some
systems (colonial wars, military occupation or permanent intervention, economic corruption--top of
vertical lines) might be termed pathological, in that
they are marked by the extreme use of an instrument
common to the diagonal to the left. The colonial wars
of Portugal in Subsahara Africa since 1961 and of
France in Indochina and Algeria in the 1940's and
1950's contrast with the routine policing of a normal
colonial system. The permanent military occupation by
the Soviet Union of East Germany, Czechoslovakia, and
Hungary, modern East European states, contrasts with
the routine indirect interventions and "anticipated
reactions" of a normal hegemonial system.[45] And, by
the 1980's, multinational but American-based corporations in West Europe may engage in the economic corruption of European politicians and officials and not
merely in the remote forms of political influence of

294

FIGURE 2

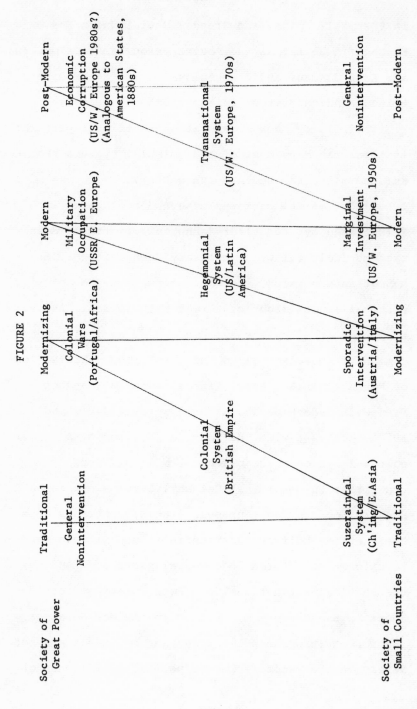

the present transnational system; if so, the relationship of the multinational corporation to the West
European nation-states may come to recapitulate the
relationship of the national corporation to the
American states a century before.

Other systems (suzeraintal system, sporadic
intervention, marginal investment--bottom of vertical
lines) might be termed prototypical, in that they are
marked by the underdeveloped use of an instrument
common to the diagonal to the right. The formal
subordination which is a feature of a suzeraintal
relationship contrasts with the real administration of
a colonial one. The sporadic military interventions
necessary in Austria/Italy contrast again with the
routine indirect interventions and anticipated reactions
of a normal hegemonial system. The marginal role of
American investment in West Europe in the 1950's pre-
viewed its larger role in the future.

The initial position of even development or
rather nondevelopment, however, was one of general
nonintervention. And if one is in a complacent mood,
he might expect that the final position of even development in some distant future might be one of general
nonintervention too.

At present, however, the United States and Latin
America are not moving toward some bland pattern of

even development but rather toward the opposite pattern
of two-step uneven development: a post-modern United
States confronts a modernizing Latin America. What
does our social modernization analysis predict about
the future of their relations? If one focuses on the
post-modern character of the United States, the prediction would be for no more military interventions but
for increasing multinational investments. If one
focuses on the modernizing character of most Latin
American countries, the prediction would be for continued receptivity to military aid and advisors (the
less modern, the more receptive) but for increasing
resistance to multinational investments in extractive
industries (the less modern, the less resistant). And
if one puts the two pieces together, the prediction
would be for continued military aid and advisors,
increasing multinational investment in manufacturing
industries, declining multinational investment in
extractive industries, and little or no prospect for
military intervention in the future. This hybrid
between an hegemonial system and a transnational one
could well become a stable equilibrium that could last
out the 1970's and more. In any event, the prototype
here seems to be Brazil.

In summary, the concept of the modern/modernizing
gap offers one explanation for the hegemonial behavior

of great powers and in particular for foreign interventions, military alliances, military aid, and military
advisors. It is an explanation which on the test of
generality succeeds more than any other one except for
the more ambiguous explanation of strategic denial.

But consideration of the modern/modernizing gap
only establishes the central tendency toward hegemonial
policies, and certain historical situations are left
uncovered. The most relevant are the modern/modernizing
situations characterized not by interventions and
alliances but by something else, most notably nonintervention. Why, for example, has the United States not
undertaken interventions or established alliances in
large areas of the modernizing world, such as Subsahara
Africa, much of the Middle East, and much of South
Asia? Why has France since 1960, a modern society as
well as a middle power, had its own hegemonial system
composed of its former colonies in Subsahara Africa,
while the other former colonial power and a modern
society, Britain, has not? Further, given a great
power and modern society whose normal practice in a
region has been interventions and alliances, why in
some particular cases has the outcome been intervention
but in other cases abortive intervention (e.g., Cuba
1961) or nonintervention (e.g., Chile 1970-1971)? In
order to answer such questions, we would have to add

to the explanation based on modernization refinements
drawn from the remaining theories, such as the
democratic, and the stylistic.[46]

U.S. FOREIGN POLICIES AND LATIN AMERICAN POLITICS

In the preceding two sections, we have considered
the two most general explanations for U.S. foreign
policies--the strategic and the economic. In the concluding two sections, we will briefly consider the
counterpart explanations for Latin American politics--
the international and the developmental. The international explanation, i.e., the argument that U. S.
foreign policies are a major determinant of Latin
American politics, is obviously the connecting link
between our two problems in explanation.

Is there any way to test the argument that Latin
American politics is best accounted for by U. S.
foreign policies? We have already argued in section
III that an approach which focuses only on individual
countries and ad hoc cases will suffer from the
problem of overdetermination.

A second obvious approach to take is a comparative analysis of different Latin American states, comparing them in regard to (1) the degrees of involvement
by the United States or of dependence upon it and (2)
the kinds of political outcomes, in order to see if
the two variables are associated.

Some familiar statistical indicators of degrees
of U.S. involvement or Latin American dependence are
(a) U.S. military aid to the Latin American state in
absolute amounts, or per capita, or per soldier, or as
a percentage of the state's military budget; (b) U.S.
economic aid absolute, or per capita, or as a percentage
of the state's total government budget; (c) American
direct investment absolute, or per capita, or as a
percentage of the state's total investment or of its
GNP; and (d) the Latin American state's exports to the
U.S. as a percentage of its total exports. The first
two indicators, U.S. military aid and U.S. economic aid,
relate to U.S. policy. The last two indicators, American
direct investment and Latin American exports to the U.S.,
relate more directly to American (private) presence
rather than to U.S. (government) policy.

Similarly, some familiar statistical indicators
of kinds of political outcomes are numbers of (a)
military coups or more generally "irregular executive
transfers;" (b) deaths from domestic group violence;
(c) riots; and (d) armed group attacks.

Comparisons of Latin American states along these
variables are susceptible to statistical methods such
as correlation and regression analysis. Examples of
such work are articles by Manus Midlarsky and Raymond
Tanter and by Philippe Schmitter.[47] Each finds

"statistically significant" correlations between particular indicators of the American economic presence, such as American direct investment or Latin American commercial dependence, and particular Latin American political outcomes, such as magnitude of civil strife. Schmitter in addition finds several correlations for Latin American policy outputs, such as military expenditure per soldier. When one turns from indicators for the American economic presence to those for U.S. foreign policy, however, it becomes much more difficult to find statistically significant correlations with Latin American political outcomes. The article by Schmitter in this volume suggests that there is no significant correlation between U.S. military aid and Latin American military rule (although he finds a correlation between U.S. military aid and Latin American military spending), and my own statistical investigation of the indicators for recent years found no significant and consistent correlations between U.S. military or economic aid and Latin American political outcomes. Even if statistically significant correlations could be found, however, there is the familiar argument that the low accuracy of many Latin American statistics coupled with the low number of Latin American countries (n ≤ 20) makes for a data base too weak to support a sophisticated statistical apparatus. For instance, the article by Schmitter in this volume includes a critique of statistics for U.S. military aid and that by Jerry Weaver includes a similar critique of statistics for Latin American military spending.[48]

A more traditional and more historical comparative approach is only slightly more supportive of the argument that U.S. foreign policy has been a major determinant of Latin American politics. The strongest support comes from the oldest comparison. Consider the Latin American states where the U.S. military impact was the heaviest in the first three decades of the twentieth century, i.e., those states which underwent U.S. military intervention and occupation. There were "the five protectorates:" Cuba, Haiti, the Dominican Republic, Nicaragua, and Panama. In each, the U.S. organized the army or "National Guard." Then consider the Latin American states which have suffered the longest and harshest tyrannical regimes in the period since World War II. These have been Cuba under Batista, Haiti under the Duvaliers, the Dominican Republic under Trujillo, Nicaragua under the Somozas, and Paraguay under Stroessner. Indeed, in Haiti and Nicaragua, the tyranny reached the point of a dynasty and passed from father to son.

What can explain this apparent if imperfect

association between U.S. military occupation in one
period and a tyrannical regime in a later one? For
one thing, of course, the U.S. military in effect
appointed Trujillo and Somoza to their military commands
and therefore to the base from which they later took
political power. (To a much lesser extent, the U.S.
government did the same for Batista in 1933.) More
importantly, however, the effect of the U.S. occupation
in the Dominican Republic and Nicaragua was to level
what remained of the traditional political institutions
and to erect a single institution, the army, which
towered over the traditional rubble, the urban rabble,
and everything else. To a lesser extent, the same
process occurred in Cuba (where, however, the relatively
high commercial development encouraged countervailing
urban political organizations for a time), Haiti
(where all political institutions, including the Guarde,
remained weak), and in Panama (where the relatively
high commercial development which grew up around the
Canal also encouraged countervailing political organizations).[49]

The U.S. military impact on various Latin
American states since World War II has been much
lighter, however, and that impact has resulted in no
clear pattern of political regimes common to several
states. In the only case of full military intervention

and occupation, the Dominican Republic in 1965-1966, when the U.S. military involvement clearly made a difference in the outcome, the result was a conservative civilian regime. In the proxy intervention in Guatemala in 1954, when the U.S. involvement again probably made a difference in the outcome, the result was a conservative military regime. The later advisory intervention in Guatemala was followed by a conservative military regime, the advisory intervention in Peru by a radical military one, and the advisory intervention in Bolivia was followed by both. And the police advisors in Uruguay have reinforced a moderate civilian regime. There is no obvious common thread connecting these disparate political outcomes. However, some current regimes do seem to be either more military (Peru) or more conservative (Dominican Republic, Uruguay) or both (Guatemala) than the regimes (or in the case of the Dominican Republic, than the rebellion) that existed at the time of the intervention.

Similarly, the distribution of U.S. military aid seems to have resulted in no clear pattern of political regimes common to several states. In the period 1962-1970, the six largest recipients of U.S. military aid were, by rank and by current regime, (1) Brazil, conservative and military; (2) Argentina, also conservative and military; (3) Chile, radical and civilian;

(4) Peru, radical and military; (5) Venezuela, moderate and civilian; and (6) Colombia, moderate and civilian. In sum, three military and three civilian regimes; or, two conservative, two radical and two moderate ones.[50] And the seventh rank was held by Bolivia, which, as we have seen, has recently had both radical and conservative military regimes. A similar lack of common regime pattern results if we look at U.S. military aid per capita, or per soldier, or at U.S. economic aid.

In brief, the comparison of Latin American states for the last decade or so gives little support to the argument that U.S. foreign policies--defined in the strict sense of U.S. military interventions, advisory interventions, military aid, and economic aid--are a major explanation for Latin American military rule. Regretfully, we conclude that a convincing case for the argument has yet to be made. And it will be a case all the harder to make in the future, if the U.S. military and economic aid programs in Latin America continue at their current, diminished level.

Insofar as American economic presence and especially American direct investment are included as an adjunct or result of U.S. foreign policies, however, the argument that U.S. foreign policies are a major explanation for Latin American military rule may become more convincing. The evidence for an association between American direct investment and Latin American military rule is mixed, but cases such as Honduras, Guatemala, and Bolivia are suggestive. The topic is beyond the scope of this paper, but it needs further investigation.

ECONOMIC DEVELOPMENT AND LATIN AMERICAN POLITICS

The argument that Latin American politics is best accounted for by levels of economic development is as familiar as the argument that the major determinant is U.S. foreign policies. Also familiar is one method of testing it: to compare different Latin American states or different political systems in general in regard to (1) these levels of economic development and (2) the kinds of political outcomes, in order to see if the two variables are associated.[51] We shall briefly present such a comparison here, in regard to GNP per capita and kinds of political regimes.

The new edition of the Yale World Handbook of Political and Social Indicators is a convenient, comparative, data source for these purposes; Table 5.5 in it ranks 135 countries by GNP per capita for 1965.[52] We will find it useful to break this list into three groups: (1) what we shall call, with some license at the lower end, developed economies, those countries above $800 GNP per capita (ranks 1-30); (2) semi-developed economies, those countries between $800 and

$400 (ranks 31-51); and (3) underdeveloped economies, those countries below $400 (ranks 52-135).

Developed Economies

In the first group (above $800), all but Kuwait are either a pluralist democracy (alternatively termed "polyarchy" or (civil polity) or a communist party-state. Only two in this group are Latin American "countries:" Puerto Rico ($1,154) and Venezuela ($882). In both of these, of course, the American economic presence is very large, and it not only explains the high figures but also distorts their meaning.

Underdeveloped Economies

Conversely, in the third group (below ($400), nearly all by 1973 were ruled by some variety of authoritarian regime (be it military or civilian, corporatist[53] or communist) or, in the case of several states which had only received independence in the decade since 1963, were ruled by the same political leader to whom the colonial government had relinquished its power, and thus they had not entered into their first "succession crisis." The exceptions (and some of them were rather dubious as examples of nonauthoritarian regimes) were Malaysia, Colombia, the Dominican Republic, Ceylon, and India. It is noteworthy that in three of these exceptions (Malaysia, Ceylon, and India), there were large minority linguistic communities, illustrating

once again that plural societies are disproportionately
hospitable to pluralist democracies or "polyarchies."
In two other exceptions (Colombia and the Dominican
Republic), civilian rule could properly be interpreted
as resting on a "peace of exhaustion" in turn result-
ing from violencia or civil war.

This group of underdeveloped economies includes
thirteen or almost two-thirds of the Latin American
countries:

Country	GNP per capita
Cuba	$393
Peru	367
Nicaragua	343
Guatemala	318
Colombia	282
El Salvador	271
Brazil	267
Dominican Republic	265
Honduras	221
Paraguay	218
Ecuador	216
Bolivia	104
Haiti	74

This review suggests once again the familiar
proposition that below a certain level of economic
development (in this case defined as $400 GNP per
capita), nonauthoritarian regimes can be expected only
under very unusual conditions (e.g., societies including large linguistic minorities or societies exhausted
by civil war), and even in these cases the idiosyn-
cratic factor of political leadership seems as
necessary as the systemic factor of social bifurcation.

Of course, countries with low economic development may
on occasion experience a democratic interlude (e.g.,
Peru 1963-1968, Brazil 1955-1964, Bolivia 1956-1964)
or, in Barrington Moore's phrase for an earlier era, a
semi-parliamentary regime.[54] The situation is unstable,
however, and when unfavorable conditions reappear, be
they the strains of international economic depression,
or of national economic development, or of national
political elections, or of something else, they tip
the political system back into military rule. Accordingly, the developmental explanation would predict
that for the next decade or so it is more likely that
Colombia or the Dominican Republic will fall back into
a military regime than it is that any of the other
Latin American underdeveloped countries will establish
a durable democratic one. And there is a heavy burden
of proof upon an advocate of an alternative explanation
for military rule in Latin American underdeveloped
countries--such as an explanation focusing on U.S.
foreign policies. He has a responsibility not only to
argue for his own alternative explanation but also to
argue against the developmental one.

Semi-developed Economies

The most interesting group of countries, in the
sense that they are the ones with the most contingent
possibilities, are those that fall between $800 and

$400 GNP per capita (ranks 31-51). This group includes
pluralist democracies and nearly every variety of
authoritarian regime--military and civilian, corporatist and communist. The semi-developed group includes
six Latin American countries. We will also list the
Mediterranean countries for comparative interest:

Latin American Country	GNP per Capita	Mediterranean Country	GNP per Capita
Argentina	$770	Cyprus	$695
Uruguay	573	Greece	687
Chile	565	Spain	561
Panama	485	Libya	542
Mexico	455	Malta	502
Costa Rica	413	Yugoslavia	451
		Lebanon	437
		Portugal	406

Why some of these semi-developed Latin American
countries are pluralist democracies and others are not
has been a matter of considerable debate. My own view
is that the best explanation lies in a variation on
the thesis by Barrington Moore.[55] Countries which have
passed through a social revolution or civil war in
which an urban middle class or bourgeoise defeated the
military forces of landed elites are then able to maintain a stable democracy or at least civilian supremacy.
In Mexico the Revolution destroyed the power of the
landed elites, in Uruguay the civil war of 1904
defeated them and diminished their power, and in Costa
Rica the civil war of 1948 resulted in the incorpora-
tion of new urban groups and the abolition of the army.

In a semi-developed country, it seems, a stable democracy or at least civilian supremacy is the bequest of a conquering bourgeoisie. To assure civilian rule, the civilians must at some point become more militant than the military. The absence of any such bourgeois heroic age in the history of Argentina and Panama would then explain the absence today of stable democracy or civilian supremacy in these two countries (and in Spain, Portugal, and Greece). Unfortunately, Chile still remains as a case difficult to explain in any of these terms.

Whatever explains the disparate regimes of these six semi-developed Latin American countries--be it an historical, organizational, or cultural approach, or some combination of them--it does not seem that the discriminating factor is the impact of the United States. The four variables of U.S. military aid, U.S. economic aid, American direct investment, and American trade do not vary in ways simply and directly associated with the variation in regimes.

If a one-step international explanation (U.S. foreign policy ⟶ Latin American military rule) does not work, perhaps a two-step explanation (U.S. foreign policy ⟶ Latin American economic underdevelopment⟶ Latin American military rule) would. Economic underdevelopment would be only an intervening variable.

The primary variable would include U.S. interventions, military aid, economic aid, and, less directly, American direct investment, and American trade. The connections between the last three or economic elements and Latin American economic development have, of course, been a matter of endless debate; I will not enter that thicket here, other than to remark that I believe the analysis of Albert Hirschman to be the most sophisticated and the most persuasive.[56] The connections between the first two or military elements and Latin American economic development have been less discussed, perhaps because those connections are far from clear. Let us stipulate, however, that the impact of the U.S. foreign policy variables on Latin American countries contributes to the underdevelopment of their economies and to the maldistribution of income within them. Even if the U.S. economic and military weight were removed in some way and the development of Latin American countries were accelerated, there would still be the second link in the causal chain. While a certain threshold of economic development ordinarily may be a necessary condition for stable pluralist democracy, it is of course not a sufficient one. As the analysis of Moore suggests, an additional necessary condition, at least at the semi-developed level, may well be a conquering bourgeoisie imbued with liberal ideas.

Otherwise, as economic advance pushes a country into the zone of semi-development, it will push it down the corporatist or communist path and not down the pluralist, democratic one.[57] And for many familiar reasons, a conquering bourgeoisie is most unlikely to develop within the authoritarian semi-developed and underdeveloped countries of contemporary Latin America. Consequently, even if economic development should bring one of these up to the level of, say, $700 GNP per capita, it is far more likely that the accompanying political system would resemble that of Argentina, Spain, or Greece than it would that of Uruguay.

These dismal observations suggest that, if there is any hope for movement away from military rule in Latin America in the next few years, it lies not in the movement of underdeveloped countries into semi-developed ones but in the movement of semi-developed Argentine and perhaps Panama into developed countries. But not too much should be made of even this possibility. After all, it took a conquering liberal bourgeoisie in the guise of the U.S. Army to establish the conditions for stable pluralist democracies in 1945 in West Germany, Austria, Italy, and Japan, when those countries were at a comparable or high level of development.

In conclusion, it seems that there is no direct connection between U.S. foreign policies and Latin

American military rule, other than in some cases of U.S. military intervention and in the proxy intervention in Guatemala. If we examine individual countries and ad hoc cases, we find that other explanations for military rule serve just as well or better. If we turn to a more general, comparative investigation, we find that there is no consistent and significant pattern.

Conclusions such as these at times have been turned into arguments with which to exonerate or even advocate the continuation of the U.S. military aid program. Such arguments, however, rest upon a failure to draw important logical distinctions. First, the argument that U.S. military aid has no demonstrable harmful effects on Latin American political systems obviously does not prove that the aid has any beneficial effects; that has not been demonstrated either. Second, the argument that the aid has no harmful effects on the political systems says nothing about the harmful effects on particular policy outputs of the systems or on particular individuals within them. Schmitter has shown the correlation between U.S. military aid and Latin American military spending; there may be other correlations with other Latin American policy areas.

In any case, there is no defensible justification for the U.S. government to give or sell guns or tanks to the present military regimes of Argentina, Brazil, Paraguay, and Bolivia, among others. U.S. government officials and military officers often defend military aid to such regimes with attractive if vacuous phrases such as "collective security," "public safety," "professional development," and "civic action." Or, if they concede that military aid does little good, they also argue that it does no harm. The image is of a program that is wholesome at best and harmless at worst. There is another picture which is a truer one, however. A famous painting by Goya shows a squad of French soldiers shooting civilians of Madrid during the Napoleonic occupation. The role of the U.S. military aid program in Latin American politics is like the role of one soldier out of the several who form a firing squad. A soldier in a firing squad who shoots a civilian may defend himself with the argument that the victim would have been shot by the other soldiers any-way, or that his own bullet was not the first to hit the mark, or even that his own gun wasn't really loaded. And it is true that the important point about the civilian is that he would still be dead. But the important point about the soldier--and about the U.S. policymaker--is that he chose to pull the trigger.

NOTES

1. A useful analysis of the concept of dependency and of its
   formulation by Latin American social scientists is Susanne
   Bodenheimer's "Dependency and Imperialism: the Roots of
   Latin American Underdevelopment," Politics and Society (May,
   1971), or the slightly different version by the same title in
   K. T. Fann and Donald C. Hodges, eds., Readings in U.S.
   Imperialism (Boston: Porter Sargent, 1971), pp. 155-181.

2. Robert A. Dahl, "The Concept of Power," in J. David Singer,
   ed., Human Behavior and International Politics (Chicago:
   Rand McNally, 1965), p. 374.

3. Hans Morgenthau, Politics Among Nations: The Struggle for
   Power and Peace (4th ed.; New York: Knopf, 1967); Thomas C.
   Schelling, The Strategy of Conflict (New York: Oxford
   University Press, 1963) and Arms and Influence (New Haven:
   Yale University Press, 1966).

4. Charles Osgood, An Alternative to War or Surrender (Urbana,
   Illinois: University of Illinois Press, 1962); Joseph de
   Rivera, The Psychological Dimension of Foreign Policy
   (Columbus, Ohio: Merrill Publishing, 1968); Robert Jervis,
   "Hypotheses on Misperception," World Politics (April, 1968),
   pp. 454-479.

5. See for example Philip Geyelin, Lyndon B. Johnson and the
   World (New York: Praeger, 1966). And Tom Wicker reports a
   remark by Lyndon Johnson to a group of reporters not long
   after he became President: "I know these Latin Americans. I
   grew up with Mexicans. They'll come right into your yard and
   take it over if you let them. And the next day they'll be
   right up on your porch, barefoot and weighing one hundred and
   thirty pounds and they'll take that too. But if you say to
   'em right at the start, 'hold on, just wait a minute,' they'll
   know they're dealing with somebody who'll stand up. And after
   that you can get along fine." Tom Wicker, JFK and LBJ: The
   Influence of Personality Upon Politics (Baltimore: Penguin
   Books, 1969), p. 196.

6. Richard E. Neustadt, Presidential Power (New York: Wiley, 1965)
   and Alliance Politics (New York: Columbia University Press,
   1970); Roger Hilsman, To Move a Nation (New York: Doubleday,
   1967) and The Politics of Policy-making in Defense and Foreign
   Affairs (New York: Harper and Row, 1971).

7. Arthur M. Schlesinger, Jr., A Thousand Days (Boston: Houghton
   Mifflin, 1965); Theodore C. Sorenson, Kennedy (New York:
   Harper and Row, 1965); Abraham F. Lowenthal, The Dominican
   Intervention (Cambridge: Harvard University Press, 1972).

8. Graham T. Allison, The Essence of Decision (Boston: Little, Brown, 1971). Allison's work also makes a valuable contribution in being an explicit comparison of alternative explanations.

9. Kenneth N. Waltz, Foreign Policy and Democratic Politics: The American and British Experience (Boston: Little, Brown, 1967); Theodore Lowi, "Making Democracy Safe for the World," in James N. Rosenau, ed., Domestic Sources of Foreign Policy (New York: Free Press, 1967); Stanley Hoffmann, Gulliver's Troubles (New York: McGraw-Hill, 1968), pp. 217-339.

10. See, for example, Jerome Slater, Intervention and Negotiation: The United States and the Dominican Revolution (New York: Harper and Row, 1970); Geyelin, op. cit., pp. 244-258.

11. William Appleman Williams, The Tragedy of American Diplomacy (New York: Delta, 1962) and The Roots of the Modern American Empire (New York: Random House, 1969); Gabriel Kolko, The Politics of War (New York: Random House, 1968), The Limits of Power (New York: Harper and Row, 1971), and The Roots of American Foreign Policy (Boston: Beacon, 1969); Harry Magdoff, The Age of Imperialism (New York: Monthly Review, 1969).

12. James Petras, Politics and Social Structure in Latin America (New York: Monthly Review, 1970); Andre Gunder Frank, Capitalism and Underdevelopment in Latin America (New York: Monthly Review, 1967) and Latin America: Underdevelopment or Revolution (New York: Monthly Review, 1969). Also see articles in Fann and Hodges, op. cit.

13. Stanley Hoffmann, op. cit., pp. 87-213; Louis Hartz, The Liberal Tradition in America (New York: Harcourt Brace, 1955); George F. Kennan, American Diplomacy, 1900-1950 (New York: Mentor, 1965), pp. 82-89.

14. For somewhat different uses of the concept of overdetermination, see Albert O. Hirschman, A Bias for Hope: Essays on Development and Latin America (New Haven: Yale University Press, 1971), pp. 350-360; Louis Althusser, For Marx (New York: Vintage, 1970); Adam Przeworski and Henry Teune, The Logic of Comparative Social Inquiry (New York: Wiley Interscience, 1970).

15. James Petras, op. cit. and Cultivating Revolution: The United States and Agrarian Reform in Latin America (New York: Random House, 1971).

16. A third answer to the problem of many explanations might be called the skeptical or eclectic solution, to simply rest satisfied without choosing between theories and to hold that the combination of interlocking and reinforcing explanations is the best explanation of all. This, of course, is a very reasonable solution, and it is supported by such concepts as accessory condition, probabilistic cause, interdependent system, and ceteris paribus. Yet, this solution also has its flaws. It is intellectually unsatisfying and even self-abnegating. Further, it suffers from what might be called the nth + 1 problem. Given n theories, the simple eclectic will accept them all and equally, for he has no standards with which to discriminate among them. But suppose someone offers another explanation, the nth + 1 theory. The simple eclectic must accept this theory too. And the same is true for the nth + 2, nth + 3 . . .

17. Samuel P. Huntington, "Political Development and Political Decay," World Politics (April, 1965); Political Order in Changing Societies (New Haven: Yale University Press, 1968); and "The Change to Change: Modernization, Development, and Politics," Comparative Politics (April, 1971); Lucian W. Pye, Aspects of Political Development (Boston: Little, Brown, 1966).

18. On the concept of praetorianism, see especially Huntington, Political Order.

19. Bodenheimer, op. cit.

20. In the second structure, there is no counterpart of the psychological theory which is found in the first structure, simply because few analysts stress the personal qualities of only one or a few men as the determinant of a country's politics over a broad range of issues and over the long-run.

21. Paul Baran, The Political Economy of Growth (New York: Monthly Review, 1957); Frank, op. cit.; Petras, op. cit. Also see articles in the following: Irving Louis Horowitz, Josue de Castro, and John Gerassi, eds., Latin American Radicalism (New York: Vintage, 1969); Robert I. Rhodes, ed., Imperialism and Underdevelopment: A Reader (New York: Monthly Review, 1970); and James D. Cockcroft, Andre Gunder Frank, and Dale L. Johnson, Dependence and Underdevelopment: Latin America's Political Economy (New York: Doubleday, 1972).

22. Huntington, Political Order.

23. Douglas W. Rae, The Political Consequences of Electoral Laws, rev. ed. (New Haven: Yale University Press, 1971).

24. Karl W. Deutsch, _Nationalism and Social Communication_
    (Cambridge: M.I.T. Press, 1953) and "Social Mobilization and
    Political Development," _American Political Science Review_
    (September, 1961); Seymour M. Lipset, "Some Social
    Prerequisites of Democracy: Economic Development and
    Political Legitimacy," _American Political Science Review_
    (March, 1959) and _Political Man_ (New York: Doubleday, 1960).

25. Seymour M. Lipset and Stein Rokkan, eds., _Party Systems and
    Voter Alignments_ (New York: Free Press, 1967); Barrington
    Moore, Jr., _Social Origins of Dictatorship and Democracy_
    (Boston: Beacon, 1966).

26. Gabriel Almond and Sidney Verba, _The Civic Culture_
    (Princeton: Princeton University Press, 1963); Edward C.
    Banfield, _The Moral Basis of a Backward Society_ (Glencoe,
    Ill.: Free Press, 1958) and _The Unheavenly City_ (Boston:
    Little, Brown, 1969); Lucian W. Pye, _Politics, Personality,
    and Nation Building_ (New Haven: Yale University Press, 1962)
    and _The Spirit of Chinese Politics_ (Cambridge: M.I.T. Press,
    1968). Also see the articles in Lucian W. Pye and Sidney
    Verba, eds., _Political Culture and Political Development_
    (Princeton: Princeton University Press, 1966).

27. For a systematic analysis of CONDECA, see John Saxe-
    Fernandez, "The Central American Defense Council and Pax
    Americana," in Horowitz, de Castro, and Gerassi, _op. cit._

28. In regard to the more obscure systems, some references may
    be useful. On France/Rhineland, see Hajo Holborn, _A History
    of Modern Germany: 1648-1840_ (New York: Knopf, 1966);
    Frederick L. Nussbaum, _The Triumph of Science and Reason:
    1660-1685_ (New York: Harper and Row, 1962); and David Ogg,
    Europe in the Seventeenth Century (New York: Collier, 1962).
    On Britain/Indian States, see William Lee-Warner, _The Native
    States of India_ (2nd ed.; London: Macmillan, 1910); K.M.
    Panikkar, _Indian States and the Government of India_ (London:
    Martin Hopkinson, 1932); and G. N. Singh, _Indian States and
    British India: Their Future Relations_ (Benares: Nand Kishore,
    1930).

29. See Karl W. Deutsch, _The Analysis of International Relations_
    (Englewood Cliffs, N.J.: Prentice-Hall, 1968), p. 117.

30. The words are nearly identical to the title of an article by
    Arnold Wolfers in _Political Science Quarterly_ (December, 1952),
    reprinted in his _Discord and Collaboration_ (Baltimore: Johns
    Hopkins, 1962), pp. 147-165.

31. A familiar example of the classical critique is Joseph
    Schumpeter, "The Sociology of Imperialisms," _Imperialism and
    Social Classes_ (Cleveland: Meridian, 1955).

32. It is also true that, in regard to the Soviet Union, an
    economic argument for U.S. hegemony can be coupled with a
    strategic one for Soviet hegemony, i.e., it can be argued
    that Soviet hegemony in East Europe and now in the Middle
    East has been only a defensive reaction to American hegemony
    in West Europe, the Middle East, and elsewhere and to
    American threats generally. But this argument does not
    adequately explain the intensity and severity of Soviet
    intervention in East Europe, including the invasion and
    occupation of Czechoslovakia.

33. On the concept of modernization, see especially Huntington,
    Political Order, C. E. Black, _The Dynamics of Modernization_
    (New York: Harper and Row, 1967); Dankwart A. Rustow, _A
    World of Nations: Problems of Political Modernization_
    (Washington, D.C.: The Brookings Institution, 1967).

34. See especially Lloyd and Suzanne Rudolph, _The Modernity of
    Tradition_ (Chicago: University of Chicago Press, 1967) and
    Huntington's own critique of the concept of modernization in
    his "The Change to Change: Modernization, Development, and
    Politics," _Comparative Politics_ (April, 1971).

35. In some hegemonial systems, however, there have been cases
    where the client states were more advanced than the hege-
    monial one: in Austria/Germany, where several Western German
    states were more modernized than Austria, and in Soviet Union/
    East Europe, where East Germany and Czechoslovakia were more
    modernized than the Soviet Union.

36. On feudalism and patrimonialism, see Max Weber, _The Theory of
    Social and Economic Organization_ (ed. by Talcott Parsons:
    New York: Free Press, 1964), especially pp. 346-358; 373-381.

37. John Gallagher and Ronald Robinson, "The Imperialism of Free
    Trade," in George H. Nadel and Perry Curtis, eds.,
    Imperialism and Colonialism (New York: Macmillan, 1964),
    p. 108.

38. Quoted in Michael Edwardes, _The Last Years of British India_
    (Cleveland: World Publishing, 1963), p. 234.

39. Quoted in John Strachey, _The End of Empire_ (New York:
    Praeger, 1964), p. 72.

40. At certain times and under special conditions, however, some
    modernizing powers stopped merely at the point of hegemony
    (e.g., Austria and Britain in the mid-nineteenth century and,
    less restfully, France in the seventeenth century).

41. Huntington, _Political Order_, p. 135. The phrase "born equal"
    is Tocqueville's; "born modern" is Huntington's.

42. Prior to becoming a great power at the end of the nineteenth
    century, the dominant American pattern was annexation, but
    it was generally annexation of hunting rather than farming
    peoples.

43. Daniel Bell has developed the concept of post-industrial
    society in numerous articles, and Zbigniew Brzezinski has
    developed a similar concept of "technetronic" society in his
    Between Two Ages: America's Role in the Technetronic Age
    (New York: Viking, 1970). For a critical review of the
    literature, see Victor C. Ferkiss, _Technological Man: The
    Myth and Reality_ (New York: George Braziller, 1969).

44. Robert O. Keohane and Joseph S. Nye, Jr., eds.,
    Transnational Relations in World Politics (Cambridge: Harvard
    University Press, 1972). Also see Samuel P. Huntington,
    "Transnational Organization in World Politics," _World Politics_,
    forthcoming.

45. Indeed, since 1968 the more modern the East European state
    (as defined for instance by GNP per capita), the more Soviet
    troops have been garrisoned within it. (The order is East
    Germany, Czechoslovakia, Hungary, Poland, and Bulgaria.)

46. Consideration of such general concepts as the modern/
    modernizing gap also tells us very little about the particular
    timing of interventions or alliances, about why a modern
    society becomes an hegemonial power at one time instead of a
    decade later or a decade before. But for many cases of
    hegemony, the timing can readily be explained in strategic,
    international terms: the hegemonial system was established
    by a victorious great power at the conclusion of a general
    war (France/Rhineland, Austria/Germany, Austria/Italy, United
    States/West Europe, United States/East Asia, Soviet Union/
    East Europe, and less clearly Britain/Middle East, and United
    States/Middle East). The timing of the other hegemonial
    systems can be explained also, if somewhat less readily, by
    various _ad hoc_ strategic arguments.

47. Manus Midlarsky and Raymond Tanter, "Toward a Theory of
    Political Instability in Latin America," _Journal of Peace
    Research_ (1967, no. 3), pp. 209-227; Philippe C. Schmitter,
    "Military Intervention, Political Competitiveness and Public

Policy in Latin America: 1950-1967,' in Morris Janowitz and J. van Doorn, eds., On Military Intervention (Rotterdam: Rotterdam University Press, 1971), pp. 425-506.

48. However, the accuracy of Latin American statistics is itself a variable. For a comprehensive analysis of the problem, see Schmitter's "New Strategies for the Comparative Analysis of Latin American Politics," Latin American Research Review (Summer 1969), pp. 83-110.

49. A similar argument is presented in Edwin Lieuwen, Arms and Politics in Latin America, rev. ed. (New York: Praeger, 1961), pp. 186-187. Lieuwen's book is more generally the major work on U.S. military aid in Latin America prior to the 1960's. Accounts for the more recent period include John Duncan Powell, "Military Assistance and Militarism in Latin America," The Western Political Quarterly (June 1965), pp. 382-392, and John M. Baines, "U.S. Military Assistance to Latin America: An Assessment," Journal of Interamerican Studies and World Affairs (November 1972), pp. 469-487.

50. It is noteworthy, however, that the Chilean cabinet has included military officers, including the Minister of the Interior, and that the radical policies of the Peruvian military have had definite limits.

51. Several well-known studies discussing the association between developmental levels and political outcomes are included in John V. Gillespie and Betty a Nesvold, eds., Macro-Quantitative Anslysis: Conflict, Development, and Democratization (Beverly Hills, Calif.: Sage Publications, 1972). Also see Egil Fossum, "Factors Influencing the Occurrence of Military Coups d'Etat in Latin America," Journal of Peace Research (1967, no. 3), pp. 228-251.

52. Charles Lewis Taylor and Michael C. Hudson, World Handbook of Political and Social Indicators, 2nd ed. (New Haven: Yale University Press, 1972), pp. 314-320.

53. On the concept of "corporatist-authoritarian" regimes, see Philippe C. Schmitter, "Paths to Political Development in Latin America," in Douglas A. Chalmers, ed., Changing Latin America: New Interpretations of its Politics and Society (Proceedings of the Academy of Political Science) (New York: The Academy of Political Science, Columbia University, 1972), pp. 83-105.

54. Moore, op. cit., p. 438.

55. Moore, op. cit.

56. Hirschman, op. cit., especially pp. 85-123; 197-252.

57. See Schmitter, "Paths to Political Development."